C000296196

# Lean Materials Planning and Execution

## A Guide to Internal and External Supply Management Excellence

# Lean Materials Planning and Execution

## A Guide to Internal and External Supply Management Excellence

Donald H. Sheldon, CFPIM, CIRM, CSCP

Copyright ©2008 by Donald H. Sheldon

ISBN-10: 1-932159-65-7
ISBN-13: 978-1-932159-65-3

Printed and bound in the U.S.A. Printed on acid-free paper
10  9  8  7  6  5  4  3  2  1

**Library of Congress Cataloging-in-Publication Data**

Sheldon, Donald H.
  Lean materials planning & execution : a guide to internal and external
supply management excellence / by Donald H. Sheldon.
      p. cm.
  Includes index.
  ISBN-13: 978-1-932159-65-3 (hardcover : alk. paper)
  1.  Business logistics.  2.  Materials management.  3.  Six sigma (Quality control standard)
I. Title. II. Title: Lean materials planning and execution.

  HD38.5.S549 2007
  658.7--dc22

                                                                    2007030816

Phone: (954) 727-9333
Fax: (561) 892-0700
Web: www.jrosspub.com

*This book is dedicated to God
from whom all blessings fall.
I also thank my family,
especially my parents,
Don Sr. and Jane,
and my wonderful wife and children,
Anita, Erica, and Geoffrey,
for their unending support.
I am truly blessed!*

# CONTENTS

# PREFACE

Lean materials, supply management, and supply-chain management are a constant challenge in most businesses. They are, by nature, among the most critical responsibilities in any manufacturing organization. Success is defined by controlling all components of operations and the synchronization of the correct parts processed into salable units and delivered to the customer when the customer wants them. Cost containment in this globally competing environment is a constant focus and the flexibility of customer requirements makes cost effectiveness require effective planning and execution. Lean systems and thinking are often the only answer that allows these sometimes competing objectives to result in effective materials management.

In this book, various approaches that are used in lean materials management are analyzed and reviewed to support a case for keeping the processes lean and short-cycled. The Toyota methods are intertwined into the discussion with examples from factories to aid in the application of ideas. Since materials control has been around for several years and has been constantly evolving, there is an expansive discussion.

Materials professionals today are a different breed than 15 or even 10 years ago. Today's materials executives are less dependent on traditional paths and more interested in using continuous improvement processes to invent new ways to increase flexibility and speed of process. Kaizen is as much a part of the lean materials world as it is the production process, and inventory is no longer a dirty word; it is an asset, like cash, to be managed wisely and carefully. No longer are the materials people isolated within the organization and thought of as the people who just "make it happen" in reactionary mode. Instead, these people are considered the professionals who strategically broker the supply chain for not only component availability, but also cost efficiency. Price is no longer the highest priority in the supply management or supply-chain decision arena. This top priority in the decision process has been replaced with overall cost. This cost includes quality, delivery speed, and flexibility.

The materials world is at the center of the manufacturing, supply management, and the supply-chain management world and is worthy of special attention. Those of us who have been in it for a few years have seen a tremendous amount of change and the velocity of change is increasing as you read. Even the American Production and Inventory Control Society (APICS) has upgraded their organization's name recently to include operations management, and they have introduced a new certification on supply-chain management because the lines are blurred more than ever between the functional boundaries.

Initially, I considered calling this a book on lean materials planning and supply-chain management. Based on the original definition, and the one to which I still subscribe, this might be accurate. However, in many circles today, supply chain is mostly about logistics, as are most books on the topic. That is not the primary focus of this book. Some books on supply management are primarily about procurement, but others actually fit the original definition of supply-chain management. I've yet to see one that truly covers supply-chain management end-to-end, but I expect we will in time. *Lean Materials Planning and Execution: A Guide to Internal and External Supply Management Excellence* was the best fit for a title. However, when I mention supply chain in this book, please keep in mind that I am referring to the original end-to-end definition and not this more recent narrow focus that is primarily on logistics.

While there are several good books available on lean manufacturing and a few good books on supply management primarily in the procurement space, none give much attention to the significant opportunity for cost reductions in materials planning and execution, which is why I decided to write this book. This guide provides an appropriate treatment of the basics and a detailed understanding of how lean materials management is practiced in today's high-performance manufacturing organizations. Since my overall objective for writing this book was to help organizations achieve high levels of performance, other world-class or class A strategies and processes are presented as well. Discussion questions are included at the end of each chapter to facilitate learning and to test your understanding of the material.

When you have finished this book, you will not have all the answers; nobody does. You should, however, understand many of the approaches and have a sense for how to find the answers still out of your grasp. After all, today lean materials, supply management, and supply-chain management require creativity and imagination.

# ABOUT THE AUTHOR

**Donald H. Sheldon** is president of the DHSheldon & Associates consulting firm in New York. He has over 30 years of management experience, serving in the positions of Director and General Manager of The Raymond Corporation's (world-class manufacturer of material handling equipment) Aftermarket Services Division, Vice President at Buker, Inc. (world leader in business management education and consulting), and Director of Management Systems and later Vice President of Global Quality and Six Sigma Services at the NCR Corporation. Mr. Sheldon consults with companies all over the globe to improve competitive advantage.

Mr. Sheldon has written numerous articles published in journals, and is co-author (with Michael Tincher) of *The Road to Class A Manufacturing Resource Planning* (MPR II) (1995), and is the author of *Achieving Inventory Accuracy* (J. Ross Publishing 2004), *Class A ERP Implementation* (J. Ross Publishing 2005), *World Class Sales & Operations Planning* (J. Ross Publishing 2006), and *World Class Master Scheduling* (J. Ross Publishing 2006). He has been a frequent speaker at colleges, international conventions, and seminars, including APICS (the Association for Operations Management). He holds a Master of Arts Degree in Business and Government Policies Studies and an undergraduate degree in Business and Economics from the State University of New York, Empire State College. He is certified by APICS as Certified Fellow in Production and Inventory Management (CFPIM), Certified in Resource Management (CIRM), and Certified Supply Chain Professional (CSCP).

Mr. Sheldon can be contacted at www.sheldoninc.com

*Free value-added materials available from*
*the Download Resource Center at **www.jrosspub.com***

At J. Ross Publishing we are committed to providing today's professional with practical, hands-on tools that enhance the learning experience and give readers an opportunity to apply what they have learned. That is why we offer free ancillary materials available for download on this book and all participating Web Added Value™ publications. These online resources may include interactive versions of material that appears in the book or supplemental templates, worksheets, models, plans, case studies, proposals, spreadsheets, and assessment tools, among other things. Whenever you see the WAV™ symbol in any of our publications, it means bonus materials accompany the book and are available from the Web Added Value™ Download Resource Center at www.jrosspub.com.

Downloads for *Lean Materials Planning and Execution* include a free downloadable glossary of terms, lean and other high-performance assessment tools, and a set of job descriptions for lean material roles.

# EVOLUTION OF MATERIALS MANAGEMENT AND LEAN

## INTRODUCTION

Materials management has been around since the beginnings of time. Efficiency follows function in every process, including material management. It is a sure bet that the cavemen developed and evolved systems for efficiency in procuring food for their survival. It is not much different today. Materials professionals are still developing methods to increase the effectiveness and efficiency of the supply-chain flow. The hunting ground just seems to be getting bigger and bigger! Recently, this evolution has been referred to as "lean" but the idea of lean is not really new. Forty years ago George Plossl and Oli Wight, the fathers of "modern day" materials management, started chapter 1 of their book, *Production and Inventory Control* (Prentice Hall 1967), with this list:

> *Three of the major objectives in most manufacturing firms intent on earning profit are: 1. Maximum customer service; 2. Minimum inventory investment; 3. Efficient (low cost) plant operations.*

They further stated that "the major problem in meeting these objectives is that they are basically in conflict." That statement suggests that they might not have had a total understanding in those early days of "modern day" materials management.

I am not sure we would all agree with that conjecture today. The conflicts are not as obvious when getting under the hood and starting to understand the underpinnings of lean materials management. As many have found, process improvements are often free and result in higher margins for products produced. Not much conflict rising out of these opportunities from today's viewpoint!

## HISTORY

Materials management started out as part of the production manager's function. It was imperative for managers to understand the location of the needed components to finish their required schedules. Without some tracking and knowledge of the supply-chain activities, there was little chance of timely success. Henry Ford was probably one of the first managers to get a tight handle on his supply chain. He was in the lean material space and didn't even know it. His approach was vertical integration, which was an advantage in those early days. "The thing is to keep everything in motion and take work to the man and not man to the work. That is the real principle of our production, and conveyors are only one of many means to an end" (*Today and Tomorrow*, Henry Ford, 1926, reprint Productivity Press 1988). Ford continues, "The motor block is the heaviest casting used in the car. It was formally manufactured at Highland Park, but it was a waste to transport these castings to Highland Park and then ship the completed motors out by rail to the branches past the very gates of Fordson." So what did he do? He transferred the motor assembly to Fordson, putting it in a building 800 by 600 feet where there were four main assembly lines or conveyors. The process of making the motors became continuous. He knew the concepts of lean materials management in the early 1900s. Toyota Production System (TPS) experts have acknowledged the thinking of Henry Ford more than once. This early concept of the conveyor belt bringing material to the worker is precisely the concept behind lean materials management. Add to it the additional process of building only what is required for customer consumption, and waste becomes a lesser evil.

Jumping ahead to the 1980s, the Japanese influence gives rise to new thinking in the material management space with the concept of just-in-time (JIT) material. Kanban systems were introduced as methods to allow rapid communication between suppliers and users/customers for material movement and to supply demand fitted exactly to the need. This eliminated much of the waste created by stocking inventory on forecasted requirements. This new thinking, made famous by Toyota, migrated the Western thinking that only a few containers meant too little inventory to the Toyota view that if many containers existed, it meant too much inventory! This was truly revolutionary in the 1980s. Few North American manufacturing organizations at that point fully recognized this opportunity.

In the West there was another revolution starting—the rise of the computer. Material Requirements Planning (MRP), invented in the 1970s, was evolving and developing in the 1980s and would greatly influence the planning of material flow and materials management. Although a far cry from today's definition of lean materials management, MRP, nonetheless, did help eliminate a tremendous amount of inventory in most production facilities. It might now be said that in those early days, MRP helped businesses go from absolutely no material control to bad control! It was a huge jump forward, however.

According to the *Production and Inventory Control Handbook* (James H. Greene, 1987; p. 4.2), MRP was used first by J. I. Case, Twin Disc, Black & Decker, and Perkins-Elmer. According to this text, the American Production and Inventory Control Society (APICS) and a few pioneer organizations started the MRP revolution in the early 1970s. MRP was a simple idea. Bills of material (BOMs) that defined the recipes of the products created the requirements. Inventory records were then accessed and requirement quantities netted against available balances. Using the MRP software, the delta between requirements and on-hand balances generated signals for purchase orders and shop orders.

This innovation slowly led to a greater use of centralized computers and more controls built into manufacturing and planning systems. Manufacturing Resource Planning (MRP II) methods were next in the evolution. MRP II happened as many evolutions do—from need. Humans often do not change radically unless forced to in some manner. In the 1980s, manufacturing was forced in a big way. Interest rates were sky rocketing and businesses were getting pressure from many fronts. Competition from other parts of the world was becoming more real and prices reflected it. This included some of the Japanese companies that were learning to build unheard-of quality into their processes. The need to cut costs and, therefore, become more competitive drove materials management professionals to look for better and more efficient methods to plan material deliveries. It wasn't just for the sake of continuous improvement; it was a matter of survival. This effort led to more discipline on data inputs and files accuracy. According to the *Production and Inventory Control Handbook* (Greene, 1987; p. 4.8), the acronym MRP II was first documented in *Modern Material Handling* in 1979. The article described activities going on in Tennant, Twin Disc, and Hewlett-Packard as integrating their financial and operational processes.

Standards of excellence within the planning processes were also developed in this period. The term Class A MRP II had become a desired recognition, and consultants like the Oliver Wight group were building businesses on Class A MRP II process with its corresponding certification. The early certifications only required that a handful of operational metrics be at 90% performance or higher. Crude, and not close to today's required competitive standards, it was one of the first definitions of high performance in the materials management space.

Materials management had changed course forever by this point. There was no going back to the days of unrecognized waste. The new emphasis had begun— make only what is needed and clearly define those needs. Those businesses were still a long way from lean, but they were getting closer. In the 1980s, because of cost constraints and competitive pressure, businesses placed more emphasis in the areas of capacity planning and increased scheduling disciplines. It was getting more and more important to build and to stock the right inventory.

With the success of Toyota penetrating Western markets in the 1980s, the world took notice of the techniques that had been evolving in Asia. The late Dr. Shigeo Shingo was one of the more important figures to revolutionize the management of production and materials. With the introduction of Single Minute Exchange of Die (SMED), many methods of lot sizing, specifically Economic Order Quantity (EOQ), became obsolete. Although some companies recognized this in the 1980s, realistically it was well into the 1990s before Western manufacturing fully understood this fact. Again, it was only through being forced into change. Competition forced major changes in thinking. The word "can't" was being tested continuously.

In the twenty-first century it is fully recognized that not only is lean materials control necessary but so is change. Without continuous improvement, companies cannot stay ahead of their competitors or, in some cases, even stay with them! Without keeping material moving into the process, and at the same time limiting the unnecessary movement, maximum efficiency is unrealistic. It sounds like manufacturing has come full circle with Henry Ford—same ideas, just at a higher level of performance expectation.

## ENTERPRISE RESOURCE PLANNING

Through normal process evolution and help from software providers and their marketing efforts, MRP II became Enterprise Resource Planning (ERP) in the 1990s. It was acknowledged that times were changing and, therefore, acronyms needed to change also. Normal ratcheting of requirements and expectations led to the upgrading of MRP II methodology. This transformation in name did not take long once started. High-performance standards followed quickly on the heels of Class A MRP II. Naturally, the scope of the Class A performance standard grew with the competitive pressures, and because the market was asking for ERP rather than MRP II, Class A MRP II upgraded its moniker to Class A ERP in the late 1990s.

The ERP model encompassed the entire business model, including linkage to the supply chain through to the customer (figure 1.1). Materials management, especially lean material management, was a critical part of the ERP business

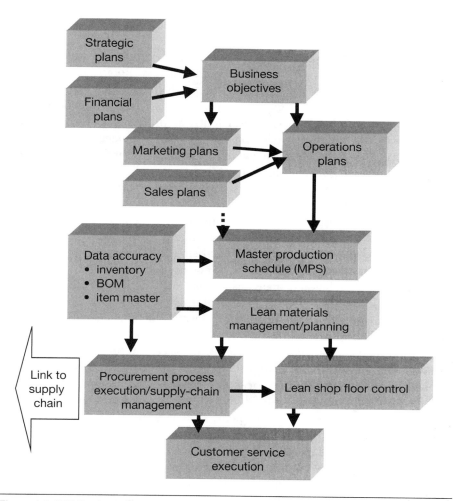

**Figure 1.1** ERP Business System Model

model. Although developing throughout the 1990s, it was late in that decade when lean materials management started defining the new role of MRP and the Toyota principles of lean manufacturing.

ERP today is often confused with software. APICS defines ERP as both process and software. Some argue with the software part of the definition, stating that software is only the planning enabler and that good ERP process starts and ends with robust process design, dependable management systems and disciplines, and repeatable execution. Lean materials management cannot be divorced from any of those keys. It is part and parcel of good ERP performance. Starting with top management planning and following through to customer satisfaction, materials management is in the middle of the fray.

When organizations do a good job with ERP execution, the materials management is at the center of the planning and success. Robust ERP execution encourages top management to have well-mapped strategies, including markets, products, and inventory strategy (e.g., make to stock, make to order), and have capacity and capital plans in place as well. Materials professionals within the business facilitate the inventory decisions by providing models and proposals. Following closely, the handshake between the demand side and the supply side of the business must risk-manage the commitment of supply-chain resource. Again, the materials management is involved because proposals to position inventory are usually suggested for scrutinization during these planning sessions. In some organizations the master scheduler organizationally reports to the materials group and, in those organizations, materials management owns the show from proposal to execution. Only approval and associated adjustments are outside their roles. In ERP environments this comes as no surprise. After all, the "P" in ERP does stand for planning and materials management is the planning center for manufacturing organizations.

The top management planning process during which the demand and supply sides of the business meet once a month for risk assessment and analysis is called the Sales and Operations Planning (S&OP) or Sales, Inventory and Operations Planning (SIOP) or even Production, Sales and Inventory (PSI) process by most companies. The master scheduler, or sometimes the materials manager, normally prepares the S&OP formats and data for the meeting. Metrics are reviewed to determine the accuracy of previous plans so that adjustments can be made to improve the predictability of the process and to minimize risks. The results of this planning process are 12-month rolling requirements that drive supply-chain signals for the next 30 days until the team gets together for a follow-up review. It is an age-old proven process in all high-performance organizations and the materials management is in the middle of it. Chapter 7 details the S&OP process and the mechanics behind it.

Once the S&OP process has authorized the supply-chain risk, the master schedule in an ERP process is released, sending the new 12-month rolling updates to the connected world through the materials plans and supply-chain links. Today this is often executed through secure and confidential web pages designed to give access and information to key suppliers and partners several times a day. Information includes forecasts of shipments, configurations of model breakdown and, often, existing stock for materials provided by that particular supplier. In less sophisticated web links, only the unit build forecast is shown (figure 1.2). This web information is the result of materials management activities. Depending on the level of detail, it is either an output of the master schedule or an output of

| Company XYZ | | Web-Based Requirements Sharing for Supplier 4577 — Date: Dec. 28 20XX | | | | | | | | | | | | | |
|---|---|---|---|---|---|---|---|---|---|---|---|---|---|---|---|
| Model | Jan Wk1 | Wk2 | Wk3 | Wk4 | Feb | Mar | Apr | May | Jun | Jul | Aug | Sep | Oct | Nov | Dec |
| ABC | 45 | 24 | 56 | 75 | 250 | 255 | 270 | 250 | 240 | 250 | 256 | 278 | 255 | 150 | 175 |
| BCD | 65 | 44 | 60 | 75 | 280 | 285 | 280 | 280 | 280 | 280 | 286 | 278 | 288 | 210 | 225 |
| DEF | 42 | 22 | 52 | 72 | 222 | 220 | 230 | 233 | 222 | 232 | 234 | 245 | 232 | 250 | 275 |
| FGH | 55 | 54 | 46 | 55 | 223 | 222 | 223 | 220 | 223 | 224 | 223 | 222 | 223 | 220 | 225 |
| LMN | 5 | 4 | 6 | 7 | 20 | 25 | 20 | 20 | 20 | 20 | 26 | 27 | 25 | 25 | 25 |

**Figure 1.2** Weekly Web-Based Communication Example

MRP. The format can be in weeks (figure 1.2), days, or even hours in some supply chains, depending on the quantities and tightness of inventory control. The detailed schedule information in SKU format would be a separate feed. In some arrangements there is only one communication, the detailed version.

There is no generic right or wrong way to communicate direction to the supply chain in an ERP environment, but it must be in the correct level of detail for the market and environment. In the automotive supply chain, the details could be communicated in hours; in other supply chains, days could be enough; still others forecast in weeks and months; however, the detailed schedule is generated in days and communicated separately. In one appliance manufacturing environment, the drumbeat is communicated each day on a web tool with requirements stated in hours. In this same environment, the 12-month rolling (long term) plans change once a month but the detailed (short term) plans are updated hourly. Several of the ERP linkages that must happen in high-performance companies have now been described (figure 1.3).

Once the link is made to the supplier, the process flow has only begun. There are still numerous communications and controls required in a high-performance ERP process. The next link is to the shop floor, both internal and to the supplier's shop. Lean is a more recognizable element in this section of the ERP model. Here, we might not use web-based tools. Simpler tools, including visible factory boards, kanban cards, lines painted on the floors, or limited rack size can be utilized. Now, lean materials management gets exciting and fun! More detailed information is found in the next chapter, but right now the objective is to continue to map the ERP process. Think for a minute about where we are in the process discussion. If looking at this from the perspective of the customer, we would be communicating the signal to the supply chain. What about when we are the supplier in the

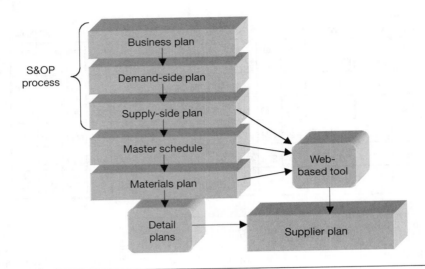

**Figure 1.3** Linkages in ERP Process

transaction? The perspective now becomes a customer signal through the demand side of the process map and the ERP business model starts from the top again. It doesn't stop until the supply chain comes to the consumer product. Everything starts with dirt and ends up a consumer product! *Some would argue that the consumer product often ends up back to dirt. At least the biodegradable ones do!* Think of it. All supply chains start with raw materials which usually involve chemicals (dirt related) or elements (found in dirt) or plants (plants get nutrition from dirt) or animals (animals connect down the food chain eventually to plant eaters or plants and, of course, dirt). ERP encompasses all of that activity through the entire food chain from dirt to dirt! Understanding lean methodology allows that massive energy expenditure to be as efficient as possible.

ERP is the model that all businesses follow throughout the supply chain. Some do it better than others, of course. Some do it and wouldn't admit it because they are not all that versed in the formalities. Lean is often substituted for a business model. Lean and ERP are not of the same genus and species. One (ERP) is a process model; the other (lean) is a tool and/or focus. Lean ERP is the high-performance organizations' focus. In these organizations, lean materials management is making improvements to the process and increasing performance through the supply chain. It is from this perspective that the discussion on lean materials management is built. Good manufacturing process requires the elements of ERP—top management planning, demand and operations planning, master scheduling, material planning and execution. Done in the most competitive format, a lean process focus is evident in each step of the ERP process model.

## LEAN AND MATERIALS MANAGEMENT DEFINED

Lean, as a performance term, has been around for several decades. One early definition of lean describes it as a generic process management philosophy derived mostly from the TPS and renowned for its focus on reduction of the original Toyota "seven wastes" to improve overall customer value. Another definition is the focus upon implementing "flow" or smoothness of work through the system rather than upon waste. Perhaps authors James Womack and Daniel Jones are most responsible for popularizing the lean principles in their landmark texts. Recently, other authors, including Dennis Hobbs, have shown readers how to implement lean effectively in a manufacturing environment to the extent that it is feasible to do so in a single text. So what is lean? The word lean means different things to different people. At the strategic level, lean is a business philosophy. Lean also refers to a set of practices and principles implemented to eliminate waste. And lean is used to describe specific lean tools. The reality is that lean has several different meanings depending upon your particular perspective. The perspective conveyed throughout this book is how it can be used to improve materials management.

So what is materials management? Materials management is the process of aligning components with process to meet customer need. Sounds easy but it is not as easy as it sounds. Many professionals have started their careers in materials to find out that there are less demanding positions to their liking. Production control is often the stepping-stone to materials, and, to the best performers, other opportunities usually develop from there. With a few exceptions, most materials people do not retire as production control or materials managers but end up in higher leadership positions. Materials management seems to be a good learning position. Oli Wight's poem, "Production Control Experts," written several years ago ended:

> *Materials management*
> *Is a concept to which I'm devoted—*
> *Instead of learning production control,*
> *I've escaped and getting promoted!*
>
> *So study each book and seminar,*
> *Attend every one you can, sir!*
> *You'll find a thousand experts*
> *—each with PART of the answer.*

Getting it right requires skill, knowledge, business savvy, and, most importantly, creativity. With the speed of communications and associated sharing of information, barriers to new performance levels are being dismantled continuously. The best lean materials managers today are not using ideas in proven ways; they are constantly using proven ideas in new ways. This might include faster processes, quicker response, improved visibility into the customer's requirements, or better organization of resources. It nearly always includes fewer finished goods as compared to just a few years ago. The Internet has opened up avenues for resource alignment that are only now beginning to be understood. The materials manager now has more respect in manufacturing than any time in the past. The creativity that can be applied to the availability of materials can give significant competitive advantage to suppliers as well as their customers. Being able to react in short time frames to customer-specific requirements can set a company apart from others in the market. In some cases, it not only ensures market share but increases margin and shareholder equity. Not small feats in this fast-moving world.

In the next chapter, techniques are discussed along with examples of how some companies have taken advantage of their creativity and supply-chain prowess to build walls that their competition has to climb over. Companies like Dell and Toyota have changed the supply-chain landscape, and those who listen and apply the logic are seeing great benefits. Materials management is a significant contributor to the bottom line in today's environment. No wonder there is so much water cooler talk about lean thinking and how it can be used in materials management.

## DISCUSSION QUESTIONS

1. Who is most often given credit for being the "father(s)" of modern day materials management?
   a. Henry Ford
   b. George Plossl
   c. Oli Wight
   d. b and c
   e. all of the above

2. What car manufacturer first started the concepts behind lean thinking?
   a. Toyota
   b. General Motors
   c. Ford Motors
   d. American Motors

3. Kanban is a method for
   a. reducing the time to transport components from plant to customer.
   b. signaling replenishment of inventory.
   c. decreasing changeover time.
   d. all of the above

4. MRP was invented in what period?
   a. 1960s
   b. 1970s
   c. 1980s
   d. 1990s

5. What manager was given the most recognition for the development of SMED?
   a. Henry Ford
   b. George Plossl
   c. Dr. Shigeo Shingo
   d. none of the above

6. SMED stands for
   a. Simple Manufacturing Execution and Demand.
   b. Society for Manufacturing Engineers and Design.
   c. Single Minute Exchange of Die.
   d. Simple and Minimized Engineering Design.
   e. none of the above

7. EOQ is
   a. used in service parts planning only.
   b. used in machine shops only.
   c. used in all businesses.
   d. often referred to as obsolete.

8. APICS says ERP is
   a. software to manage a business.
   b. the process of planning and executing a business plan.
   c. often referred to as obsolete.
   d. a and b

9. The ERP business model starts with
   a. business planning.
   b. master scheduling.
   c. MRP.
   d. a mission statement.

10. S&OP is also known as
    a. SIOP.
    b. PSI.
    c. MSI.
    d. a and b
    e. none of the above

11. An example of inventory strategy is
    a. MTO.
    b. MTS.
    c. ATO.
    d. a and b
    e. all of the above

# 2

# APPLYING LEAN TO THE PLANNING PROCESS AND HOW IT AFFECTS MATERIALS PLANNING

## INTRODUCTION

Lean approaches to process improvement are found throughout well-managed businesses today. It is just the way good businesses are run. Materials management is no exception. The opportunities for the use of the lean approach are numerous and frequent. The lean terminology most often used in materials management and supply-chain direction is discussed first. This terminology list includes: pull systems, 5-S, kanban, kaizen, and Single Minute Exchange of Die. These execution processes are only as effective as the overall planning process. To be 100% effective, even robust lean execution processes require good planning methodology as prerequisites although it is not often acknowledged in the lean "production"-centered books (as opposed to materials planning books). Materials and supply-chain management adds a whole new element to the production execution equation for success.

## PULL SYSTEMS AND PLANNING

The term "pull system" refers to the way that the material requirement system generates the signal for material to move. Pull systems have been around for a long time. Logically, pull systems are what we use when we start out to build something and procure after the fact. Say we are going to plan a New Year's Eve party. The pull system is the customer requirements for the party. This drives the decisions of what to kit in preparation for the party. Some items need to be there at the last minute (such as chicken wings and pizza ordered from the local deli) and some can arrive earlier but still are not ordered until we have a final decision on the timing and number of guests. The "pull" is the last-minute signal to order and pick up the wings or to go to the store to buy the crackers and cheese. The pull signal can also be characterized by the initial invitation signal sent to guests. The lean production-oriented books always talk about the trips and signals to the store, but a robust planning process is also required for optimum performance. Without a plan to have the party, the lean pull systems would not work effectively. Additionally, the deli needs to know that on New Year's Eve there is typically more demand for wings than on any random weeknight. This might appear to be obvious, but in manufacturing there are many signals to manage, and the more that are clear and timely, the more effective the results will be. Most businesses have highs and lows in demand. Planning for these is a major step in the preparation for successful lean execution. The requirements for good planning are described throughout this book. In chapter 4, the descriptions of a good master scheduling process support this planning requirement, as do chapters 8 and 9 on Sales and Operations Planning (S&OP) and demand management. First, discussion focuses on the lean methods and how they can be an integral part of the materials management process. The first is the famous 5-S approach that came from early Toyota Production Systems work.

## 5-S

The 5-S approach was developed in Japan and came from the early Toyota Production System (TPS) work. It is an approach to organization and housekeeping. It was originally applied to the production floor, and later office areas, to achieve improved levels of organization and cleanliness. Initially, the focus was on quality improvements driven by the Toyota discovery that most quality issues stem back to safety, organization, and neatness. Like many simple ideas, 5-S has now transitioned into many other applications, including materials management (figure 2.1).

Starting with the premise that quality often circles back to a lack of organization and neatness, it is not a difficult transition to the belief that opportunity in lean materials management lies in these concepts also.

1. **Seri (sort)**—Materials management is constantly dealing with the issues associated with the complex and changing environment of requirements and customer needs. Engineering changes are commonplace, as are specialized requirements for key customers. Good

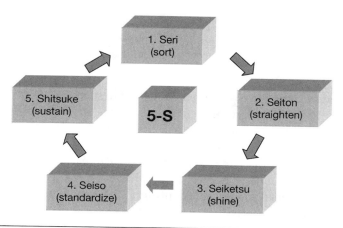

**Figure 2.1** 5-S

materials management practice includes sorting of materials into categories. The application of the ABC stratification is such an example. Taking the inventory requirements and sorting them by criticality and value results in improved cost effectiveness. Sorting of data might be even more important to the materials manager. This includes good query tools, reports, and access to information for proper sorting. Tools like Cognos®, and other measurement dashboard assists, are becoming required tools of the materials professionals and their organizations. *Any organization that has not dedicated resources and the time to ease the process of sorting data to give flexibility to the materials organization for problem solving and improvement is missing the boat!*

Deal with obsolete materials as they are determined. When materials are rejected or otherwise sidelined, good materials managers use this as a trigger for action. One organization I worked with in China allowed only 4 hours to lapse before rejected material had to be disposed. If the 4-hour mark passed, the plant manager and engineering manager were summoned, and the problem was resolved immediately. This immediate attention was helpful from many angles. It limited the impact, maintained awareness, and kept management keenly involved.

There are various applications for the philosophy of keeping items sorted. Inventory is probably the best example. Good warehouse operations manage units by location, not total quantity. Golden zoning is a structure designed to ensure that the units are in the right location. This might include considerations such as: ergonomics (having items at arm's reach) and efficiency (having the fastest moving items closest to the door and moving obsolete items out of the way altogether).

2. **Seiton (straighten)**—Closely associated to sorting is the straightening of the areas, inventory, and data. There are numerous applications in the lean material management space for this topic. One of the most important is material storage. In lean materials management application, inventory is minimized. Space is limited and needs to be utilized properly. When there is any storage required, it is straightened and is located only in the designated area. When lines are painted on the floor, they are there for a reason. The business should follow the rules or change the lines. Figure 2.2 shows pallets out of place, which is an example of how *not* to keep areas straightened.

    The order of things is a sign of how much importance is placed on discipline. Materials managers that have (sometimes) hundreds of suppliers and a dependency of thousands of component requirements have to be organized. Playing by the rules is the only way items throughout the business stay straight. When entering a business, we can tell a great deal about the management there by these signs. In figure 2.3, the rolls are in order and lined up. It does not take any longer to set them down in line than to do it haphazardly.

    Shadow boards are another method for orderly supplies, tools, and other needed items. In areas where tools are stored, it is especially important to keep areas neat. In figure 2.4, it is easy to see that some tools are missing by the black background outline.

3. **Seiketsu (shine)**—The third "S" focuses on cleanliness. The spirit of this message is not just cleanliness but tenacity surrounding the goals of cleanliness. This culture-changing characteristic is only found in the best of the best organizations. When materials managers insist on this model within the warehouse, stores, and point-of-use inventory areas, the result is better control throughout the supply chain, and it rubs off on the supporting activities. In one Indianapolis warehouse, I worked with the manager, and Henry was a stickler for cleanliness. This 500,000-square-foot warehouse floor was always shiny (figure 2.5). Although not a great idea, it was so clean that one could actually consider eating off the floor! When asked how his group was able to keep it so clean, he responded, "It's

**Figure 2.2** Pallets Out of Line — Not Following 5-S

**Figure 2.3** Pallets in Line — Following 5-S

**Figure 2.4** Shadow Board Used for Tool Storage

easy, we clean the entire warehouse floor twice every day." Some suggest that that kind of tenacity is a waste. He argued that it was part of the reason his operation was one of the most cost-effective warehouses in the company. It is probably not a good idea to argue with him!

In this example, the standards are higher than many other warehouses, but this is exactly the spirit of the Japanese meaning behind seiketsu. Without high expectations, the discipline is no better than an average facility. The best operations lower cost by having the expectations higher than normal and having the maintenance of these standards completed simply as part of the daily routine, which leads us into the fourth S, seiso.

4. **Seiso (standardize)**—How do materials managers get their organizations to implement the 5-Ss with rigor? The good ones create a standard that expects it. Managers must walk the talk. The objectives and metrics around housekeeping and workplace organization must be the same in all departments and functions within the organization. Label and color-code items that are important in the process focus. Having fire extinguisher locations designated with red and white arrows hung at certain distances is one such indicator. In the warehouse, different container sizes might have different but consistent colors for easy identification. One warehouse had some items

**Figure 2.5** Indianapolis Warehouse

stored in multi-packs (e.g., 10 in a box). Wherever items were multi-packed, the pallet was painted red to help minimize mistakes. Another example has been adopted by several companies. Inventory accuracy measurement data hangs in each controlled area on standardized performance boards. Many have the picture of the process owner included on the board for that controlled area. Standardizing process makes it easy for everyone to comply. There must also be management systems in place that ensure this sustainability, which leads us to the final "S."

5. **Shitsuke (sustain)**—Once process improvement has occurred, it becomes of utmost importance to maintain or sustain the improvement. There are several keys to remember. The most prominent management system is probably documentation. Nobody likes paperwork, but if process is to be repeated, each player in the process needs to thoroughly understand the process the same. This can only happen if it is written down. Every player has his/her own experience filter through which he/she screens his/her activities. These filters are a result of varying experiences in each player's past. Procedure interpretations result from these experiences and it becomes difficult to maintain consistency after variations on habits have developed from these "filtered" procedures.

The next shitsuke consideration after documentation is accountability management systems or infrastructure. When expectations are assigned and detailed to monthly, weekly, and daily (and in some cases hourly) buckets, the organization moves closer to autopilot. Each daily schedule, for example, needs to generate acute awareness. If emphasis is on schedule accuracy, accountability is easily achieved by requiring the process owner(s) to report variation and actions to eliminate barriers to high performance each day. Other management systems are weekly performance reviews attended by the plant manager or another upper manager in the organization. These management systems are key to establishing a culture of continuous improvement and discipline. Lean materials management cannot excel without such management systems driving sustainability and improvements. Chapter 13 is dedicated to describing the management systems associated with scheduling.

This is only an introduction to the 5-S idea. The successful lean materials manager incorporates this concept into all activities. This includes data organization, office housekeeping, as well as measurements and management systems with the supply chain and factory. Good materials managers educate their workforce and staff for a clear understanding of the 5-S principles. This pays off in reaching higher levels of discipline and efficient execution.

## Red-Tagging

One of the more effective methods of getting an area cleaned up initially for the new housekeeping model is to red-tag everything that is not used. The criteria can vary, but a common rule is to red-tag items not used in the last 6 months. If this does not move enough, try 3 months as the window of acceptability. When these objects (tools, equipment, furniture, parts, components, garbage, rags) are tagged, they are moved to a common area for disposition. Management has 15 days to evaluate the worth and then the items are thrown out, sold, or donated to a local charity. One organization I worked with used to have silent employee auctions. In these auctions, employees had the opportunity to make a secret-entry bid for an item. The highest bidder got the item and had 2 days to settle up and remove the item. A red-tagging practice is beneficial because it emphasizes the need to have only useful and required tools and equipment at the work area.

Items that are used infrequently are often taken out of the immediate work area and pulled as needed. This allows the maximum efficiency of the workspace and supports the culture of best-in-class housekeeping and workplace organization.

## Kanban

It is doubtful that there are any materials managers left in the industrialized countries that have not heard of kanban. Most of them have probably used it in at least a few applications. That probability is a testament to the influence Toyota has had on the manufacturing world. Kanban is a pull system triggered by a signal, either from a card, a light sometimes called an andon ("lantern" in Japanese), a transfer mechanism, or other signal device. Kanban is the simplest and most important idea the lean materials managers need to incorporate into their systems designs. In one plant in Brandford, Ontario, Canada, the entire process flow is driven by a drop area kanban. Utilizing squares painted on the factory floor, inventory is "pulled" into each process step by available space within the square: fabrication fills the square in the next process, welding; welding fills a square for assembly. Over time, by controlling the size of the square, the inventory can be weaned down to almost no buffer between operations. In still other operations, there is no buffer at all. The trigger for material movement is the movement of the unit ahead. When one moves, the next one takes its place.

Kanban is an idea that works on nearly every level. Most organizations have abandoned material planning on fasteners that have them in their bill of material (BOM). Instead, bins are placed at point of use sized for the appropriate amount of inventory for a few hours or a few days of assembly. For example, longer bolts would have larger bins. Often, since hardware items are not normally manufactured by the assembly plants, the hardware is brought to the point of use by the supplier. This can happen daily, weekly, or once every other week, depending on the size and amount of hardware required. The supplier can either invoice each month or the assembly plant can simply send a check for the amount of hardware required in the BOM for the amount of product shipped out the door that month. Obviously, ample trust needs to be built between the supplier and the assembler in most of these scenarios; therefore, the best lean materials managers are continuously building these relationships with the right suppliers.

This relationship goes well beyond fasteners and hardware. Other easily administered items include packaging, paint, raw materials, and even finished-goods storage. A plant in Somerville, Massachusetts, eliminated $70,000 of corrugated packaging by having the materials delivered and loaded into the trailer in the same sequence and quantity as the customer's master schedule. Materials were delivered twice a week; the trailer simply backed up to the dock and the packaging materials were not unloaded from the trailer until they were needed. At the end of the third day the trailer was unloaded, and the next trailer was ready and waiting. I do not know how many times I have been told by clients that corrugated suppliers will not deliver to the master production schedule (MPS). I know several that do.

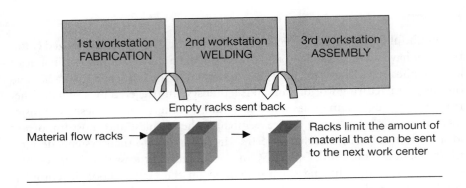

**Figure 2.6** Fixed Cart Kanban

Another company near Binghamton, New York, uses a trucking company to consolidate loads to its customers. Products are manufactured and "shipped" by having a local trucking company pick up the materials and hold them for full truckload quantities. The customers have agreed to this process to save freight and everybody wins: the manufacturer, the trucking company, and the customer. Obviously this does not work in every situation but it is the use and application of these simple ideas to the environment that creates competitive advantage. Good materials managers look for these opportunities to use new ideas and old ideas in new ways.

Many companies have adopted the fixed cart pull system in which material carts or racks facilitate specific, controlled amounts of inventory. If there are 3 racks that hold 10 parts each, only 30 pieces can be in the process as buffer at one time. When the racks are full, the supply line has to hold up further production until a rack is empty (figure 2.6).

This works much like the drop area kanban, but the limiting factor is the cart size instead of the floor space designated for the buffer. The 2-bin pull system is closely related to the fixed cart kanban system and is frequently used in hardware applications. The size of buffer, like most kanban systems, is limited easily by the size of the storage area. In this case, the buffer size is determined by sizing the tote pans or storage bins that are allowed. Take, for example, a company that has hardware required in an assembly operation, including nuts, bolts, and washers. If, for example, quarter-twenty nuts were a popular item used frequently in assembly, the bin size might be larger so that it could hold a couple days' supply of nuts. When the bin is empty, it is forwarded on to the supplier; a second bin, located behind the first, begins feeding required consumption. The empty bin is filled by the supplier, returned to the area, and is ready for the next kanban signal (figure 2.7).

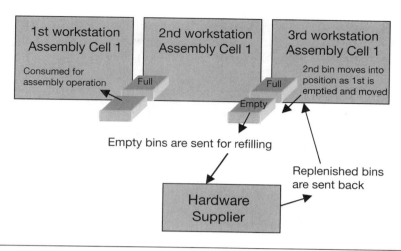

**Figure 2.7** 2-Bin Kanban

Perhaps the most popular form of kanban is the pull system card. In this kanban variation, a card is held in the area with the buffer inventory. At some pre-arranged point in the buffer consumption, the card becomes a trigger to the supplier to send the next container. If there is transportation time required during the replenishment process, the card surfaces in the assembly process in a timely manner so that there is enough inventory left to make it through to replenishment. Sometimes it is a card stuck on the top of the last bin (similar to the 2-bin system) or it might be at the bottom of each part bin and is sent as the bin is emptied. There are many possibilities for kanban usage. It is not used only with "C" items such as hardware. Kanban pull cards also work to limit expensive items on the floor. In an assemble-to-order scenario, one of each possible configuration component might be stored and triggered at the point of consumption for replenishment. It is helpful for limiting costly inventory and, accordingly, lead time for the customer.

## MRP AND LEAN PULL SYSTEMS

Why would Material Requirement Planning (MRP) even be needed if pull systems are in place? A friend of mine, John Darlington (whom I met while working in Cheadle, England), a disciple of Eli Goldratt and the "Theory of Constraints," many years ago wrote an article describing MRP as a dying process. We have had several friendly debates about it although we have never actually worked together on a project. The evidence might suggest that he was either wrong or way ahead of his time because MRP is still alive and well! Like most applications, MRP's use

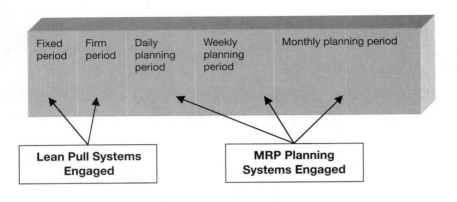

**Figure 2.8** Lean versus MRP Application

has evolved. MRP used to be the heart of both the planning and the execution processes. Today, it might be described more accurately as a planning tool. Lean has moved in on the execution space in most high-performance organizations (figure 2.8).

The reasons are obvious. Lean pull systems are reactionary. This is acceptable within the shorter-term requirements and when the lead time is short. In many businesses there are longer lead time components that require some planning prior to the receipt of the customer order. When this is the case, there is little choice except to plan for materials prior to the actual customer purchase order (PO) (figure 2.9). This stocking process is usually referred to as inventory strategy. In reality, the inventory does not have to be brought into the facility prior to the customer PO. Instead, the actual pull signal can be the driver of final action. This fits the reactionary lean pull systems scenario and becomes a cost-effective process. MRP is not dead; it is just not as valuable to the process after the PO has been received from the customer or as the ship date closes in. In the "old days" MRP, using the BOM, would bring the components in based on planned dates. Often these dates would be inaccurate and excess inventory would result. The best of all worlds is to utilize both lean pull signals and MRP.

How much inventory and where it is in the process is driven more by market need as compared to the lead time of the process than it is by dictates from management. The lean process role and application is to drive the process steps to shorter, more flexible reactions. The more this is done, the more planned inventory can be converted to planned signals, in effect, transforming make to stock (MTS) or assemble to order (ATO) to make to order (MTO) or engineer to order (ETO). When MTO inventory strategy falls into the acceptable market lead time, inventory investment decreases.

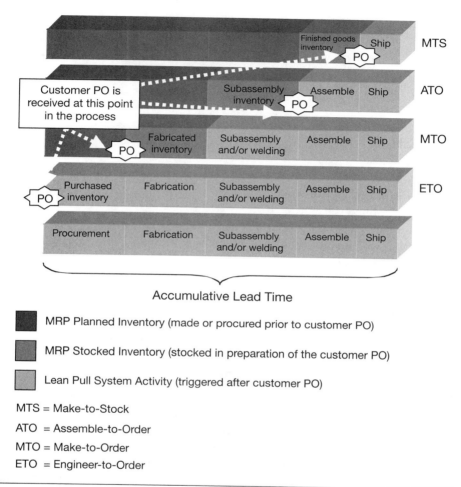

**Figure 2.9** Inventory Strategy

## WASTE IN MATERIALS MANAGEMENT

Lean is both a methodology and a performance goal. With the focus almost entirely on elimination of waste and increasing flexibility and speed, lean thinking starts from the premise that there is waste all around us. There is probably no more appropriate topic connecting lean to materials planning than through the topic of waste. Waste is the reason the lean methodology exists, and there is plenty of it to focus on in the materials field.

**Categories of Waste**
1. unnecessary material movement
2. unnecessary worker movement
3. space
4. time
5. material
   a. scrap
   b. rework
   c. lost
   d. damaged
   e. mistakenly ordered
   f. unnecessary
6. insufficient effort (poor quality)
   a. work quality
   b. material quality
   c. process design quality
   d. standards
7. untapped creativity and knowledge

When applying materials management aspects, lean certainly is an easy fit.

## Unnecessary Material Movement

Unnecessary material movement and the essence of materials management is found in nearly every corner of nearly every business. Starting with the premise that *any* material movement is an opportunity for the elimination of waste, ample opportunity arises. Many warehouses that examined forklift movement, for example, discovered that oftentimes the trucks are running empty. Also, the storage location of certain products makes a marked decrease in wasted movement. The management team at one manufacturer, where carousels were utilized for storage, discovered from studies that receipts and picks could be implemented on opposite ends of the carousel. This change eliminated several unnecessary moves. Some concurrent activity was also possible, decreasing lead time to pick and kit components. Of course, the most effective elimination of picking and kitting lead time results in storing the components in the cell where they are consumed.

## Unnecessary Worker Movement

Materials managers are often involved in kaizen events such as these, if not to facilitate then to initiate the training and scheduling. Cycle time is a key to flexibility and reaction time. Frequently, the shorter the cycle time, the less inventory

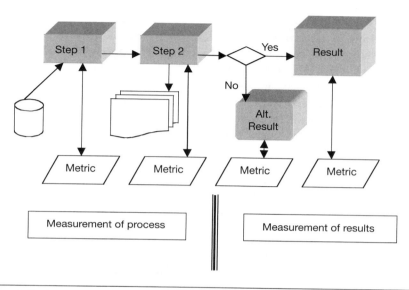

**Figure 2.10** Addressing Opportunity

is required because machine lines can react quickly to incoming orders. When a facility does hundreds of parts per day, just small increments of time per part can make a huge difference (figure 2.10).

Unnecessary worker movement is not limited to big movements such as walking or even a few steps. One of the greatest opportunities in manufacturing is the cycle time of machines driven by human triggers. Good materials managers watch for cycle times between machine strokes while walking through the shop. Watch the palm buttons. How long does it take between the end of the machine cycle and the trigger of the next cycle? What could be done to make it easier for the operator to start the cycle sooner? Often it has to do with required movement. This is not a case for harder work. This is a classic case of the opportunity for smarter work. People should not have to exert "all out, all day" for the process to be successful. As my father, Don Sr., always said, "Don't ask people to do something you wouldn't do yourself."

A plant experience in Kodama, Japan, is a good example of unnecessary worker movement. In this plant a machine was moved approximately 6 inches within a work cell to eliminate an arm movement that caused the worker to swivel in his stance. This small adjustment proved a significant advantage at the end of the day because several seconds were gained in the process. The icing on the cake included ergonomic advantages as well. Perhaps it would not be noticeable to the outside observer, but to them they had discovered real gold.

In the materials management environment there are extensive opportunities to witness unnecessary people movement in the warehouse environment, just as there is unnecessary material movement. Going to get paperwork, walking to the office from receiving, even in pick operations moving only horizontally and vertically can generate unnecessary time and movement, thus, diagonal movement can be less wasteful. Perhaps it requires the pick platforms to be moving up at the same time they are moving forward. It is done safely in many warehouse environments when the right equipment is utilized.

## Space

In the business in which I grew up, growth was a constant issue that created space issues. Once the decision to subcontract operations for capacity growth was made, the space constraint was eased. However, in the early years of growth the business thought that everything had to be done in-house. Every growth spurt in sales and new products brought the shifting of machinery and work cells to gain capacity. Space was at a premium all the time. That is pretty typical. Many times inventory is taking up a great deal of space in a facility. It is not uncommon for a manufacturing organization to have more than 25% of the available floor space dedicated to part storage. What a waste!

In most businesses today, inventory turns are a critical measurement reviewed by top management (usually at the monthly S&OP review). Investments in manufacturing space are not best utilized by piling inventory in it. This is not a new topic. Most companies have, at this point, realized that inventory is an opportunity. It is so not only because of the obvious cash requirements but also because of the space needed. There are many operations around the world that have outside warehouse space leased to take care of overflow. Many of these extra outside warehouse costs are opportunities, examples of waste waiting to be a focus of process improvement. Inventory strategy (MTS, ATO, MTO, and ETO), when planned and executed properly, can provide a huge advantage.

## Time

An important focus of lean, wasted time is a major element of materials planning, specifically scheduling. For the best utilization of equipment and schedules, downtime needs to be minimized. This includes setup or changeovers, machine repairs, unrealistic standards (both favorable and unfavorable), and absenteeism without backup support. Waiting for parts, tools, manpower, paperwork, or schedule direction is a terrible waste of time that happens in businesses every day.

Unnecessary meetings can eat up valuable time and resources. Additionally, it is especially wasteful when attendees show up late for meetings that are necessary.

How much time is wasted in your organization on unnecessary meetings or waiting for people to show up?

It might be said that wasted time is normally quite obvious in most organizations when we know where and how to look. I am amused when I go into factories that are running material long distances in the plant from some warehouse or from one functional department to another and yet still clock labor standards with a stopwatch. In my experience, it is both foolish and unnecessary. This is like throwing away dollars to save pennies! Wasted time is easily mapped. I prefer the mapping approach that uses real timelines and lists value-added activities on the top of the line and cost-add activities on the bottom. Putting the line on a large white board makes the exercise easier. Using yellow sticky pads works best for the activities. Normally the time units do not have to be seconds as would be the case with the stopwatch. Too many times, hours or even days are the starting point. With today's lean material managers looking for increases in flexibility and responsiveness, hours wasted is costly.

## Material

Although materials managers do not usually have direct control over scrap in the factory, scrap is a materials issue. Frequently, inventory planning is affected because of either unexpected scrap or scrap that was not properly transacted for in the process. The result, inflated balances and inventory shrink, can add to the waste in any operation and does not even address the waste that scrap represents. Data accuracy measures drive this to the surface early in the process. From the perspective of the experienced materials professional, lost or damaged materials do not go unnoticed when data accuracy measurements have proper accountability and management systems.

## Effort

Lost labor as a result of poor quality is quickly identified through proper first time quality (FTQ) measurements. Process design quality is one area that gets special attention through a BOM and a standards review often required in material organizations that set high standards. New product introduction is one of the most frequently abused processes resulting in wasted effort. High-performing organizations have strict disciplines on process gates, making sure inappropriate behavior is discovered and minimized in the process. Considering the risks and process variation normally associated with new product introduction, it is a worthwhile focus.

## Creativity and Knowledge

Creativity has always been an unrecognized manufacturing resource and, therefore, a waste opportunity. When we engage the entire materials workforce in problem solving, it becomes much more likely that good ideas will be generated. Creativity comes in many forms. Many, if not most, of the best ideas implemented in manufacturing businesses and materials departments are not ideas of management or engineering. A number of them are contributions from the people in the warehouse, the office, or on the factory floor. Engaging the entire workforce (from the head down—not just their backs) is a big step forward in driving improvement and waste elimination. Former Toyota Motor chairman Eiji Toyoda was quoted in Masaaki Imai's book, *Kaizen, The Key to Japan's Competitive Success* (McGraw Hill 1986): "One of the features of the Japanese workers is that they use their brains as well as their hands." Most of the suggestions made by workers are implemented at Toyota.

Most high-performance organizations today are engaged in some sort of project management focus. Six Sigma is a measurement of quality (3.4 defects in a million opportunities or a yield of 99.99966%), but the methodology is more than a measurement. Many organizations thus focused are engaged in project promotion. It requires that they prioritize efforts and engage all of their people in continuous improvement. Creativity comes from this engagement. Some people jump at the opportunity with little coaxing, while others need some form of invitation. When management offers that, less creativity is wasted. Too many organizations do not recognize the potential in this waste area. The key is performance improvement, however, not projects completed. I go into many organizations which describe themselves as focused on Six Sigma that are just that—focused on the Six Sigma program and losing sight of the reason for the program, which is quality, cost, and service improvement.

## KAIZEN

Getting the organization to engage in the elimination of waste is an important step in establishing a culture of continuous improvement. Toyota was one of the first organizations to introduce the world to a concept of focused and fast improvement. The Japanese call it kaizen, which means improvement. Materials management is a perfect opportunity for kaizen given the diversity of processes and systems expertise resident within most materials organizations. Materials management is responsible for the control of most of an organization's resources, including scheduling of the machine, process assets, and management of the inventory assets. The opportunity doesn't get much more obvious than that!

There are two generally practiced approaches to kaizen: the 1-day kaizen blitz (the most frequently used) and the week-long kaizen focus. The approach is very logical. There are two ways to focus on improvement: results only (payback) or from process (measures). Both are valid and should be put to use. Although the kaizen approach is used effectively in both areas of focus, generally it is used in the process focus. The best kaizen executions are ones that get into the details of a specific aspect of a process. Kaizen blitzes generally follow the 10,000-foot brainstorming session after the details of root cause are thoroughly understood. It could be said that kaizen events are generally more tactically related than strategic in nature but not exclusively.

## 1-Day Kaizen (Blitz)

Step 1—Identify the area of focus for the event. This might be a specific process within the warehouse or a piece of a process such as the data accuracy process for inventory and all its associated transactions. A good way to ensure an appropriate topic is to review the business priorities or business imperatives for the current year. Improvement topics should be directly linked to these objectives.

Step 2—Designate a team and team leader. The team needs to be the right team—people who know the process and are capable of making good decisions regarding its improvement. The team leader should be versed in problem-solving techniques such as process mapping and cost-add/value-add analysis. In Six Sigma organizations, the leader is typically a Six Sigma black belt.

Step 3—Define the charter. The charter describes time frame, scope of kaizen, objective of the event, and resources available.

Step 4—Schedule the event including support as required. Sometimes this impacts the MPS, requiring modifications. The event should be scheduled a few days in advance in case the team leader or team members require preparation time.

Step 5—Execute the 1-day kaizen. Each team member is expected to contribute to the problem-solving and improvement event. A 1-day kaizen needs only to be one shift. Usually if more than one shift is involved, the shifts work together, coming in on a shared-shift schedule for the event. Starting the day shift a couple hours late and ending a couple hours late works well.

Step 6—Document and otherwise control the process for ongoing gains. Even though the kaizen is a blitz, the results should be ongoing, which requires updated documentation.

Step 7—When the kaizen is successful, the results should be celebrated. Management should give plenty of accolades for a job well done.

Step 8—Plan the next improvement. Many times during the brainstorming session within the kaizen, some ideas are sidelined for later use. These become the opportunities for the next improvement effort either through kaizen or simply defined projects.

## The Week-Long Kaizen

The week-long kaizen is similar to the shorter version except the projects tackled can be more complex. The steps for a successful week-long kaizen are:

Step 1—Document the "is" condition. Understand the existing situation from a factual position. Map the process in question and look for all decision points, inputs and outputs.

Step 2—Identify waste in the process. Once the process is well-mapped, it is time to test for value-add versus cost-add activities.

Step 3—Brainstorm or otherwise find solutions. Look for alternatives to the existing system and test for favorable results.

Step 4—Analyze logic around the possible solutions. Evaluate the reasonability of solutions. Do preliminary pre-tests if possible.

Step 5—Implement the solution. Once solutions seem reasonable, implement and monitor.

Step 6—Verify the improvement. Once the new process changes are in place, make sure the results are as predicted.

Step 7—Measure the results. Always measure everything!

Step 8—Make this the new standard. Once confirmed as an improvement, document and assign ownership and accountability for the new process.

Step 9—Celebrate. Celebrations do not have to be big and elaborate. Just getting the kaizen team together for the acknowledgement of a good job is often enough to inspire future team effort.

Step 10—Initiate another kaizen event. Start the process over again. Team members should be changed. Those who like the format and want to join again are good people to engage. Some will be ready to get back to their old job and should be allowed to do so. Keep the membership rotating through the best players.

**Table 2.1 Effects of Cycle Time Reduction**

| No. of parts or assemblies produced weekly | Cycle time reduction per part | Total savings per week |
|---|---|---|
| 10 | 5 minutes | 50 minutes |
| 1000 | 10 seconds | 2.8 hours |
| 1000 | 75 seconds | 20.3 hours |
| 10000 | 2 seconds | 5.6 hours |
| 100000 | 0.5 second | 13.8 hours |

## Typical Kaizen Projects in Materials Management

There is an unending list of possibilities for kaizen events in materials management.

- Achieving single piece flow through a process
- Variability reduction kaizen using statistical problem-solving tools
- 5-S kaizen in the warehouse or materials office area
- Obsolete inventory focus for finding solutions for use-up
- Excessive inventory focus for finding alternative uses for this inventory
- Supplier visit kaizen for help with data accuracy or schedule adherence
- Cycle time reduction from order receipt to work being done on the factory floor (table 2.1)
- Engineering change system controls improvements
- Database management and accuracy
  - locations balances
  - BOM accuracy
  - routing record accuracy
  - lead time accuracy
  - standards accuracy
  - item master field accuracy
- Item master policy review
- Supplier certification design or improvements
- Supply chain management
- Customer service improvements

Some production (non-materials) kaizen events are helpful in supporting materials management interests. Setup reduction is always a big win for the material management folks as they can then reduce lot sizes and associated inventory as setups are shortened. This gives setup reduction a place in the materials management hit parade.

## SETUP REDUCTION/SINGLE MINUTE EXCHANGE OF DIE

Setup reduction is a major opportunity in nearly every manufacturing facility in the world! Also referred to as changeover reduction, this is a great focus area with almost unending potential. Manufacturing machines that convert product to salable goods are only making money when the processes and machines are actually converting needed product. Any time machines with customer-driven work to do are sitting idle, there is lost opportunity cost being incurred. If a machine is able to convert products in one hour that equate to profit when shipped, the machine is actually earning the profit for the company at that rate per hour. While the machine is in changeover and idled, no profit is produced; in fact, quite the opposite, costs are being incurred.

There is more to the story. Normally, if a machine has a lengthy changeover standard, it is changed over less frequently to avoid downtime. This creates a natural requirement for additional buffer inventory to "fund" the longer run times or to complete schedule cycles back to other needed products. These same organizations often have several "rules" that are administered daily by the master scheduler to minimize the number of changeovers—not good!

Small lot orders, even one-piece orders, are the direction most high-performance businesses find the most profitable, taking all costs into consideration. These costs include inventory carrying charges as well as changeover times amortized on their typical lot size.

Lean thinking and techniques focus on the elimination of waste. Changeover time is a great example of that waste. One method to minimize this setup time that has been successful in literally thousands of businesses worldwide is Single Minute Exchange of Die (SMED). Developed by Toyota and credited to Dr. Shigeo Shingo, the SMED approach is an easily learned and communicated process methodology for many activities, including machine changeover and preventative maintenance.

SMED starts with the understanding that all activity originates from two distinct processes, internal activity and external activity. To illustrate the differences, think of a simple drill press like many hobbyist carpenters have in their home workshops. If a drill press operator is drilling 3 pieces of part A requiring a 3/4-inch hole and then had to change to drill 3 pieces of part B requiring a 1/2-inch hole, there are some planned activities that are executed. Please note that these might not be in the best sequence. It is just a list of activities that must happen in some order.

a. The 1/2-inch drill bit is sharpened
b. The 1/2-inch drill bit is brought to the machine
c. "B" parts are brought to the drill press
d. Completed "A" parts are moved to the shipping department
e. The 3/4-inch drill bit is sharpened for the next use
f. The 3/4-inch bit is returned to its storage bin
g. The 3/4-inch bit is removed from the drill press
h. The 1/2-inch drill bit is inserted into the drill press

Using the SMED methodology, each of these steps required by the process falls into either internal activity or external. Internal activity occurs when the machine is off, and the external activity takes place while the machine is running. Therefore, external activity allows the machine to continue earning money. In the above-listed activities, if the machine operator shuts the machine down before any of the activities, these activities are considered internal activities. In this methodology, avoid or minimize internal activities if at all possible and keep the machine running. The only steps that require the machine to be stopped are steps g and h. All the others could be completed with the machine still running although someone's help could be required. This is the idea behind SMED. Ensure numerous changeovers are possible with the machine running.

To the trained materials professional, it is clear why setup reduction is of benefit to a manufacturing organization. Lot sizes are smaller, the plant is more flexible and less inventory buffer is required. Using this lean concept, SMED keeps costs down and is easy to understand and administer. Dr. Shingo, in conjunction with SMED, used an improvement approach that has been adopted by many firms around the world. His method was to initiate an SMED project by consistently establishing the first-time objective on a particular setup, reducing the changeover time by 50%. Once this is successfully accomplished, the next assigned team has the same goal, reducing the setup by (another) 50%. By the time the third team is chartered to reduce an additional 50%, the setup is reduced to approximately 10% of the original setup time. This approach is quite effective (figure 2.11).

## LEAN INVENTORY STRATEGY

Lean is often considered to be a method of reducing inventory. The two are definitely connected, but lean is not defined by the process of reducing inventory. The flexibility and speed requirements of well-implemented lean do not negate the opportunities for buffer inventory in any given process. Even TPS incorporated "buffer zones" that linked process steps for the temporary storage of inventory. This is not a case for lots of safety stock; quite the contrary. It does need to be said,

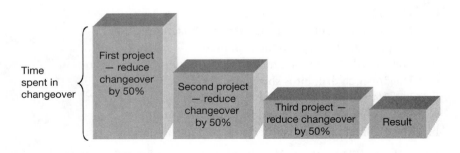

**Figure 2.11** SMED Approach

though, that eliminating inventory for the sake of eliminating inventory can actually be counterproductive if the objectives are reduced cost and improved customer service. *Inventory can be a strategic weapon and needs to be thought of as such.* The key is in understanding why inventory exists. Of course, this should be followed by continuous improvement actions to minimize the need for the inventory buffers.

Car manufacturers, including Toyota, do not make the bulk of their finished goods inventory after the receipt of the PO from an end-user consumer. Instead, they build to a forecast, frequently adjusting the plan. The reason is easy to understand but often ignored. *The lead time to build a car and transport it to the end-user consumer is longer than the market wants to wait. Anytime that situation exists, the lead time has to be changed or inventory needs to be resident within the process.* Figure 2.12 illustrates that planning of inventory is necessary when this situation exists.

If the accumulative lead time is 3 weeks and the customer is willing to wait only 3 days, a time fence line has to be created at the 3-day mark. All activity prior to that must be planned. There is no need to spend energy arguing about this. The sooner organizations recognize this life-fact, the easier it is to develop improved plans regarding inventory. Understanding the inventory strategy is the acknowledgement of this planning requirement.

Many businesses receive an added bonus when they acknowledge inventory strategy. This advantage comes from improved recognition of relationships between specific configurations and lead times. Companies that have a more advanced view of configuration control and inventory strategy tend to have more than one strategy per product grouping. In other words, each product group actually has more than one inventory strategy. Some configurations could be MTS, some MTO and even some ETO. This approach often saves cost and unnecessary inventory expense. The higher the awareness, the easier it is to recognize opportunities to move strategy from one to another, perhaps MTS to ATO, saving inventory

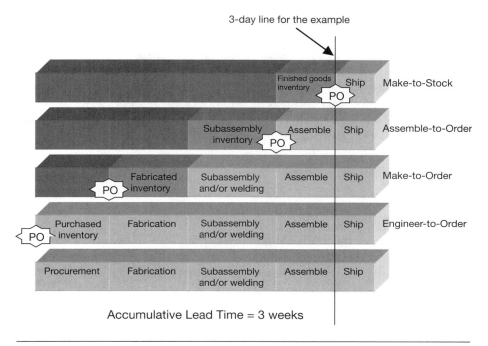

3-day line for the example

Finished goods inventory | Ship | Make-to-Stock
PO

Subassembly inventory | Assemble | Ship | Assemble-to-Order
PO

Fabricated inventory | Subassembly and/or welding | Assemble | Ship | Make-to-Order
PO

Purchased inventory | Fabrication | Subassembly and/or welding | Assemble | Ship | Engineer-to-Order
PO

Procurement | Fabrication | Subassembly and/or welding | Assemble | Ship

Accumulative Lead Time = 3 weeks

**Figure 2.12** Forecasting as Inventory Strategy

in the process. It can move the other way, too, if one particular option or feature becomes popular and requires shortened lead time beyond present capabilities. It should go without saying that the opportunity for lean process and approach becomes second nature in this scenario. Eliminating waste is one of the fastest ways to reduce lead time, allowing adjustment of the inventory strategy again.

## Make to Stock

MTS has earned a bad reputation. It is like saying that "all inventory is bad," which is not necessarily a 100% true statement. While some of the MTS reputation is well-deserved, all applications of MTS are not bad. It is dangerous to start from that perspective. *The optimum is to have the accumulative manufacturing lead time match the market required lead time.* Since this doesn't always happen to our satisfaction, alternatives need to be found. Take groceries, for example. Are we willing to wait in the store for cereal to be manufactured, boxed, and sent to the store? Probably not. On the other hand, we might be willing to wait a few minutes for the butcher to make a specific cut for our Christmas dinner. The grocery store understands the market and stocks accordingly. When Grafco PET Packaging supplies bullet bottles, the market is normally unwilling to wait; they must be ready to ship at a moment's notice. Alternatively, some of their customers buy specialty bottles and supply forecasts to Grafco. This allows them to make the bottles to order and not necessarily stock them. Production capacity is forecasted to need. In reality, the automotive food chain entertains a lot of MTS strategy even though it is one of the leaner and more efficient supply chains in manufacturing. Vendor managed inventory (VMI) normally incorporates some MTS strategy. It is usually made from a blanket order, which some would argue makes the process MTO. *In reality, in most markets the blanket is simply a firm forecast. The actual order is the schedule release that follows the blanket with more exacting requirements, usually in short lead times.* In most applications of VMI, it is really just MTS strategy in MTO's clothing.

## Assemble to Order

The ATO strategy is much more appealing to most lean-thinking managers and for good reason. There is naturally less inventory involved. Dell Computer is probably the best known example of a company that utilizes ATO strategy to their advantage. The key is their market lead time as compared to their reaction time— the two lead times, are compatible. It is the suppliers that allow it to happen in a timely manner. Suppliers are exercising at least some of their process in anticipation of the final schedule from Dell. There are many other examples of ATO strategy in our lives. And many more organizations are exercising MTS strategy but have lean or Six Sigma projects opened to develop shorter lead times allowing MTS to be converted to ATO. A solid component of continuous improvement in most businesses is shortening lead time. And shortening it is not just about customer service; the gains come from cost decreases, quality control, and inventory reduction. In the end it is about choosing the right inventory strategy to meet the existing situation and immediately planning continuous improvement. ATO many times represents the first step in optimizing inventory strategy over MTS. There are higher-performing strategies when the luxury of market need and manufacturing lead times will allow.

## Make to Order

In too many cases, ATO strategy is just moving the cost of inventory to the supplier. If we have enough clout and volume to support the cost, sometimes it works well. When the market conditions are right, MTO offers a better scenario for cost reduction and meeting custom requirements specifically to the customers' desires. If we receive the order prior to the manufacturing commitment, it becomes much easier to manufacture an item in a wider range of configurations. If the customer can wait, it is beneficial to plan for variation and make it after the PO is received. Many companies do exactly that.

MTO does not necessarily mean that the shelf is empty at the receipt of the order. In fact, many companies have raw materials and some components in stock all the time to reduce overall lead time to their customers. It allows immediate production as soon as the order comes into the process. One business mapped and improved their processes to the point that they were able to commence production within 90 seconds of the receipt of the customer order—90 seconds! They generally shipped custom products in the sporting world for the likes of Wal*Mart within 48 hours. This was acceptable and allowed them to customize products for specific store chains. Most MTO applications include having some raw material in position as well as having a few components with longer lead times available to be used at a moment's notice. This is not a license to offer any possible configuration, however. There still needs to be limits around the configuration possibilities or problems could arise.

## Engineer to Order

This last strategy is left to the really weird possibilities. ETO offers an almost unlimited configuration possibility. That is what makes this inventory strategy so much fun. By corralling the strange, the mediocre and the mundane become extremely easy and profitable again. Too many organizations manage all of their respective product families as one big grouping. That includes similar products in the same family that should be MTS, ATO, MTO and/or ETO. The real problems become obvious when the customer wants complex configurations and the promises are for short lead times targeted at a totally different set of configurations. It happens all too often. If the other strategies are well-defined, the leftovers become ETO by default. It is when they are not defined that troubles begin. The lean-thinking materials manager is always striving to keep offerings well-defined. Marketing or sales should be tasked to review product strategies at least once a quarter, more often in some businesses. The materials manager or master scheduler should take the lead in making this happen. Usually, all similar products are well-served to be treated in separate product families based on not only similarities, but also inventory strategy. This is covered in detail in a slightly different context when we discuss master scheduling. Another important aspect of lean materials management is lot sizing. Lot sizing is directly related to the flexibility of the production process. A well-known and successful process improvement methodology for setup reduction is known as SMED, which has been previously explained. Driving lot sizes to smaller quantities allows for more flexibility from the perspective of the customer. This flexibility requires the process to provide quick changeovers.

## DISCUSSION QUESTIONS

1. The terminology for lean includes the following terms.
   a. 5-S
   b. pull systems and kanban
   c. kaizen
   d. SMED
   e. a, b, and c
   f. all of the above

2. Seri, one of the 5-S elements, means
   a. to keep organized.
   b. to sort belongings, including but not restricted to data.
   c. to clean thoroughly.
   d. a and b only
   e. all of the above

3. Golden zoning is a practice of
   a. making an area especially clean.
   b. having an area for customers to see.
   c. warehousing items in an area with considerations for ergonomics or usage.
   d. marking high-efficiency areas.

4. Seiketsu is the 5-S element that focuses on
   a. polishing the workplace.
   b. getting the area organized.
   c. making discipline a part of the culture.
   d. none of the above

5. Shitsuke is the 5-S element that focuses on
   a. cleaning.
   b. organizing.
   c. discipline and sustaining process.
   d. sorting.

6. Kanban is a pull system technique.
   a. false
   b. true

7. Supply-chain management includes the ability to link suppliers directly to the MPS of the customer.
   a. true
   b. false

8. Fixed cart kanban includes the following expectations:
   a. Carts are in the process with limits on how many parts can be transported.
   b. There are a planned number of carts available to workers depending on the MPS.
   c. The carts have no linkage to the MPS but instead are linked to the customer demand.
   d. a and b
   e. all of the above

9. MRP is needed in most manufacturing businesses.
   a. true
   b. false

10. Creativity is considered a standard focus for waste in materials management.
    a. true
    b. false

11. Inventory is a strategic weapon.
    a. true
    b. false

12. Buffers are inefficient and should be used rarely.
    a. true
    b. false

13. Kaizens can and should be used in materials management as well as production.
    a. true
    b. false

14. SMED is a consideration for materials as well as production.
    a. true
    b. false

15. Different types of kaizens used include
    a. 24 hour.
    b. 1 week.
    c. 30 day.
    d. 90 day.
    e. a and b only

# 3

# LEAN AND EXCELLENCE IN SUPPLY MANAGEMENT

## LEAN AND CHOOSING SUPPLIERS AND SUPPLY-CHAIN PARTNERS

In recent years, lean thinking has taught us that costs eliminated anywhere in the supply chain are good for everybody involved. Partnerships are special working relationships that allow and foster sharing of technology, forecasts, and financial information. In this context, partnership does not refer to the legal term and does not suggest any special legal implications, although they are not excluded from the process. When members within the supply chain trust each other and work closely, there is a greater opportunity to eliminate waste and duplication.

During a Class A training course, when asked "what is the most important measurement for supplier value," the automatic answer is usually "quality." It is a conditioned response; everyone has "read the book" or "got the tee shirt." The answer "price" runs a close second. In reality, "price" is the top priority in practice, unfortunately, even in many of the companies answering "quality" as the top priority. High-performance organizations have price as a consideration, but it is not the number one concern. In most cases, continuous improvement is a good sign for supplier value. Knowing that a supplier is constantly striving for improved quality, responsiveness, and/or cost reduction gives most customers a feeling of confidence. Probably the real number one reason, however, is trust or reliability.

## Partner Development Criteria

Consider the following criteria for developing partnerships. These are not necessarily in order of priority.

1. **Criticality**—When lean thinking is implemented in the supply chain, the communication between suppliers is constant and complete. Choosing the suppliers carefully is paramount to success. Some suppliers are easy picks because they are joined at the hip with their customers in terms of shared technology, financial information, and forecasts. For example, a supplier who is involved in the development of the customer's product right from the idea stage is a natural. In some other cases, it is not as easy. In some commodity markets, the best suppliers supply both you and the competition. This makes for strange bedfellows. Risk of having information get to the competition through the supplier, even unintentionally, is a definite consideration before partnerships are defined too closely. Certainly criticalness of the supplier is a number one qualifier. Critical or extremely important single-source suppliers should be considered for partnership potential. This might include single sources, best quality sources, or location of the source. If the supplier has done a good job, often they raise the "criticality" bar to assure more security in the relationship. This can actually be good for both the customer and the supplier when done for the right reasons.

2. **Reliability**—Before considering any supplier for a partnership agreement, reliability needs to be both examined and experienced. Eliminating waste within the supply chain necessitates the elimination of redundancy and duplication of efforts and sources in most cases. Reliability of the partner is the only acceptable parameter if waste is to be driven to the lowest levels. For example, if the supplier is providing the main frame for assembly, and a lean process flow is being implemented from their facility to yours with no buffer beyond a couple hours, reliability is a huge factor. It probably goes without saying! It rarely makes sense to have two suppliers for these main components, especially if expensive tooling is involved.

   Being able to look away from a supplier and be confident that they deliver when required and what is needed is a huge asset. Reliability comes in many forms.

   • *Quality*—Reliability of quality process and product is table stakes today. Without it, suppliers should not be on the approved list. Quality of process is defined by having repeatable processes, management systems to assure compliance, and metrics in place to warn of process variation as it develops. High-performance organizations measure first time quality (FTQ) and it is a good indicator of quality process. FTQ is a measure required by Class A process to audit adjustments and tweaking done in all operations. The assumption is that if the process requires adjustment to stay within spec, there is opportunity for improvement and elimination of waste.

- *Integrity of promises*—Reliability is only meaningful if it includes reliability of promises. Promises in this category would include dates and times met on new product design commitments for components, quality improvements, cost reductions, and most importantly, perhaps, delivery of product to the customer's door. Delivery times, in many lean-thinking manufacturing companies, are stated and measured in time within the day, not dates. Sometimes this means several deliveries within the same day, depending on the location and agreements. Along with this comes the trust that when problems arise there is an early warning system to allow plan realignment with minimal loss.

- *Responsiveness to schedule changes*—The supplier is not the only source for schedule changes. More often, customers are the source of process variation. Be aware that the lists of requirements discussed in these criteria apply to not only suppliers, but to you as well. After all, everybody is a supplier. It is your responsiveness to customer need that requires equal or better responsiveness from your suppliers. Confusing? The further you look down the food chain, the more responsive the parties need to be.

3. **Competence**—Just as with reliability, competence has many faces. There is no reason to develop a partnership with a supplier who lacks reliable competence. Being reliable is good; being reliably competent is great. There are a few expectations in this space:

- *Technical expertise*—If a company makes the highest quality goods, it should also understand the technology behind these products. Only a few years ago most businesses could afford full research and development (R&D) staffs. Today, with the competitive markets and lean thinking, most companies are relying on suppliers for technical assistance in their field of expertise. This only makes sense. Total cost is incurred throughout the supply

chain, not just in the factory. If the company engineers are designing the components as well as the final assembly configuration,
there is a duplication of resource sitting at the supplier's site. The
easiest component-design-related resource to eliminate is yours.

- *Financial stability*—Supplier profitability has not always been on
the top of priority lists with customers. It is not generally the
focus of everyday concern. Customers who have experienced a
bankruptcy of a single-source critical component supplier think
differently. Financial stability is the enabler to allow design
improvements, capacity investments, and risk-taking for the sake
of improvement.

- *Improvement history and plans*—With competence comes the will-
ingness and tenacity to stay at the head of the pack. All great companies have a continuous improvement track and measure
progress and results regularly. Some progress is visible to the
customer, but not all of it. When considering the possibility of a
partnership handshake with a supplier, ask for evidence of their
internal process improvements. Some partnerships include shared
training and project work, which can have great value.

4. **Location**—This topic is often controversial. Most companies in the
United States are either thinking about or have done some sourcing
off-shore. The North American Free Trade Agreement (NAFTA) had
some influence, but China's favored-nation status with the United
States has also been a driver. Many readers may be convinced that
these are good advancements and would prefer to keep this topic off
the list of qualifiers for determining potential partnerships. There are
no firm, fast rules about the importance of supplier location. There
are always trade-offs. Distance equals cost and adding either is bad.
However, it does play a part in the decision, at least it should.

Location is on this list not because there are recommendations
that always apply, but because the risks are many and the rewards are
not always as significant as planned. People are good at getting components across great distances (thanks to rail and ships) at a relatively
low cost. We are also good (thanks to priority freight companies) at
getting components across great distances quickly. But there is an
obvious gap when reviewing abilities to get components across great
distances quickly and cheaply. The "not cheaply" part of freight transportation is not always baked into the planning cake initially when
making decisions to source on the other side of the globe, often
resulting in poor decisions

There is another way to look at location as a competitive advantage. One client I work with is a blow-molder engaged in lower-volume packaging needs, mostly for the food and drug industry. Opposite from the off-shore approach, their strategy is to build plants across the street from their customers. In the past few years, they have built two new plants and are getting ready to break ground again. This strategy has created and funded their growth.

Many organizations that are moving off-shore for components are starting to require buffer within a radius of the customer's facility. This, of course, also comes at a price. Again, there are always trade-offs! Materials managers are the people ultimately responsible for getting required components to the right place at the right time for the right cost. Adding a global boat trip to the equation is asking for trouble and cost, and it needs to be calculated carefully into the decision process. Too often it is not.

Leaning out material flow in the supply chain may expose several factors that begin to add difficulty when lengthy lead times and process variation, including border crossing issues, customs delays, and uncooperative weather, affect schedules unexpectedly. When the costs of priority freight, for example, are incurred after the implementation of the sourcing decision, it is often too late for reconsideration. Better research should occur prior to the supplier transfer. This includes calculating inventory requirements for transit time and buffer to offset potential issues. With the increases in inventory comes the opportunity to orphan inventory through engineering change. Plug all of these aspects into the decision. If the math supports the sourcing of inventory from the other side of the globe, move ahead. Sometimes it does make good sense.

5. **Price**—Notice that price is last on the list. This does not mean it is not important; after all, it is on the list. Price is important, just not as important as reliability and technical competence. The three-legged stool (purposely leaving location out of it) would be pretty wobbly without any one of the legs (figure 3.1). Price does not need to be the lowest. The price paid for a product needs to provide good value. Few high-performance companies have made their success on price alone. Most of the best companies in terms of growth and stakeholder return are not the lowest priced in their markets. The common denominator is value. Value is built from product quality, service behind the product, and people behind the products and services.

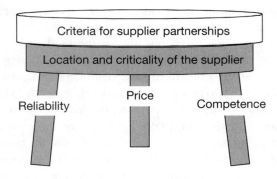

**Figure 3.1** Three-Legged Partnership Criteria Stool

## IMPLEMENTING SUPPLIER PARTNERSHIPS

Once suppliers are chosen for partnership development, the obvious question is how to go about successful implementation. Project management is a proven process, and each supplier-partnership implementation should have a separate project with a team leading, measuring, and supporting the progress.

- **Define the scope of the project**—The first step is to define the scope. When does the group get to buy pizza and celebrate their victory? How long do they have to get the project completed? What are the deliverables from this partnership in terms of information sharing?
- **Choose the team**—The team is important. It cannot be lower level individuals exclusively, although there is good reason to have people from within each company who understand how the information systems work (figure 3.2).
- **Develop the implementation plan**—The elements of the plan should include:
  1. Define the expectations in measurable terms—the "should be" state.
  2. Collect data that describe the current "as is" condition.
  3. Develop plans to close the gap. Process map the information flow, product flow, and technology or knowledge flow that occur both today and in the future model.
  4. Implement the changes and test for success.
  5. Document and audit the results.

The Six Sigma DMAIC (define, measure, analyze, improve, control) process improvement methodology is effective in this application. DMAIC is a classical

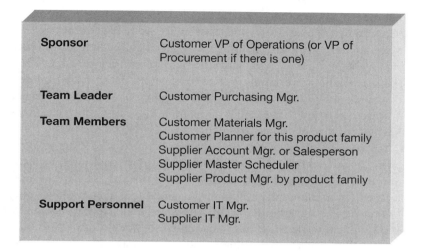

| Sponsor | Customer VP of Operations (or VP of Procurement if there is one) |
|---|---|
| Team Leader | Customer Purchasing Mgr. |
| Team Members | Customer Materials Mgr. Customer Planner for this product family Supplier Account Mgr. or Salesperson Supplier Master Scheduler Supplier Product Mgr. by product family |
| Support Personnel | Customer IT Mgr. Supplier IT Mgr. |

**Figure 3.2** Typical Partnership Implementation Team

Six Sigma approach that insists on all elements of robust problem solving when implemented correctly.

- **Create and assign actions in Gantt chart format**—Document all the expectations. Do not lose track of the original "promise" dates even when rescheduled. Maintain two columns: original and revised dates.
  1. Drive actions to move the relationship to the desired state.
  2. Measure the results and adjust as necessary.
  3. Document the policies and rules of engagement.
  4. Monitor results.
- **Celebrate**—Too many teams forget to celebrate success. This does not require fireworks, but if the desired outcomes were met, some recognition is in order. The celebration spotlight helps educate others in the organization on what good behavior looks like. It is not just about the team members but also the rest of the organization. There will be many additional partnership agreements to implement.

## REVERSE AUCTIONS

Reverse auctions have taken root in many markets and are probably here to stay, at least for the foreseeable future. The interesting thing about these web-based events is that they seem to go against everything the best supply-chain professionals have learned in the last 30 years of developing supply-chain improvements. Nonetheless these events do have a place in a world-class materials manager's tool kit.

Reverse auctions are events in which invited suppliers share an Internet web gathering for the purpose of bidding for the right to service a customer's business need. The specifications are supplied prior to the event and usually include starting price and quality specifications along with drawings on technical requirements. In more recent auctions, companies have built flexibility and responsiveness requirements into the auction criteria.

Bidding consists of lowering (thus the label "reverse") the agreed-to price. Adding a required lead time for the supplier to have materials on the customer's dock from the point of signal is an excellent use of the process. On this topic, for example, the lean-thinking material manager might include a response criterion of "24 hours from receipt of order to the delivery of goods to the customer." This forces the suppliers to thoroughly evaluate how they build flexibility into their processes. Service is where real value is added in today's competitive markets. Getting the cheapest price is not the way to lean process. In fact, when price is the only focus, it ignores the spirit of lean thinking.

In an unscientific study within our client base, more than 80% of the auctions result in maintaining the original supplier. This has led some suppliers to decide against participating when their best customers schedule reverse auctions. From the supplier perspective this is risky and, yet, in the right circumstances, it is the correct decision. It is expensive and risky to change critical suppliers. This risk has to be included in the strategic thinking of the customer as reverse auctions are considered.

Often reverse auctions are designed to squeeze some of the price out of the market. Intelligent professionals have opposing views on this topic. Businesses need to use caution in their approach to and application of reverse auctions. These web exercises can bite unexpectedly. In one situation a critical supplier chose not to participate. The customer chose another supplier, but the transition was so painful the company returned to the original supplier. The result was a complete lack of trust between the two important supply-chain partners.

The reverse auction topic is intriguing and is a bit like gambling for both the customer and the suppliers. The rules of the game are not fleshed out completely. In the next few years, the strategies in reverse auctions will be fine-tuned. Most high-performance companies today use reverse auctions to some degree in certain applications. Experienced lean materials managers and procurement professionals have to think through each case individually.

## VENDOR MANAGED INVENTORY

Suppliers are like the air hose or lifeline to a deep sea diver. If the line gets severed or is not managed properly, there are devastating results. In high-performance businesses, lean thinking begins internally but goes well beyond the four walls to the supply chain. In the beginning days of "just in time" (JIT), the forerunner to lean, many larger companies, especially in the auto industry, tried stocking inventory at the suppliers across the street, thinking that if the cost passed upstream they would be free of the curse. In a short time the market found out that the cost did not go away. In the world of modern vendor managed inventory (VMI) there is similar thinking in some corners. As the saying goes, if we ignore history we are destined to relive it.

Costs in the supply chain are passed along eventually. If each rung on the supply-chain ladder is not healthy and profitable, eventually everyone pays. That either comes from temporary lapses in service as the weak link drops out and is replaced or ugly surprises in price increases when reality hits. Lean-thinking materials managers understand that it is up to the stronger customers to help manage the full supply stream. If the similarities to the diver's lifeline are recognized, it is easier to understand the urgency. Too many short-sighted materials managers view supplier inefficiencies as "the supplier's problem," but inefficiency in the supply chain is everybody's problem. In many of the best-in-class examples, customers send teams into their supplier's facilities to teach problem solving or to help with continuous improvement projects, frequently at no charge. One company in the Boston area sent a 12-member team into a supplier's facility to work setup reduction. The suppliers' product was corrugated material, and the objective was to align packaging materials tightly with the master schedule drumbeat so that the customer could reduce the lot sizes in the order cycle and eliminate their packaging inventory. The work focused on setup reduction at the corrugated supplier's operation. Did the return justify the cost of these 12 problem solvers? They thought it did.

Often the result is not desirable. The customer who does not have "their act together" sends help into the supply chain. Often this help has the finesse of a large hammer! Nothing is more frustrating than a customer who doesn't know how to manage a master schedule or maintain discipline within order management shouting orders to others in the supply chain or explaining how to manage the supplier's schedule. At this point the supplier can get defensive or even drop out, finding alternative ways to satisfy their stakeholders. *The first step in good supply-chain management is to get your act together!* There are two foolproof steps.

1. Make sure inventory strategies are perfectly aligned with supply-chain capabilities (e.g., MTS, ATO, MTO) and market needs.

2. Keep schedule changes within the fixed fence as stable as possible. The rules of engagement need to be pre-defined and disciplined.

If these two prerequisites are followed, the journey is easier for everyone. Properly executed, VMI results in suppliers bringing materials into the supply-chain process in anticipation of need. This is efficiently completed by partnering with the customer and by the total sharing of data surrounding demand flow.

Consigned inventory is another deviation of this process that assumes some inventory is required to buffer demand variation. Consigned inventory has a cost and needs to be deemed necessary and advantageous.

## CONSIGNED INVENTORY

Sometimes it makes sense to have inventory on sight at the customer's facility. *Consigning inventory is not often the first plan of attack, but is, instead, a calculated alternative approach that is based on customer need and defined by lead time and configuration variables in demand.* Consigning inventory can be a service to the customer and, thus, is a competitive advantage. From the customer's perspective, it can be valuable, but it is not a given. There are specific situations calling for consignment over VMI. Consigned inventory buffers can be dangerously close to waste and, therefore, an unnecessary cost if not thoroughly considered. Those considerations should include:

1. As a supplier, your facility is farther away from the customer than other suppliers (competitors), and freight transportation time and cost are disadvantages to your position in the supply chain.
2. The supplied product is widely available from other sources.
3. Your product as a supplier is not distinctly differentiated from your competition's product; thus speed and cost are major factors in remaining competitive.

Interestingly enough, cost or value of the supplied product does not come to play as often as we might expect. Probably the most frequent consigned product is hardware, including fasteners, nuts, and bolts. Consigned inventory is a required service in this highly-competitive supplier market. In fact, the service goes well beyond simply providing consigned stock. Today, the larger customers are delegating the filling of bins and restocking of assembly areas to the hardware supplier. This is a beneficial situation for both the supplier and the customer. However, the result is one of those "golden handcuffs" examples; the customer is happy because they have reduced the staff and they have no inventory control issues concerning hardware, but it is also difficult to change suppliers because of systems knowledge and familiarity, which is an advantage for the supplier.

On the other side of the equation it makes sense to have expensive items consigned because of the lack of distinction between suppliers. Facility location is another factor in play. In one application a supplier of gold components found that the naturally high per-piece price of gold products made it undesirable for the customer to stock multiple configurations even though they offered them to their customers. The greatest competitor to the gold supplier was located closer to the customer, affecting delivery lead time and freight costs. To offset location, this gold component supplier chose to pre-pay freight on the customer's shipments to remain competitive. When small less than truckload shipments were made, the freight costs were extremely high. Their final solution was to ship larger loads, amortizing the freight cost over a larger base. Obviously some calculations are needed to understand the optimum level between too much inventory and too much freight. Consigned inventory, in this particular example, is a strategic advantage. Keeping some inventory at the customer's site resulted in reduced freight, and customer service was improved. Everybody was happy with this arrangement.

## TIME FENCES IN LEAN MATERIALS MANAGEMENT

There are several theories and approaches to fence rules in scheduling. Class A ERP–defined "rules of engagement" normally include specifics for each product family in terms of time fence rules. One of the prerequisites to the rules normally includes having a product family for each inventory strategy within one product grouping. (For example, there might be two separate families for the same grouping, Product Family *Stainless A's* MTS and also Product Family *Stainless B's* MTO.) Without these rules/handshakes, it is more difficult to have high performance with the optimum efficiency of operations. In a normal process the lead time elements might look like the example in figure 3.3.

The process might look different than this but usually procurement and at least one conversion process exist as raw material is converted into salable product. If the process is simpler, some interpretation is needed. Figure 3.4 depicts how the time fences are allied to the lead time.

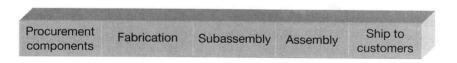

**Figure 3.3** Accumulative Lead Time

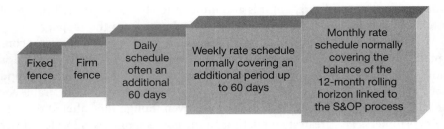

Each time period expands the planned flexibility due to expected demand plan fluctuations. This may expand 15-50% overall. The last time fence (out in time the farthest) may not have any defined flexibility limitations other than to be negotiated on an exception basis.

**Figure 3.4** Time Fence Norms and Flexibility Built into the Planning Horizon

The "fixed" fence is sometimes referred to as the "frozen" fence. Schedules are never completely locked. Because of this, most companies have abandoned the term "frozen." In figure 3.4 the inference is (by the height of each representative time block) that more flexibility is built into the schedule. At each time fence, the rules change slightly, and all the players in the supply chain are aware of the rules and the latest schedule. Flexibility is part of this handshake at each time fence break.

Flexibility is a great competitive advantage. Rules need to be developed for optimum planning flexibility and execution. In figure 3.5 some ideas for flexibility are depicted. Keep in mind that this chart does not deal with configuration possibilities. That needs to be defined also and is closely connected to the inventory strategy (e.g., MTS, ATO) rules. The factors involved (figure 3.5) are written and communicated between the partners with the common goals of flexibility, speed, and cost efficiency.

At times customers are a tremendous help if they are cognizant of supply-chain costs. Master scheduling changes that are outside the agreed-to rules can add cost rapidly.

## LOGISTICS AS A COMPETITIVE ADVANTAGE

Freight cost is normally a huge expense in any supply chain. No matter what is produced, it has to be moved somewhere, sometimes frequently, and probably by truck or additional modes, including rail or ship. Accordingly, transportation cost is a huge opportunity for waste elimination and lean thinking. Any time a truck

| Time frame | Schedule | Lower limit | Upper limit |
|---|---|---|---|
| 0-2 days | 100 per day | 100 per day | 100 per day |
| 3-4 days | 100 per day | 88 per day | 112 per day |
| 5-64 days | 100 per day | 80 per day | 120 per day |
| 65-125 days | 100 per day | 70 per day | 130 per day |
| 126-365 days | 100 per day | no limit | no limit |

**Figure 3.5** Sample Flexibility Requirements Table

is moving loaded rather than dead-heading or every time distance is minimized in transport, improved cost can result.

Today's freight haulers, the same as most businesses, are trying to differentiate themselves. These organizations can become partners as well in limiting supply-chain costs. Frequently it is the smaller, regional freight haulers that have the most flexibility; therefore, they should not be eliminated from the testing. If there are clusters of suppliers in certain regions, "milk runs" can eliminate costs by consolidating several suppliers' shipments into one trailer load. Process mapping is the proper tool to use to tackle this normally complex opportunity. Here is a short list of activities to remember when focusing on logistics as a customer service and/or cost-reducing opportunity:

- Understand the total transportation requirement. Look at and map the total freight picture, both in and out of the facility. Look for activity clusters in which freight can be combined with other shipments.
- Engineer common, shared components wherever it can be done sensibly.
- Do not have inventory made ahead of time and keep inventory in the supply chain moving. If it does not need to move, maybe it shouldn't have been made. Increase inventory velocity. Queue time adds little value.
- Sometimes consigned inventory is a good solution that saves freight. This, of course, has to be weighed against cost of inventory.
- Optimize stocking locations if utilizing distribution centers. Make sure they are aligned with the customer base and, if appropriate, the supplier base.
- Use of re-usable containers is often a cost savings option.

- Evaluate cross-docking versus warehousing of inventory for cost opportunities.
- Stock in generic packaging and specific-need packaging only after the receipt of the order. This creates flexibility in inventory. This is especially helpful when the same part is used for several applications in original equipment manufacturing.

In many instances there are opportunities to have the freight hauler involved in supplier-partnership implementation. Even team membership of the logistics provider could make sense. Many high-performance companies have included these logistics providers in the problem-solving efforts that have resulted in improved solutions.

## SUPPLIER PERFORMANCE RATINGS AND CERTIFICATION

Supplier rating and certification might be one of the most rewarding and fun topics in supply-chain management. It is without a doubt a topic with a broad impact to the procurement success. Good performance is built on metrics and management systems. Supplier rating is the heart and soul of a robust supply-chain process. Metering supplier effectiveness is most efficient when three elements are considered: quality, delivery, and service. Although it is beneficial to be objective and minimize subjectivity, rarely are supplier ratings totally objective (table 3.1).

### Table 3.1 Supplier Ratings

| Rating Category | Weight | Rating System |
|---|---|---|
| Quality | 30% | 95% sustained = Certified supplier |
| Perfect orders | | 90% sustained = Qualified supplier |
| Packaging quality | | 80% sustained = Approved supplier |
| Count accuracy | | |
| Delivery | 40% | |
| Promises met | 100% | |
| Flexibility in schedules | | |
| Value-add services | 30% | |
| Short lead time | | |
| Technical support | | |
| Consigned inventory | | |
| VMI | | |
| Supplier fills the bins onsite | | |
| Other value-add processes | | |

The application of the model normally includes written criteria for each level within the topics of quality, delivery, and value-add services. It can be developed in conjunction with the supplier or independently. It is always best to have the supplier review the criteria prior to implementation. If small adjustments are necessary, the ownership in the end product is improved.

There are times when a supplier is "the only game in town" and criteria are not met with full approval as a supplier. Because of business need, the choice to jettison the supplier is not always an option. Although not a favorable position, unfortunately it is not an unusual one. The immediate mission objective is to change this position. Although not always apparent, the options that should be considered include:

- Convincing an alternative favored supplier to add the additional product line
- Looking out of the immediate area for an alternative supplier
- Adding the capability to your facility
- Encouraging the existing supplier to improve

## CLASS A ERP

Class A ERP is a specific level of proficiency in the enterprise resource planning space. This criterion is deep-seated in manufacturing and is the down-to-earth blocking and tackling needed for process disciplines and effective management systems. Class A ERP is referenced further in later chapters. Class A ERP certification is powerful in supply-chain management. Some customer companies have actually subsidized Class A ERP education for their suppliers. As a result of the training, several benefits are enjoyed because of improved performance. Not only do the Class A criteria include service fidelity, but they also cover internal operational objectives, including data accuracy and schedule adherence. Suppliers who adhere to these strict standards internally make reliable supply partners.

There is no magic potion in the supply-chain management space, but over the years many organizations have learned the valuable lesson—namely, do not accept poor suppliers any longer than necessary. This is an easy thing to say and not always easy to do but it must become a business imperative.

## MATURITY PROFILES

Suppliers who have worked on their performance and have achieved significant improvements in flexibility and speed deserve some recognition beyond just the normal supplier certification process (figure 3.6).

| Certified supplier | Qualified supplier | Approved supplier |
|---|---|---|
| a) Minimum of 3 perfect receipts | a) No rejected material for 6 months | a) Last receipt perfect |
| b) No rejected material for 6 months | b) Quality, delivery 95% | b) No rejected material for 3 months |
| c) Quality, delivery 95% | c) Monthly performance review | c) Quality 95% |
| d) Value-add services 95% | d) Annual audits | d) Delivery 90% |
| e) Audits optional | | e) Audit every 6 months |

**Figure 3.6** Maturity Profile Specifics

Within the supplier rating system there is normally a maturity profile that rates the progress of the supplier base. There is some leeway in these ratings as evidenced by many high-performance organizations. Figure 3.6 suggests categories and rating criteria for a supplier maturity profile. Each progressive level brings added expectations and performance requirements. Only suppliers who perform at the advanced levels of performance are certified. Lesser levels of trust are also signified by "approved supplier" and "qualified supplier." The objective is to remove as much cost from the supply chain as possible by building trust between the supplier and the customer. This happens through consistency in rules and strict adherence to the audit schedule until criteria are met.

## METRICS IN PROCUREMENT

The metrics in a high-performance procurement focus on system linkage and synchronization. Although supplier metrics are often looked upon as a significant part of supply-chain management, the metric emphasis is more extensive than evaluating the supplier. The real opportunities come from making sure that the business system is maintained to the latest master production schedule (MPS) and that the suppliers are absolutely in line with the latest schedules. Unless the suppliers are hardwired to the revisions, when the master scheduler changes sequence or requirements in the MPS, little gain is seen from the change in the MPS. If the communication is not real-time or there is not some synchronizing process regularly administered, the supply chain and the customer need can quickly get out of alignment. *For that reason, the procurement process metric should look at the percent of complete orders that are received on the day that they are required.*

## Class A ERP Procurement Metric

The widely-accepted Class A ERP metric measures the percent of complete orders or releases from purchase orders that arrive on the day or hour (depending on the schedule interval) that the parts are required. For this metric, the definition of "the day or hour the parts are required" is found in the ERP business system as the "required" date/time. The required date/time is the latest date/time in the system at the time the material is received. "Complete" means the exact quantity to the latest order or release and 100% usable parts—no rejects. Any reject makes the order a miss for the day. If there are multiple stock keeping units (SKUs) on one purchase order, the full order is the definition of the requirement. This metric is at a higher standard than many procurement process measurements are, but the lessons learned from it are beneficial to the business. Frequently, the supplier is not the problem at all, but rather it is the schedule stability. Without this understanding and the strict measurement process, it is more difficult for the lean materials manager or supporting purchasing professionals to discover the root cause of the observed schedule adherence issues.

The traditional supplier metric that measures the integrity of the last promise to the customer is a reasonably lower-level metric and is a good source of data for the procurement people; however, when it is used without other support data, this limited metric does not meet the correct metric requirements for process linkage to the MPS and does not achieve the required level of detail to consistently point to an accurate root cause. The schedule adherence and customer service level metrics are:

- **Supplier quality**—Percent of perfect receipts measured in quantity and form, fit and function.
- **Flexibility**—Proven ability to react to schedule changes within the rules of engagement previously agreed upon. Additional value is achieved through the ability to provide flexibility outside the normal rules.
- **Value-add services**—Special value-add activities, including R&D of new products, VMI, consignments, small quantity deliveries, and on-site replenishment, can add a great deal to the supply-chain effectiveness.
- **Delivery fidelity**—The delivery performance should always be measured to the last MPS date in the customer's ERP business system. The date used for the metric is the receipt date.
- **Speed**—Short lead time.

Obviously, these metrics are in addition to the form/fit/function quality requirements which are the minimum table stakes to do business with any supplier. If these categories are all at the top of the score chart, the supplier is clearly an impressive asset in the supply chain.

## DISCUSSION QUESTIONS

1. Criticality is an important component of supply-chain management. The use of criticality as a descriptor in this instance refers to
   a. importance of the supplier to the customer.
   b. importance of the part to the customer.
   c. lead time constraints.
   d. all of the above.

2. Competence is also on the list of criteria for supply-chain management. In this application competence refers to
   a. excellence of the supplier.
   b. excellence of the customer.
   c. excellence of the logistics agent.
   d. ability to meet lead time standards.

3. Is the location of suppliers a consideration in supply-chain management?
   a. Location is considered after price and quality.
   b. If the supplier has a warehouse close to the customer, location is not a factor.
   c. Consigned inventory at the customer trumps location considerations.
   d. Sourcing should not require water transportation unless all costs are taken into consideration.

4. Elements of the implementation plan should include which of the following?
   a. Define the expectations in measurable terms—the "should be" state.
   b. Collect data that describe the current "as is" condition.
   c. Develop plans to close the gap. Implement the changes and test for success.
   d. Document and audit the results.
   e. all of the above

5. VMI and consigned inventory are names for similar processes.
   a. true
   b. false

6. Reverse auction refers to
   a. disposing of obsolete inventory.
   b. disposing of excessive inventory.
   c. competitively sourcing material to specifications over the web.
   d. negotiating requests for quotes.

7. A "milk run" is an expedited trip to the supplier to pick up materials.
   a. true
   b. false

8. Reusable containers are a component of logistics management. Often these returnable shipping materials are too costly to be considered.
   a. true
   b. false

9. In a company with a supplier certification process, an approved supplier is one that has the customer's full trust.
   a. true
   b. false

10. Measuring the supplier promise fidelity is the main measurement for success in high-performance supply-chain management.
   a. true
   b. false

# 4

# DATA INTEGRITY IN LEAN ENVIRONMENTS

## INTRODUCTION

Most materials managers worldwide understand "garbage in, garbage out," yet many businesses do not invest the time and effort necessary to eliminate data inaccuracy, which invites an opportunity for cost, waste, and chaos. Even companies focused on the elimination of waste through lean philosophies too often ignore data accuracy. Some important lean solutions, 2-bin systems for example, force data accuracy through quantity control. Bin size becomes the control, but the information connection back to the computer business management system also needs to be robust.

Inventory is one of the necessary building blocks for the material planning business system engine to operate. Without reliable data elements, including inventory balances, bills of material (BOMs), routings, lead times, and standards, the formal system breaks down. As a result, informal buffers, including expediting and manual intervention, become the backbone of any residual reliability. Process capability or operating on a desired "autopilot" mode requires robust and reliable data integrity. The good news is that data accuracy is one of the easiest goals to achieve within a business. Data accuracy is an enabler for the Enterprise Resource Planning (ERP) system to work properly and to achieve the planned results.

The best lean materials management standards have high expectations for data excellence. These data elements include inventory record accuracy, BOM accuracy, item master inputs including lead time and standards, and, depending on the system and application, routing records. Inventory location balance record accuracy is probably the easiest to achieve and yet, ironically, the least robust in many businesses.

## INVENTORY BALANCE ACCURACY

When organizations discuss inventory balances, the usual reference point is either dollars or the total count of on-hand inventory for a certain item number. Any data accuracy discussion that starts with dollars is uninformed at best and risky at worst. Even total count misses substantial cost-saving and waste-eliminating opportunities. In high-performance businesses, the reference point for inventory accuracy is more detailed. In organizations with high data integrity standards, the definition of inventory accuracy not only includes the total item counts but also the counts in each location. For example, if there are a total of 100 pieces of item "123-456" and there are 30 in location A, 30 in location B, and 40 in location C, the accuracy is in knowing how many are in each of those locations.

In more than a few less sophisticated business system applications, inventory is listed in one all-encompassing system location. While infinitely better than not maintaining a balance, it is not an efficient way to manage a business asset. Discussion of cycle counting efficiency omits the inefficiencies of searching for parts when they are required. Many times, without specific company-wide knowledge, searching is required for normal business to be executed. In some businesses survival mode has stock keepers developing stand-alone spreadsheet applications in the warehouse to maintain balances and locations. Obviously, this does not reflect lean materials management.

In most businesses the picking sequence is more efficient if the locations are known to the system. It is then easy to maintain the balances more accurately. The accuracy cannot be achieved without effective data integrity processes (transactions) at the location balance level. There is the belief that this adds cost, but that is not the belief with those who have experience with an accurate warehouse. It is no more costly to do inventory transactions correctly than to do the transactions incorrectly, and when done correctly, the benefits are many. Others have read the lean books and are convinced that warehousing inventory is wasteful and that working to make the area disciplined is compounding the waste. They usually are managers who have some undisciplined centralized storage and their goal is to move it into point of use; or managers who do not have centralized warehouses and do not appreciate the need for factory-floor discipline for control of their point-of-use inventory.

Both of these manager types can benefit greatly from understanding the need for disciplines in this important asset as well as robust process design.

## Inventory as an Asset

Inventory is a dirty word in most organizations. Once we have "been to the seminar" and/or "read the book" we quickly become a disciple for the "no inventory" program. It is a fallacy in many manufacturing and service organizations. Inventory in the majority of manufacturing or service companies is positioned because of the need to offset variation in their processes. Some of the sources for variation include:

- demand forecast inaccuracies
- scrap reporting errors or omissions
- inconsistencies in amounts produced compared to amounts requested
- normally ill-behaved customers
- machine downtime
- process yield rates

Understanding this concept is the first step in eliminating unnecessary burdens. Inventory is a great thing when a customer is ready to buy it. Waiting for that customer to want the inventory is often not so pleasurable.

## Allowing for the Elimination of Buffer Inventory

In many businesses lower inventory is a priority for top management and generally for good reason. When it is the only focus and the business goal of lower inventory is periodically brought to the top of the priority list, the materials people get excited about the cause and, not surprisingly, inventory goes down. Area planners have little they can do quickly to lower inventory, but they can influence levels of new material that is ordered. This same inventory is (hopefully) the specific component inventory required by customer requirements. The planners, as a result, might not order the parts that are required. When an inventory reduction focus is simply forced on the planners without corresponding strategy, frequently the result is increased shortages and no associated decrease in process variation. To make matters worse, the organization still has the wrong "stuff" (the inventory already "in the barn"), inflating inventory monetary values. The shortage and expedite mode that follows translates into self-induced burden cost. The root cause of the problem is often not the buffer itself but rather the inaccuracy leading to the need for buffer inventories. I visited a major manufacturer recently that had regular freight bills in the range of $600,000 per month! Imagine what fun things could be bought with that much money! Priority freight would not be on the top of most managers' wish list!

Companies frequently reconcile inventory through physical inventory counts or periodic cycle counts. Unfortunately, too many of these organizations are really engaged in merely "fixing bad balances." Like perpetual cleansing, the counts are simply designed to clean up ongoing errors that occur with no accountability. This is not the case in high-performance lean operations. In these businesses the cycle counts are designed to understand ongoing transaction accuracy habits and to make adjustments.

For example, assume that a business has a posted accuracy of 95%. In this imaginary business there are cycle counts that schedule counts through the entire warehouse, from one end to the other, every month. Here is the situation in this imaginary warehouse:

- cycle counts are relatively accurate each time
- inaccuracies are adjusted when found
- the counting cycle is four weeks, wall-to-wall
- the posted inventory accuracy is 95%

With this situation, one can assume that at least a 5% variation factor is added each and every month. If cycle counts were stopped, logically the accuracy falls to 90% in two months and 85% in three. When the process variation is really understood, it is much less satisfying to brag about a 95% performance level, especially in an environment in which cycle counts are done feverishly. The whole picture needs to come into focus and a determination made about how much variation is added daily. The cost can be significant when numerous counts are required simply to repair inaccuracies every month. It is much like "inspecting" quality into the inventory accuracy process.

Understanding and eliminating the root causes for inventory inaccuracy is a much more productive use of resources and eventually results in significantly less expense to maintain accuracy. One of the easiest ways and most successful methods to uncover the barriers to consistent accuracy of inventory records is to implement control groups as a prerequisite to a robust cycle counting process.

## CONTROL GROUP METHOD: EFFECTIVE STEPS AND RESULTS

Lean materials managers understand control group methodology. An inventory accuracy control group is a select group of fast-moving parts or component materials that are repeatedly counted to determine, reconcile, and eliminate the causes of inventory record inaccuracy. It is important to select items/materials that have high activity; this ensures exposure to error-causing events and/or inaccurate process inputs. The control group should also be representative of the total population of parts/materials and locations where these important components are stored. This means that the control group is spread out over several controlled areas within a facility.

## Control Group: Step 1—Item Selection

To start an effective control group, it is wise to choose 30-50 item numbers from high-activity locations. The items chosen should also be a reasonable representation or sampling of the kinds of materials or parts used in the process. It is also beneficial to pick stock keeping units (SKUs) from various areas rather than all from the same stocking zone.

The ultimate objective of this control group methodology is to ensure a controlled process and accurately account for inventory movement. It is essential to ensure that variation causes can be determined. Individual item location balances (rather than the total item balance of all locations) make up the 30-50 balances required for this step.

Some managers want to know exactly how many to count in the 30-50 locations. Although this is a wide range, choosing how many locations to count in any specific control group is simple. There should be a mandatory requirement enforced to reconcile all variation to root cause each day for all inaccurate balances found and to initiate actions for elimination of the inaccuracies. If there are too many inaccuracies to track and the team is not able to reconcile the root cause with actions for elimination of these causes daily, then too many location balances are being counted. On the other hand, if enough location balance variation is not found with the number of locations being counted, more location balances should be added to the control group. This will make more sense as the control group methodology is explained more completely. Keep in mind the objective is not to fix balance issues; it is to understand and eliminate root causes.

On the morning of day one, count all of the items/locations in the control group. Next, match the count quantity to the perpetual record file (on the computer) and reconcile any differences. Reconcile in the context of this Monday morning count means to assure accuracy and adjust as necessary. The objective is to be assured that the computer record is accurate when the control group process begins, because it is essential to have an accurate starting point for the implementation of the control group. If any of the balances do not correspond with the perpetual computer record, count them again to ensure accuracy in the count. Make sure that the records are absolutely accurate. Once confirmed accurate balances are documented, move to the next step.

## Control Group: Step 2—Recounting the Same Locations

On day two, the same process is repeated. Count the same control group of item location balances and match the quantity counted with the perpetual inventory records just as was done on day one. The purpose of this second count is to see if the process variation causing inaccuracies has shown its ugly head. Often there is variation occurring regularly, and since only high-activity locations are used in this exercise, finding variation should not be difficult. For example, in the control group counted, four location balances have become inaccurate since the previous day's count. Some important information is known. It is at this point that the value of this process becomes apparent. In this case and all others, we know:

1. These four inventory balances had activity. Because we picked high-activity location balances for this test we can be confident that there was picking or put-away activity in each of these locations during the test.
2. Transactions were not aligned with physical movement of inventory. The simple fact that four of the balances in the example were out of sync with perpetual is an indicator that the required transactions, for some reason, were not in synchronization either.
3. The most important piece of information is the simplest. *The error occurred in the last 24 hours.* Too many times it is impossible to know when the error occurred, making it difficult to diagnose. Knowing it is current helps to determine the root cause.

*It is critically important to find, document, and initiate actions to eradicate the root cause(s) of any errors from the control group within 24 hours of detection.* Without this timely action, it is sometimes impossible to find out what process control collapsed or was missing to cause the inaccuracy. The objective of a control group is to find the variation or problems in the transaction-processing system and fix them immediately.

It is a good idea to use the individuals who perform the inventory transactions in the control group activity to eliminate the accuracy errors. This ensures user understanding of any changes to the process, understanding of the process controls, and ultimately results in process predictability. While much variation in manufacturing can occur from process issues, in this space it is often process discipline that is at the center of inaccuracies.

Although it is important to find the source or root cause of the problem creating the inaccuracy, it is even more important to eliminate the barriers to high-performance inventory record accuracy. Possible problems include:

1. Parts were moved without the proper corresponding inventory transaction.
2. Parts were received incorrectly from a supplier.
3. The supplier sent a different count than was documented on the packing slip, and no verification count was made.
4. Improper new employee training resulted in inaccurate picking.
5. Scrap generated was not properly recorded with a corresponding transaction.

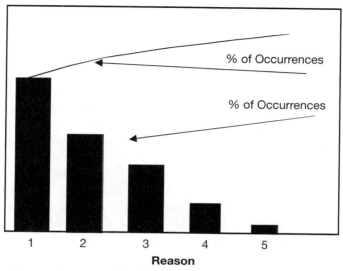

% of Occurrences

% of Occurrences

**Reason**

**(Sample) Reason definitions:**
1. Parts moved without the corresponding transaction
2. Inaccurate picking from warehouse
3. Parts not received correctly from a supplier
4. Scrap not accounted for in production
5. Production personnel sending parts back into the
   warehouse with inaccurate transactions

**Figure 4.1** Pareto Chart

Once the reasons for errors are understood, a measurement document should be created to depict and communicate the facts surrounding the inaccuracy of inventory records. A Pareto chart provides an adequate visual display of errors and the frequency of occurrences. Pareto analysis allows the targeting of the greatest offenders of accuracy, thereby utilizing assets in the most efficient manner (figure 4.1).

Reasons for inaccuracies vary from company to company, plant to plant, and department to department. Reason codes can differ from the sample model, but it is an extremely useful exercise to accurately document the errors causing variation in the process in a consistent manner.

## Control Group: Step 3—Determining Root Cause

Once facts are gathered concerning the reason(s) for record inaccuracy, good managers interested in accuracy find the root cause for the flaw. Often what warehouse or inventory managers discover at this stage is that the procedures are not understood, process disciplines are not being enforced, suppliers are not holding quantity to the same level of accuracy that they do dimensional tolerances, or there are inaccuracies in the BOM records because of the absence of proper standards. All of these can be easily corrected. The prerequisite is the acknowledgement of this variation.

There is no fail-safe or mistake-proof method of determining root cause; in fact, root cause can be deceptive. The best way to be sure the root cause has been properly identified is to determine that action can be implemented as a result of knowing the data. Many times problem solvers believe they have achieved root cause only to find out that there are more underlying causes not revealed by the data.

One approach that ensures the successful discovery of the root cause is to apply the proven "5-why" method, also referred to as "5-why diagramming." This detailed problem-solving methodology is also one of the simplest to use. When reasons for inaccuracy are initially determined, ask why five times or until there is a clear requirement for corrective action. For each reason a "reason tree" begins to develop. These reason trees are the basis for understanding real root cause. This exercise can take a great deal of wall space or flip chart pages if done correctly. A 5-why diagram is easy to use and is effective in peeling back layers of a given problem or opportunity (figure 4.2).

## Control Group: Step 4—Eliminating the Reason for Inaccuracies

Knowing the root cause for inaccuracy leads to the next logical and necessary step—eliminating it! Corrective actions must result from the findings if the control group is to be effective. Often these actions are in the form of improved documentation of procedures, more frequent audits of active procedures, and better training on proper procedures and company policies. Sustainable process requires a robust management system. In many high-performance organizations, process owners report performance at a management system event called the "weekly performance review" process and find it effective. The weekly performance review process is a formal event at which management examines progress reports. The meeting is held the same time each week and is regarded as an important part of the business management. There is more on the weekly performance review in chapter 14.

## Control Group: Step 5—Ten Error-Free Days

The expected result of root cause analysis and resulting corrective actions is achieving 100% accuracy in the original control group. Step 5 is to achieve control group accuracy for ten consecutive error-free workdays. Ten error-free days is

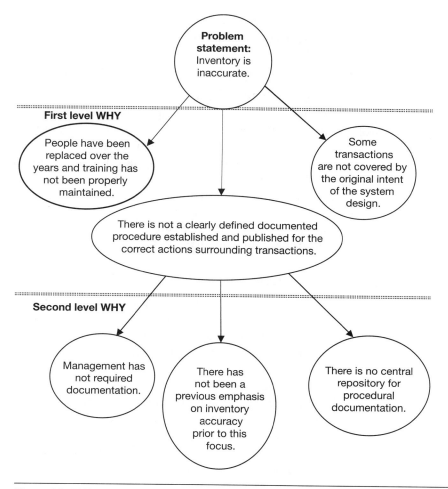

**Figure 4.2** 5-Why Diagram

an indication that the process is in control—for the control group! Since the control group is a representation of the total population of inventory balances, it is a reasonable assumption that the errors that were uncovered and eliminated in the control group were also being committed throughout the facility.

It is important to understand the realities—sometimes there is a heightened awareness of the original control group after a few days of counting the same parts over and over. Heightened awareness can lead to artificial process control that is not sustainable over time nor necessarily applied consistently over the entire base of parts or inventory. The people working around the control group part locations see the activity daily and naturally have a tendency to be more aware of these locations. This false security needs to be discovered, if it exists, and that generally means testing with a second control group.

## Control Group: Step 6—Initiating a Second Control Group

Having the original control group at 100% accuracy is great indeed! It is good, however, to verify that the newly-installed process discipline is in control outside the original control group. Verify the process control success by sample testing with a second control group. The same process from the original control group (Control Group A) is repeated. The only difference is the list of locations. Companies often choose a larger quantity of locations/items to count in the repeat testing because the errors should be infrequent or completely eliminated. The same rules apply—if the errors are in line with the ability to keep up with daily reconciliation to root cause and actions, the correct number of counts is being made. Remember, the idea is to find and fix errors if they exist.

## Control Group: Step 7—Establishing a Cycle Count Process

After the second control group verifies process control, a standard/traditional cycle counting program is appropriate. In a standard cycle counting process, a planned schedule ensures that all parts are adequately counted annually. One popular method has the count frequency of each part dependent on value and/or volume usage of each individual material or part.

Many high-performance organizations hold educational sessions on the topic of problem-solving tools prior to establishing process improvement teams. This can make the teams much more effective and can lead to faster improvement. Teams that conquer the use of these tools are typically the teams that go on to solve other, more challenging problems, which fosters continuous improvement. By using the control group methodology correctly, the results can be favorable.

## Physical Inventory

For many companies, a complete wall-to-wall physical inventory is appropriate once accurate control groups are showing that process controls are in place. This is particularly appropriate for companies starting out with low levels of data integrity prior to a successful control group approach to root cause elimination. Although it is virtually impossible to count a wall-to-wall inventory at 100% accuracy, it can be a significant improvement as a starting point for the cycle counting process to begin. *The good news is that this is the last physical inventory the company has to take! High-performance businesses do not take annual physical inventories* (figure 4.3).

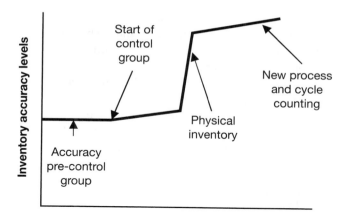

**Figure 4.3** Post-Control Group Physical Inventory

## *Eliminating the Physical Inventory Forever*

It is the control group and the recognition and elimination of root cause that allow the effective use of a one-last-time physical inventory. The control group, when executed properly, drives actions that eliminate the error causes. Once robust process is in place assuring accuracy, the normal annual physical inventory can and should be eliminated. The annual physical inventory is not a value-add exercise. Like inspecting quality into a process, which has long been known as the least effective method of assuring quality, the physical inventory is really designed to fix balances, an annual cleansing so-to-speak, but it does nothing to maintain accuracy. Also, since it is virtually impossible to make a wall-to-wall physical count 100% accurate, especially in a massive factory- or warehouse-wide effort, it also can cause some problems that didn't exist prior to the count. The cause of inaccuracies is occasionally the result of an adjustment initiated at the physical count.

Many manufacturing organizations in the United States believe that the elimination of the physical inventory count once a year is not possible due to imaginary laws or regulations. It is a fact that nearly all high-performance organizations in the United States legally (and ethically) do not execute an annual physical wall-to-wall inventory. There are some countries that do have regulations governing the requirement and, of course, in that case there is no choice.

## *Process Owner of Inventory Accuracy*

In a high-performance organization the process owner for inventory accuracy is typically the warehouse manager, who is the leader with the most inventory to watch and care for. In some cases the right person is the materials manager. It depends on the organizational structure. There are often several inventory owners in various parts of the factory or compound, and each of them can and should serve on the accuracy team, but the leadership position for this important effort is necessary and belongs to the keeper with the most to gain. The decisions made in the redesign of process affect all areas, and one team (including representation from all inventory storage areas) with one leader allows the best opportunity solutions to be implemented with consistency. Responsibility for metrics and performance is a part of process ownership. Measures define the goals within data accuracy. These measures are a result of the cycle count process.

## CYCLE COUNTING

Cycle counting is the process of randomly sampling the inventory location balances in a "planned fashion." Although the checks are random, there is a planning element that ensures that certain parts are "randomly" selected within certain time periods.

Many organizations have their inventory stratified by value. Called ABC stratification, this layering can be used for cycle counting and other inventory control purposes. Using ABC stratification, the inventory is layered into categories by value and worth to the organization. Parts are counted at planned intervals depending on value. ABC inventory stratification is covered in detail later in this chapter.

Note that systematic counts of inventory do not necessarily have to utilize ABC stratification. Other methods of cycle counting involve planned counts of racks or locations within the storage areas. In these alternative approaches, inventory counts are planned by area rather than value. This might be exercised through planned counts of bays or racks, moving from one end of an area to the other in a calculated time frame. Either cycle count approach is acceptable but can differ in the implementation cost depending on the availability of software tools and layout of inventory locations. An appropriate application of this technique might be when the value of inventory stored does not vary much. Appliance manufacturers often have all inventory in an A category of value and, therefore, use alternative methods. Cycle counting is the process of planned periodic checking for process control of location balance accuracy. It is a necessary evil in the beginning stages of inventory integrity.

Starting the cycle counting process before proper controls are in place is a misuse of cycle counting, most likely with the sole intent of "fixing" inaccurate balances. This approach alone does not result in process control. Cycle counting is not the goal; it is one step on the way to world-class data management.

## Inventory Accuracy
### Results of Physical versus Cycle Counting

| Goal | Cycle Counting | Periodic Physical |
| --- | :---: | :---: |
| Timely detection of errors | yes | no |
| Reduction of item ID errors | yes | no |
| Minimum loss of production time | yes | no |
| Sustains overall inventory accuracy | yes | no |
| Reduce obsolete/excessive inventory | yes | no |
| Allows valid MRP plan | yes | no |
| Correct statement of assets | yes | not sure |

**Figure 4.4** Cycle Counting Results Comparison

One misnomer also associated with the metric for successful inventory control has to do with the method of measuring accuracy. Auditors are mainly concerned with monetary accuracy. Not that they do not care about piece part count accuracy, they just do not use that information by itself. This allows mistakes in inventory shrinkage (when the physical count converted to monetary value is less than the current dollar amount record on the accounting books) to offset counts for other part counts that are inaccurate on the high side. Some organizations have been known to claim high accuracy based on minimal inventory shrink. The truth is scary. Little process assurance is evident from the inventory shrinkage value alone. Actual part counts documented as hits or misses and not converted to currency tell a much more complete story (figure 4.4).

Figure 4.4 (physical versus cycle counting comparison) shows some of the reasons why a physical wall-to-wall inventory is not an acceptable substitute for cycle counting.

- **Timely detection of errors**—Cycle counting inventory on a regular basis identifies errors more quickly than a yearly physical count.

- **Reduction of item ID errors**—Cycle counting is typically executed by trained personnel. Since wall-to-wall counts often involve other non-warehouse people, annual physical counts can contribute to errors in balances.

- **Minimum loss of production time**—The yearly physical inventory usually requires some stoppage of production. Cycle counting is scheduled regularly without affecting production schedules.

- **Sustains overall inventory accuracy**—When errors are found during the physical inventory, it is difficult to understand causes. There is a massive amount of information to deal with in a short time period after a wall-to-wall. The chances of root cause detection are much higher when some items are counted more frequently.

- **Reduce obsolete/excessive inventory and allows a valid materials requirement plan (MRP)**—Since errors can go undetected for a year between balance checks using only annual physical inventory counts, replenishment signals on inaccurate balances are also inaccurate. Balances that are in error to the low side (balance shows less than there is in inventory) can cause a premature replenishment signal and result in excessive inventory. Whenever there is a chance to have high actual inventory levels, there is increased exposure to obsolescence. Cycle counting reduces this risk by more frequent checks.

- **Correct statement of assets**—When inventory record accuracy is not in control, both monetary and part number perpetual balances are not reliable. The cycle count process gives an organization a better chance of maintaining accuracy.

## The Objectives of Cycle Counting

There are several objectives to cycle counting. They are:

1. to verify accuracy/identify errors
2. to identify causes of errors
3. to correct conditions causing errors
4. to measure accuracy
5. to maintain a correct accounting of assets

These objectives should be thoroughly understood and written into job descriptions of personnel responsible for the cycle counting activity.

## ABC Stratification

Many organizations, including the leanest facilities, have cycle count processes based on using an ABC stratification of the inventory. Using this approach to cycle counting, the first step is to have the item master or part number files stratified by value. This normally includes both monetary value per item and usage per period of that same item.

All modern ERP business systems have an equation for calculating the break points for inventory class assignment. The equation asks for value cutoffs and volume factors. The Pareto principle applies here. (Pareto principle says that generally 80% of the impact is caused by 20% of the factors.) This application of the Pareto principle results in some generally accepted patterns:

- The top 10-15% of the value-based (cost per piece and usage volume) part numbers after stratification are often automatically assigned to the status of an A class item. These are items that require the most attention and investment in maintained accuracy. These are the items that have the greatest impact if errors in counts occur.

- The lowest 60-80% of the value items (cost per piece and usage volume) can usually be assigned the status of C class items. On the reverse side of the scale from A class items, C items are parts/materials that have low impact. Examples include hardware or common fasteners.

- The balance of the items is assigned as B class items. B items are looked at more frequently than C items and include items that are not in the A category of value but have more impact than low-impact C items. An example might be a lower-cost colorant used in the plastics industry that has a week lead time—a low impact in relationship to cost but could be a problem if requirements are not replenished for an order in a timely manner.

Most organizations use the business computer system to stratify their inventory into categories followed by some manual massaging according to impact rather than cost alone. Such impacts might include frequency of use, lead time, and items that are rationed. These assigned ABC stratification codes are a factor in not only cycle counting but also pull signals, stocking strategies, safety stock, replenishment treatment, and review time required by planners. From the standpoint of simply cycle counting, the following rules are normally followed:

A items—counted every quarter
B items—counted every six months
C items—counted annually

The more effective stratification assignments also include the impact to the business. For example, inexpensive hardware can actually become an A item. If this hardware is specific to the application and comes from a supplier thousands of miles away it becomes critical. One organization in Shanghai, China, provides a good example. Some low-cost hardware was only available in North America in a particular configuration, consistent quality, and hardness. It was listed in the item master file as an A class item simply because it was not easily procured, and it had a long lead time required to ship it from overseas. There are many other such examples of assigning stratification codes that do not exactly follow the generic computer equation. Not only is it *not* cheating to "massage" the list after the ERP system calculation, it is *expected* in high-performance organizations with high-performance material management. High-performance organizations do not blindly utilize the computer-generated equations for stratifying inventory.

## INVENTORY ACCURACY METRICS

Surprisingly, many companies today still do not fully recognize the power of data accuracy and how easily it can be achieved. When organizations address the situation, they find it is not people that have to be addressed first, it is always the process. People nearly always perform at the expected norm.

If the freeway speed limit is a certain speed but is not closely monitored or is enforced at speeds considerably higher, and there is not a present and obvious danger, most naturally drive at the maximum speed that the process allows. This is what frequently occurs in a factory or warehouse. People do not see the dangers of taking shortcuts. Many times these people actually think they are helping the cause by reacting to a customer request by "short-cutting" the paperwork or transaction process. In fact, management sometimes rewards this "hero" behavior.

In these cases it is the process, not people, that is the problem. After all, people are somewhat predictable. It is the metric process that creates the necessary feedback loop. The world-class accepted calculation is simple for determining the location balance record accuracy for Class A performance requirements. All counts or checks (with the one exception of control group counts) are counted in the measurement process. For example, normally some extra inventory counts are requested for locations to confirm accuracy when suspicions of accuracy arise. People requesting these counts might be planners, schedulers, or even line managers. These and any other checks should also be included in the base for calculating accuracy. I have always referred to these counts as the "foul smell" counts —counts that are requested because of a foul smell coming from the item or location record to someone who cares. Usually the planning department is the one that gets the suspicious whiff first and requests the counts.

The calculation for inventory record accuracy is simple. It is calculated as the total number of accurate location balances (allowing acceptable tolerances) divided by the number of location balances checked within that period (figure 4.5).

The tolerances noted in the numerator are the ABC stratification tolerances that are published and generally accepted:

**Minimum Acceptable Class A Accuracy Standards**

| | |
|---|---|
| A items | ±0% |
| B items | ±2% |
| C items | ±3–5% |

$$\frac{\text{Total location balances accurate within tolerance}}{\text{Total location balances checked}} \times 100 = \text{Percent performance}$$

**Figure 4.5** Inventory Accuracy Calculation

Tolerances above 5% are not allowed in high-performance environments. In fact, few lean, high-performance manufacturers today allow tolerances above 2 to 3%. The only time 4 to 5% is allowed, for example, is for inexpensive items such as pounds of inexpensive resin in a silo or small washers worth $.002 per piece. Recently, new challenges were presented in which a business had products that included o-rings the size of a pencil lead. Difficult to count, these components are so light that breathing on them can blow them around! We experimented with 10 people counting what we believed to be 100 units in a plastic bag. The result was 10 different answers—using counting scales. These situations make it necessary to have scales designed for the product being counted and to have tolerances adjusted for reasonability without losing out on high expectations.

The more open 4 to 5% tolerances are rarely required in today's high-performance organizations. Little tolerance is allowed in regard to accuracy if it can be successfullly counted; if it can be counted, it can be accurate. Inventory weighing scales today are precise enough that accuracy is expected even on small parts. Lean pull systems such as kanban and 2-bin systems have a cleansing effect and effectively recalibrate inventory periodically anyway.

In one distribution center the warehouse manager put the most skilled Six Sigma resources on the application to help ascertain the best method for achieving accuracy using scales. In this particular application, the scales were not effective in the way they were being used. Some of the parts in this warehouse were so small that the time to count out the sample size and the number required for the sample was too massive. Like the example mentioned earlier, they also had difficulty getting the sample counts accurate when large samples were required. Their quality manager, along with the resident black belt, came up with a system that saved time in the warehouse and increased the count accuracy (figure 4.4). In this application a sample scale is networked with a normal counting scale. The result is a perfect scale used for each application. When the parts are small and require a large sample size on the normal counting scale, the smaller scale is used and the sample accurately completed with 20 to 25 pieces. The parts are actually dumped out onto the larger scale for counting quantities. The sample size is transferred from the smaller scale via software links. It works great and has an accuracy of better than ±.5%! This is obviously close enough for this application, especially since the parts were often less than one cent a piece (figure 4.6).

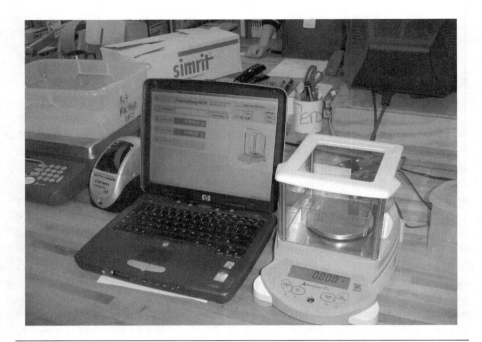

**Figure 4.6** Using More than One Scale for Accuracy and Speed

The confidence at this warehouse rose to the point that they initiated a labeling process that "certified" the accuracy of the counts (figure 4.7). This worked so well that they then required their suppliers to implement similar processes in their facilities, ensuring increased accuracy of material counts coming into their warehouse from outside suppliers.

In terms of metrics, each controlled area within the facility should be measured separately and posted visually for all employees to see. (A controlled area is any location holding inventory by process design or habit for more than 24 hours.) At the end of the week, these separate measures should be combined to calculate the overall facility inventory accuracy. This is accomplished by increasing the total base in the metric calculation to include all locations counted. The numerator in the calculation is the total number of locations that were counted and found to be correct throughout the facility. This allows everyone in the business to recognize the effectiveness of process control in terms of inventory location balances. It also allows for individual understanding of each area's contribution prior to the consolidated performance view. The same metric is used in each specific area, but the counts and base are limited to their area-specific data.

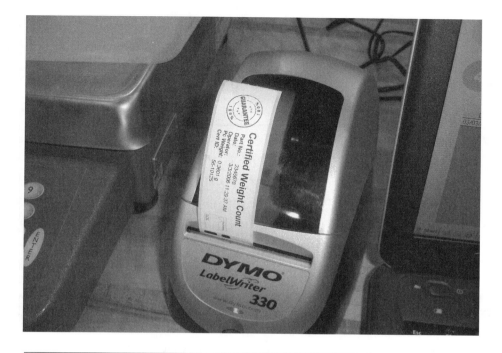

**Figure 4.7** Label Being Printed for "Certification" of Accuracy

# BILLS OF MATERIAL AND ROUTING RECORD ACCURACY

In addition to inventory location balance accuracy, it is essential to have accuracy in other records used to plan inventory flow and availability. Two such examples are BOMs and routing records. These factors can also impact inventory accuracy.

## Components of Bills of Material Accuracy

BOMs are the recipes for the manufacturing process. They also are the records to drive proper assemblage of components for kits in a distribution environment. There are several components necessary to achieve accuracy in BOM records:

- part number accuracy of parent level
- part number accuracy of all components
- unit of measure accuracy and consistency
- quantity per part accuracy
- BOM structure as it compares to the actual process

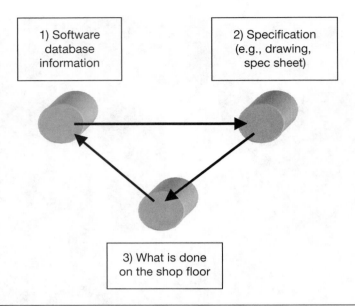

**Figure 4.8** BOM Accuracy Match Requirements

The secret to an effective accuracy process as it relates to BOM records is easy to understand. There are three applications of BOM records that need to be synchronized (figure 4.8):

1. what the computer record shows as the BOM
2. what the drawing or specification calls out as the BOM structure
3. what actually is done on the factory or warehouse floor

When all three of these files match, the result is an accurate BOM record that is used to manage change in the product, to flow inventory, and to maintain predictable quality. BOM accuracy can be especially important if backflush transactions are used to impact inventory balance changes.

## The Process Owner of Bills of Material

The materials manager or people in the materials organizations do not have to own all data accuracy processes in a high-performance organization. In most manufacturing organizations, engineering, and therefore the engineering manager, is responsible for the design of products and for detailing specifications required of those products. The BOM is the production translation of this specification into manufacturing terms. This record is used to order and flow materials into place and to assemble the components or raw materials into usable/salable products.

Some smaller organizations or companies that do not focus on new product introduction as a main core process do not have a separate R&D engineering department. In some cases they might utilize manufacturing engineers or even production lead people to make some of the traditional engineering decisions. In these organizations someone other than engineering must be designated as the BOM accuracy process owner.

One frequent comment from engineering on this topic is, "I (engineer) can be held responsible for the drawing and maybe even the computer record, but I can't control what the factory floor or warehouse clerk does." That may be true, but in reality when specifications are not followed engineering has little chance of succeeding. It is in the best interests of engineering to have their specifications followed. As engineering gets involved in the audit process, they often find variation of which they have not been entirely aware. This can even result in *higher* quality as engineering designs more manufacturability into the product. The bottom line—engineering should be the process owner and audit and report performance at the weekly performance review.

When production deviates from specification, the resulting action taken to eliminate this condition should be noted. When the computer is out of synchronization with the specification, again, accuracy performance should be reported and resulting actions recorded. While engineering is not always the one to administer the fix, they can be the overseers. Everybody gains and most learn from the process focus.

## Measuring Bills of Material Accuracy

The threshold of acceptability for Class A performance in BOM accuracy is 99%. This means that 99% of the BOM records must be perfect. It does not mean that all BOMs are 99% accurate.

It is not unusual to have several thousand BOM records on file within a manufacturing database. Many times these same organizations have situations in which a great majority of the product produced only uses about 20% of the part numbers. This can mean that a random BOM sample in work in process would skew toward frequently used records simply because they are in the system more often. The majority of the high-usage parts is verified quickly and they have the potential to be randomly selected time and time again because of the frequent use. This is obviously not a valuable use of resource once the accuracy is verified. There are a few high-performance ERP techniques that can be used, some dealing with the issue of frequently-used BOM records and the effect on the metric.

## Simple Random Sample Method

In a simple random method, a sample is taken daily of released BOMs until both the confidence and verified accuracy are high. Usually this is executed by production workers under the direction of the process owner (usually engineering) for BOM accuracy. A random selection of assemblies is, perhaps, chosen in the morning and these orders (e.g., work orders, shop orders, pick tickets) are flagged for audit. In some organizations paper travelers are used; for example, colored paper signals the audit requirements. In other paperless shops a flag is added to the dispatch screen for BOMs that are to be audited. Workers are trained to scrutinize these jobs for accuracy in all vital areas. A flag on the item master is logged for each BOM as it is checked for accuracy. This eliminates the chance of checking the same BOM too often.

Any error within the BOM makes that BOM inaccurate for the purpose of the measurement. If ten BOMs are checked and two have errors somewhere in the structure, the performance is reported as 80%. For this exercise a BOM is one level in the structure, not all levels if there are multiple choices.

## Deducting for Accuracy Method

In many environments checking BOMs for a few weeks results in an accuracy level that is high enough that errors normally are not detected through the daily random sampling. This could be a sign of verified BOM accuracy for released BOMs. At this time it could be appropriate to move to another method of measurement. One method is accuracy deduction. While some statisticians might get heartburn from it, it does its job.

When the normal audit method reaches the level at which errors are seldom found, the performance is (appropriately) continuously reported at 100%, and the enthusiasm about finding errors is lost. Occasionally, in these same environments, there is still a "feeling" that 100% isn't an accurate result because there are often problems when new products are launched or when infrequently produced items are manufactured. This is an opportune time to simply find and post errors as they are detected and stop the process of sampling BOMs on a daily basis. The question of how to measure this is still unanswered.

In this method each error discovered is given a value of 2% and is subtracted from 100%. For example, if there is one error, the performance for the day is 98%, and five errors result in 90% performance. A person with statistical tendencies might be wringing his/her hands nervously after that measurement definition. Remember the objective isn't to post a number; the objective is high performance. When errors occur, it is better to have solid recognition of those errors. That forces reporting at the weekly performance review and eliminating root cause. Some people, especially Six Sigma black belts, are not inclined to use percentage metrics consistently and want to simply keep track of inaccuracies and post the raw number with an objective of "0" inaccuracies instead.

## Simple Make-to-Stock Environments

In the simpler make-to-stock (MTS) environments, there can be fewer end-item configurations. In these environments (with less than a few thousand BOM structures), it might make sense to sample the entire BOM database. Often in these environments there are few obsolete BOMs maintained so it is in the best interests of high performance to cycle through the entire BOM record file. It is completed by item number order or it can make more sense to audit BOMs in the order of volume usage.

Some companies have hundreds of thousands of BOM records. These companies often utilize a make-to-order (MTO) or engineer-to-order (ETO) manufacturing methodology, which greatly increases the number of possibilities. They often ask the question, "How do companies in an MTO environment surface or segregate the proper database for audit?" Creating a firewall between the general database and the ones that are known to be probable manufacturing repeats could be the answer.

### Creating the Firewall for Make-to-Order and Engineer-to-Order Environments

Many organizations create a firewall between some of their data, thus greatly reducing the cost of data maintenance. The firewall is normally created by defining a "readiness code" field in the item master. For example, a "P" might be the readiness code designated for "production-ready" records. For an item to meet readiness, it has to meet minimum criteria for accuracy.

A leading manufacturer of capital equipment in the 1980s had over 150,000 BOM records. Some of these BOMs were not used frequently but could be called up occasionally in "same as except for" applications. Businesses in MTO environments often find themselves in this situation. It makes little sense to audit these seldom-used BOMs or, in fact, to perform any maintenance on this data. The company knew ignoring these BOMs without a supporting system for BOM structure integrity could result in disaster. Understanding the possible outcome, the company created a firewall to segregate their known data from unknown data.

In their environment, a "P" (production-ready or releasable) designation in the readiness code field on the item master could only be applied when the item could meet the following rigid minimum criteria:

1. The record must have a complete and unique part number (not assigned to another item).

2. The record must have a cost standard loaded (even if it is estimated).
3. If it was a parent number (higher level in a BOM), a recorded audit reflecting the latest revisions and part number changes must be present and available.
4. If it was a manufactured item, an audited routing record reflecting current machine and work centers must be loaded. It must also reflect accurate lead times from the routing.
5. The record must include a stocking code indicating if it is a stocked item or an MTO component part.
6. The record must include a lead time if it is a purchased part.

By forcing these requirements for an item prior to the release into production, all seldom-used items are converted to a "P" (production-ready) status prior to that release. In this example, a "P" also was an indicator that the item would *always* be revised each time an engineering change is authorized that connects to this item number (unless the production-ready status was changed). The company benefits greatly in terms of maintenance costs for seldom-used parts or assemblies, because it was not acceptable to be constantly maintained. The environment at this organization was one of constant high-volume change activity.

Some organizations use additional codes in the same item master field for seldom-used items. In this example, think of the production-ready code on the item master assigned as an "X." This designates "one-time-only" (seldom)-used parts. An "X" item, like the "P" item, would have to meet all the criteria for release, but as soon as it is no longer needed, it would again be treated as a non-maintained item. An engineering change would not update this item until the item was needed again. In this example, the firewall procedure would stop any item not designated as a "P" from being released or ordered. Even an "X" item would be reviewed every time it was released. It saves on engineering maintenance and costs for "one-time-only" items. To summarize, a "P" status item is maintained and kept current through every engineering change connected to it. A "non-P" item is behind the firewall and is reviewed each time (if) it is used in production.

This process allows engineering to invent and utilize the database any way they want without any risks to production or inventory control. As long as they stay behind the firewall with their experimental BOM designs, they are not bothering anyone. Many organizations find this a rewarding system for several reasons.

## ROUTING RECORDS

Routing records are the process steps or maps that material and components follow through the conversion process from raw material into salable finished goods.

In some organizations, routing records are important. In other environments, they are not important at all other than for cost standards.

## Where Routing Record Accuracy Is Paramount

In heavily-regulated organizations such as pharmaceuticals, the routing is impor-tant as a definition of process. It has to be accurate and has to be followed to the letter due to government regulation and liability concerns.

In traditional metal fabricating companies and long cycle time processes, rout-ing accuracy is also important. Routing accuracy in these businesses must be in the 99+% range also. In these environments, raw materials progress through several conversion operations and may travel reasonably long distances, which makes routing records a necessity for the planning process (table 4.1). These routings tend to support longer cycle times and more queue time as jobs move through func-tional departments, for example, the "saw department" or "lathe area."

Lean materials managers in today's high-performance organizations are opt-ing for short cycle times during which material travels in small batches and shorter distances and operations are close in proximity. Table 4.2 depicts what routings might be in these environments. In this example, no labor transactions are recorded because the time to do the process is extremely short; only inventory transactions are recorded.

Reviewing the record accuracy of routings is done similar to BOMs. Engineering, usually the manager of manufacturing engineering or processing engineering, is the responsible department and process owner for the accuracy audit and reporting. In smaller businesses where people wear many hats, again, someone from production could possibly be the right person for this process ownership.

### Table 4.1 Routing Record

| Operation | Instruction | Machine center |
|:---:|:---:|:---:|
| 010 | Saw to length | 7230 |
| 020 | Flame-cut notch | 7620 |
| 030 | Deburr/grind | 3410 |
| 040 | Form | 4620 |
| 999 | Receive into stock | 9999 |

### Table 4.2 Simplified Routing Record

| Operation | Instruction | Machine center |
|:---:|:---:|:---:|
| 010 | Make part | 3 |
| 999 | Move to shipping | SH |

Many of the newer computer systems have combined the BOM record and the routing record into one integrated record file in the system. These are usually referred to as bill of resource (BOR). The BOM structure in this application is expanded to include the process in which the component part is used. Sequencing and timing can be more efficiently planned. Again, this is not as beneficial in process flow or lean environments where inventory moves fast through several processes.

## SUMMARY ON DATA ACCURACY IN LEAN ENVIRONMENTS

There are other elements of data that drive decisions daily in lean manufacturing organizations. Each field in the item master could be a topic of discussion in this chapter. The most important ones have been outlined. As data accuracy is identified as a root cause for other metric performance issues (and it often is), actions must be driven to eliminate the causes for the process variation. Process ownership for each field in the item master should be assigned at the start of the Class A implementation, even before the problem causes are identified.

## DISCUSSION QUESTIONS

1. Routing accuracy is one of the most important areas of data accuracy in most firms.
   a. true
   b. false

2. Most companies refer to inventory accuracy in dollars or total count accuracy, which is the correct approach.
   a. true
   b. false

3. BOM accuracy should be measured as the percentage of BOMs that match the engineering specification to the MRP BOM.
   a. true
   b. false

4. In newer ERP systems there is not always a router and BOM stored in separate files. Instead there is a _____ file.
   a. router
   b. data
   c. BOM
   d. BOR

5. Why is it important to have a firewall for engineering change?
   a. It is too expensive to maintain all the part numbers all the time.
   b. There are too many part numbers in most environments.
   c. Engineers need to occasionally experiment with configurations.
   d. all of the above

6. If it is decided to count 50 items in the control group and there are too many mistakes to reconcile each day, what should the warehouse manager do?
   a. Add more cycle counters and stop picking for assembly.
   b. Get all the warehouse workers together to remind them that it is important to keep an accurate inventory.
   c. Temporarily count fewer control group items.
   d. Temporarily stop the control group.

7. The tolerance on "A" items is normally
   a. ±0
   b. ±.5%
   c. ±1%
   d. ±2%

8. In lean environments often the router file is only one operation, "make part."
   a. true
   b. false

9. Physical inventory is a necessary evil in high-performance organizations.
   a. true
   b. false

10. It is often beneficial to take a physical inventory immediately following a successful control group process.
    a. true
    b. false

# 5

# MASTER SCHEDULING IN LEAN MATERIALS MANAGEMENT

## INTRODUCTION

Master scheduling is probably one of the most important and yet least appreciated processes to help control costs in business today. Top management ignores it, middle managers take it for granted, and line management often unknowingly subverts the schedule's integrity by causing unnecessary changes to it. In contrast, high-performance businesses and lean materials managers treat the master scheduling process as the heartbeat of the supply chain and utilize the best practices in this area to minimize cost and maximize customer service. Techniques in master scheduling cover a great deal of business process territory, including links to demand planning, financial planning, inventory strategy, customer service, and rules of engagement.

## THE MASTER PRODUCTION SCHEDULE

The master schedule is the driver of requirements in an Enterprise Resource Planning (ERP) business system in manufacturing companies. This accounting of known and unknown requirements is the company's determination of firm and forecasted signals empowered to drive procurement and manufacturing requirements. Therefore, it is of utmost importance to the materials managers, especially ones with high performance as an objective. This master production schedule

(MPS) can dictate the amount of inventory, timing of procurement, and can even influence lot or order size. This is an extremely important set of requirements and makes the disciplines and rules governing the schedule crucially important to most businesses concerned about lean manufacturing, measured specifically as cost, effectiveness, efficiency, and customer service.

In high-performance businesses, top management engages in a planning process referred to as the Sales and Operations Planning (S&OP) process. It is also known as Sales, Inventory, and Operations Planning (SIOP) or Production, Sales, and Inventory (PSI) planning. The master scheduler plays a critical role in the development of the spreadsheets and performance metrics evaluated in the S&OP. Probably even more important is the requirement in high-performance companies that the master schedule link directly with this top management planning process. In the S&OP planning process, the chief executive officer, president, and vice presidents of both demand and supply engage in risk management within the planning horizon of 12 rolling months. No one understands the risks of creating the right product using only forecasts for the demand signals better than the master scheduler. Chapter 8 covers the topic of S&OP in greater detail.

In high-performance manufacturing organizations, especially in more complex product production, the two most influential positions are normally the plant manager and, you guessed it, the master scheduler. The master schedule defines the activities required to meet the top management S&OP but also dictates the requirements from customer demand. Sounds like quite a job and it is! Figure 5.1 depicts the relationship of the master schedule with the rest of the ERP process flow. Top management planning decisions feed into the MPS, drive emphasis, and create the forecasted demand. The MPS, in turn, feeds back vital data concerning customer activity and coordinates the interaction of the two inputs. This feedback affects the next S&OP cycle (figure 5.1).

The MPS is the detailed schedule that resides within the ERP business system that drives the inventory strategy, supply-chain actability, inventory levels, customer service, and machine and capacity utilization. The main categories that are driven fall into two areas, known requirements and unknown requirements. This seems too simple to even discuss, but it is the essence of understanding the MSP. In figure 5.2 the shaded areas represent these known and unknown requirements.

Where darker shaded areas are seen, there are normally detailed stock keeping unit (SKU) level requirements driven from either firm orders from customers or firm orders driven from planned requirements. If each shaded rectangle illustrated in figure 5.2 represents 1 day, the conclusion drawn is that backlogged orders only go out 6 days and, even then, capacity is not completely filled for the 6 days. Only Monday and Tuesday are close to being filled (Tuesday might even be a little over capacity per the diagram). This is the basic structure of the MPS in its simplest form. Inventory strategy has a substantial impact on the structure of the

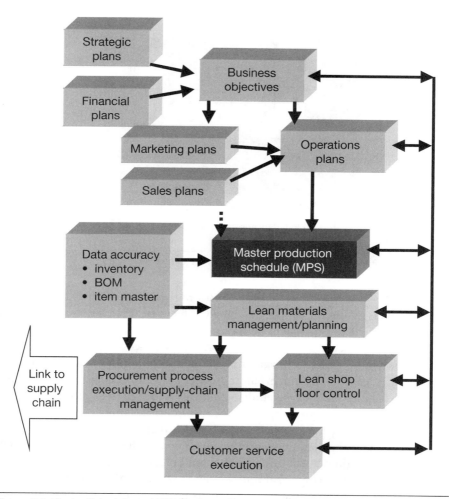

**Figure 5.1** Master Schedule and ERP Business System Model

MPS. Inventory strategy must be thoroughly understood to execute master scheduling properly.

## INVENTORY STRATEGY

Inventory strategy is the buffer inventory plan for each product family in a manufacturing planning process. Sometimes buffer is planned and held at the raw material stage (make to order [MTO]), sometimes it is planned to be held at the finished goods stage (make to stock [MTS]), and sometimes it does not exist at all

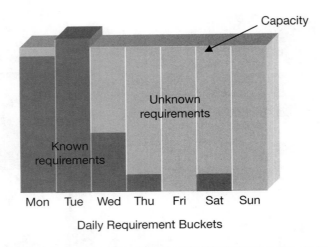

**Figure 5.2** Master Schedule Known and Unknown Requirements

except in the forecasted plan (engineer to order [ETO]). If the flexibility and responsiveness within the supply chain match the need, there is no reason to have buffer, but few manufacturing organizations meet the criteria completely. In these cases, the plan is decided based on product family process capability. Figure 5.3 gives a sense of how these strategies fit together. Keep in mind that most companies do not engage in just one inventory strategy. It is most common for companies to have three or four inventory strategies with separate pricing, rules of engagement, and service requirements for each product family.

It is necessary to review inventory strategy when setting up the MPS. The entire manufacturing planning world revolves around these strategies. Although many companies do not acknowledge this thinking, all companies have to make these decisions. Too many organizations say they are one type and actually are doing something totally different. Others do not recognize that their strategies differ from one product line to another. It is common for top management to believe that their business methodology is one inventory strategy, often MTO. It is just as common to discover after investigation that these businesses do not fully understand what is going on in the detail planning process. Maybe it's not fair to be so critical, but most of the time, especially in so-called "MTO" environments, there are buffers distributed in various places within the process. These have to be recognized and understood. These buffers are probably there for a reason. It's paramount to know what is in place and why it was initially positioned.

With the proper acknowledgement of actual buffer strategy, management has more control of the risks taken and nobody gets surprised by inventory that, by design, is *built* into the process. Inventory strategies change the method used for

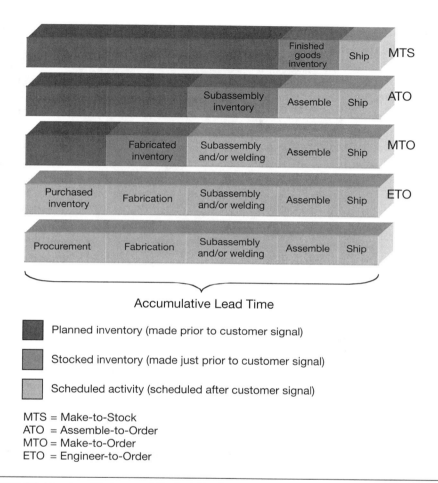

**Figure 5.3** Inventory Strategy and Product Family

master scheduling suppliers and components. Inventory strategy is smart policy but the internal, agreed-to rules need to be understood by all the players—what products, how much, and when. Frequently, finished goods inventory is scrutinized because it is visible and easily understood. Sometimes inventory does not need to be built in advance of the customer order. This is the whole point of inventory strategy. Lean thinking has gotten attention in the press recently and deservedly so, but inventory strategy has been around for years and covers some common ground with lean thinking.

It is important to realize that acknowledging rules of engagement and utilizing good inventory strategy are not designed to say "no" to the customer. Inventory strategy is acknowledged so that everyone in the business has the same shared goals. Its role is to acknowledge and understand what it costs when we say "yes" to the customer.

The acknowledgement of an inventory strategy is not difficult or complicated. In fact, it is often dictated by the data. When lead time requirements from the customer are shorter than the total accumulative lead time of the supply chain and manufacturing process, some of the process must be planned. That means some of the lead time in the process is committed to through forecasted requirements. Inventory strategy should be mapped out, agreed to by both the demand- and supply-side management, and rules of engagement documented. When the market practices or strategies change, update the handshake between the parties. Remember, the objective is lowest cost with highest service. To acknowledge the realities of inventory strategy is to allow for the most cost-effective and highest customer service processing of orders. Managers who think that all inventory is bad are not well-versed in the proper use of assets, acknowledgement of process variation, and customer service process design. Proper acknowledgement makes for a more robust and cost-effective master scheduling process. Each inventory strategy makes a difference in the scheduling approach and techniques used.

## PRODUCT FAMILIES

Through process evolution in ERP management, companies have determined that there is an optimum level of detail for planning at the top management level. This level of detail is usually labeled "product family."

As shown in figure 5.4, there is an optimum level of detail for the product family designation. It is difficult, at best, to define a generic formula for pinpointing the correct configuration that would work at all manufacturing companies. It just isn't that simple. It is also common for a company to revise the product families several times before they settle down to consistent groupings. The financial, demand, and operations plans *must* share these common planning groupings for efficiency of top management planning. It is this insistence that allows the real power of the S&OP process to work and the master schedule to be most effective.

## BILLS OF MATERIAL

The SKU level scheduled by master scheduling is determined by the bill of material (BOM) structure. The BOM is the recipe for how the product goes together and what components are required. The BOM records are one of the most important assets of an organization. Not only do they influence the manufacturing process, they also impact the planning process in several ways. It is universally

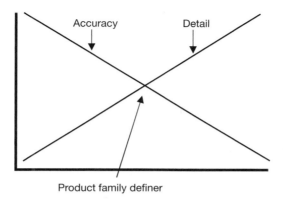

**Figure 5.4** Accuracy versus Detail Comparison

accepted that the more BOM levels designed into the structure, the more lead time (and cost) is present. The levels impact the inventory strategy requirement.

BOMs are not merely the recipe for the finished product. Planning BOMs are nearly always used in high-performance operations in some form. Planning BOMs drive components to be positioned in anticipation of a customer order. Good master scheduling utilizes planning BOM methodology. Examples include engines and transmissions for auto manufacturing. These more complex sub-assemblies require signals to be in position when the customer order is actually received.

## Planning Bills of Material

Planning bills are a huge asset to good master schedulers. These planning short-cuts make it easier for master schedulers to maintain the plans without thousands of SKU-level forecasted orders to manipulate. If in January the forecasted plan for the month of July has 100,000 units forecasted and planning bills are used, the requirements driving the Material Requirements Planning (MRP) would consist of one BOM (the planning bill) with a quantity of 100,000. The planning bill would take the expected mix and indicate proper ratios within the structure (figure 5.5).

In this example, the common parts are separated from the rest of the possible variable components for product family 123-XXX. This ensures that if some buffer is required due to mix variation, the common parts are not also buffered at the same level; thus, cost is reduced. The S&OP plan already takes risks into consideration. There is no need to double up on buffer stocks by adding buffer of common parts through additional planning. If the top management S&OP plan calls for 100,000 to be planned, that is all that should be planned—no more.

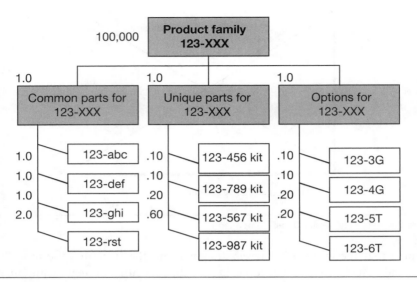

**Figure 5.5** Planning BOM

"Mix" issues, however, create a different scenario. If the S&OP plan calls for the 100,000 in the month of July, there is often no further definition of the detail requirements such as options and features within the demand plan. In reality, there could be several different SKUs offered within that one product family, 123-XXX. This is where the planning bill methodology shines.

For example, there are four different configurations (SKUs) within the 123-XXX product family. The SKU-level items are 123-456, 123-789, 123-567, and 123-987. In figure 5.6 these are listed under "Unique parts" for 123-XXX. In that section of the BOM, each configuration's unique parts are loaded as a kit without any common components.

If the SKU-level mix within the product family can migrate up or down, as is the case with most product families, buffer might be required, especially if there are long lead times for components or short lead times for customers. In the case of 123-456 above, the mix is normally 10% of the total requirements for the family. The master scheduler loads the requirement ratio at .1 or 10%. This action alone does not create buffer. Buffer is controlled easily at the top level (123-XXX unique components BOM). If there is a designator of 1.1 or 110% for BOM, it automatically drives components at a 10% buffer and fluctuates with the S&OP plan as it is maintained at the top level for each month. By driving only the unique parts at a "required plus buffer" level and common components only at required levels with little or no buffer, the flexibility is maintained with the least inventory.

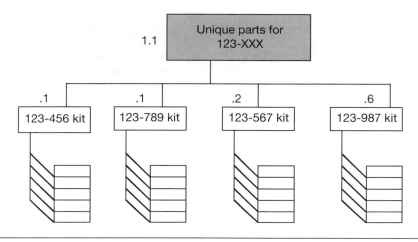

**Figure 5.6** Unique Components within a Planning BOM

In some organizations the opposite is true. Common parts are seen as low-risk and are driven at buffer levels and unique parts are planned at minimums. Both flexibility and cost become problems in this scenario as mix changes and expediting becomes the norm. Additionally, inventory is not always as low as it could be. Master schedulers need to remember that the decisions for buffer are really made at the top management S&OP process in most high-performance organizations. To duplicate buffer is not in the spirit of good planning and control. The master scheduler is normally the person who develops the plan for the top management S&OP. That sets the stage for total confidence in the plan.

Planning BOMs are a helpful tool for master scheduling and should be in the master scheduler's toolbox. In different time frames associated with time fence rules, BOMs are typically used in various ways (figure 5.7).

In the daily planning period, the requirements are normally driven at the SKU detail level based on actual orders loaded, either planned or firm. Depending on the business, this can be a few days or several. It depends on inventory strategy, lead time for components, and lead time requirements from the customers. It is the same philosophy used in each company but with a little different configuration. By using the planning BOMs in the future time periods, it becomes a much less maintenance-intensive process.

Obviously, the mix ratios in the planning BOMs determine how much inventory is being driven. It is also reasonable to question changes that might take place in the mix as products move through their product life cycles. Changes do occur and need to be part of the thought process as the master scheduler communicates with marketing and sales. Some master schedulers have a set time each month, for

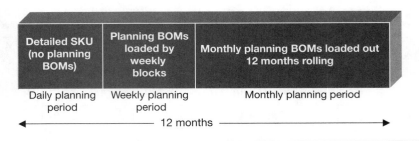

| Detailed SKU (no planning BOMs) | Planning BOMs loaded by weekly blocks | Monthly planning BOMs loaded out 12 months rolling |
| --- | --- | --- |
| Daily planning period | Weekly planning period | Monthly planning period |

← ———————————— 12 months ———————————— →

**Figure 5.7** Time Frames for Using Planning BOM

example the third Friday, to review ratios with the demand manager. Other companies need only to review these requirements drivers once a quarter. Good materials managers strive to keep the planning BOMs as accurate as possible. There is no reason to be panicked about the accuracy, but it is important for proper supply-chain signals. With netting of requirements against forecasted inventory availability, planned requirements are not duplicated if not consumed.

Every month the S&OP gets updated, and frequently there are required changes made in future months to keep the master schedule in synchronization with the top management S&OP plan. By using the planning BOMs, the changes can be made without getting into the details—provided that the S&OP, the master schedule, and planning BOMs are all in the same product family groupings. It is imperative that these three processes, including the S&OP foundations (the demand plan, operations plan, and business plan), share the exact same product family configurations.

## CAPACITY PLANNING IN THE MASTER PRODUCTION SCHEDULING PROCESS

Two types of capacity need consideration: demonstrated and theoretical capacity. In high-performance master scheduling, it is critically important to distinguish the two. In many businesses there are highly-energetic people who, with the best of intentions, think that the carrot has to be out in front of the donkey's nose for the cart to be drawn at top speed. The master schedule, in such a scenario, would be maintained at a higher rate than the actual demonstrated capacity. This can be true in lower-performance manufacturing plants but normally is not prevalent in high-performance facilities. There is no place in master scheduling for overstated requirements. The most important job a master scheduler can do is to keep the schedule tight and realistic. Without an understanding of demonstrated capacity, this is not possible. Capacity is a major concern for the master scheduler, perhaps

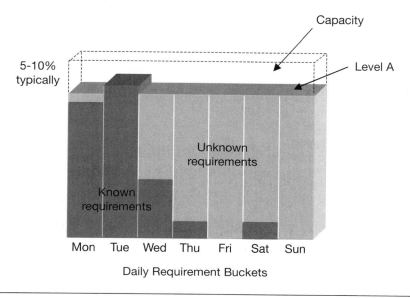

**Figure 5.8** Master Schedule and Buffer Time

the most crucial factor governing the scheduling process. A high-performance master scheduler consistently uses demonstrated capacity and is not fooled easily by opinions and emotions with no data or facts backing them.

Additionally, unless demonstrated capacity is consistent and repeatable, the argument can be made that some small amount of buffer time should be considered as well. In Frigidaire's Kinston, North Carolina, plant, this buffer is called "over-speed." Most high-performance facilities schedule some buffer time. Capacity is not lost because if the schedule is on time then work is pulled up from the next period (figure 5.8).

In figure 5.2, "capacity" was shown at level A. In figure 5.8, there is an imaginary level of capacity slightly above the filled bucket value of capacity scheduled for consumption. The inference is that the master scheduler should not always schedule to the maximum demonstrated capacity. To do so is to fail at master scheduling. Demonstrated capacity means that the process can generally yield to this level. It does not mean that the process always delivers at that level. Good master schedulers take their responsibilities seriously. When they miss schedules, it is a reflection on their accuracy and performance. High-performance master scheduling requires that schedules are hit 95+% of the time. To accomplish this, it is a requirement that demonstrated capacity is understood thoroughly, and schedules are continually synchronized with reality. In high-performance applications, this must happen at least once a week. It is not uncommon for synchronization to occur daily or even hourly, although if the process is properly initiated, this frequency interval should be minimized. In companies that initiate the process efficiently, synchronizing the schedule is not that difficult; many times only small schedule tweaks are needed. This practice should not be compromised. Any consideration of an alternative practice is generally not in accordance with effective master scheduling process.

## CUSTOMER ORDERS AND SCHEDULE LEVELING

In most businesses it seems that customers are generally ill-behaved. Orders do not come in at the same rate every day. Some days orders are heavy and on other days orders are light. Sound familiar? Customers do not work from a level schedule typically. They, after all, are reacting to their customers as well. Ultimately, it is the customers at the retail level that drive the entire supply chain. Figure 5.9 illustrates an example of the normal process variation.

In reality, figure 5.9 depicts how orders come into most businesses' order entry process. It does not matter what the position is in the food chain; consumer spending affects demand and consumers can be finicky, and usually are. This seesaw chart does not reflect how most companies want to run their operation on the supply side. For that reason, some smoothing is performed regularly. This smoothing is initially executed through decisions made at the S&OP process, specifically in the operations plan; however, the real schedule leveling takes place at the MPS. This is where planned orders meet firm customer orders.

### Massaging the Daily Schedule

The daily adjustments to the schedule, when things are working smoothly, are normal and not particularly disruptive in a high-performance operation, but as

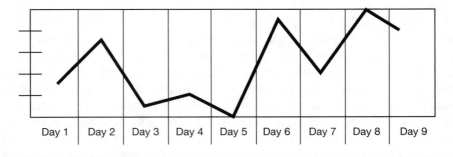

| Day 1 | Day 2 | Day 3 | Day 4 | Day 5 | Day 6 | Day 7 | Day 8 | Day 9 |

**Figure 5.9** Normal Customer Order Fluctuation

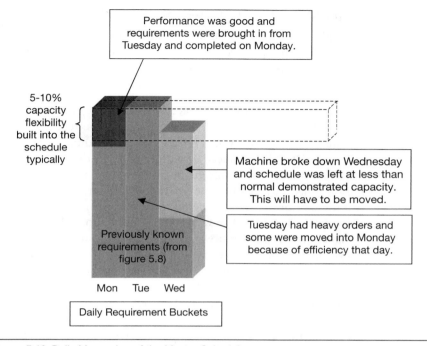

**Figure 5.10** Daily Massaging of the Master Schedule

many businesses know, every day is not a "tweak" day! Sometimes unplanned activities occur, including down machines or weather-related disruptions. I have even known clients with bomb threats! In today's world, the master schedule can have any number of possible surprises. Top performing organizations have established "rules of engagement" or a pre-designed process for dealing with these unplanned anomalies. Actually considered as daily schedule massaging by these master schedulers, it is accomplished in stride without the need for fanfare. Figure 5.10 shows the results of a process with normal uneven demand complicated by a machine-down situation. If the original planned schedule is filled to the demonstrated capacity minus 5%, there is some flexibility to move and shift orders without substantially impacting customer promises (figure 5.10).

Constant massaging is necessary for many high-performance master schedulers. Continuing with figure 5.10, the move from Tuesday into Monday is caused by customer variation, a process input that nearly all businesses experience regardless of market or product. The Wednesday problem is more avoidable, machine downtime. Robust preventative or productive maintenance is always a crucial element to minimize machine downtime.

## Rules for Master Production Schedule Level Loading

Level loading at the global level occurs in the operations planning and is detailed in chapter 8. Daily and/or hourly level loading is also necessary in most businesses. The following rules are appropriate after the operations plan monthly level loading has been accomplished.

1. Schedule materials available (not received—available) at least one period prior to the required need. If the scheduled time/requirement buckets are in days, allow supplier releases (only as authorized at this time) of material 24 hours ahead of requirements. If the schedule is in hour time buckets, schedule it for availability 1 hour prior to need. If the schedule is in minutes, schedule the material to be available 1 minute prior to need. I've yet to see a schedule in seconds but I can visualize it. It sounds like waste but to execute to high levels of performance, material flexibility is required. Most businesses overdo it, however, by bringing in material long before the need. These businesses frequently perform at less than 15-20 inventory turns. Be reminded that monthly quantities equates to only 12 turns! Unless the items are cheap components, it is not necessary to have a month's supply.

2. Schedule each product family separately. Product family designation is best established by considering inventory strategy, common constraints, and shared components and process. Along with the obvious reasons of shared constraints within a product family, it is helpful because inventory strategy affects product family selection. Inventory strategy dictates the level within the BOM, and the MPS drives material, which facilitates proper scheduling. For example, assemble-to-order (ATO) inventory strategy does not schedule at the finished goods SKU level. Instead, ATO scheduling is performed at the subassembly level, driving availability of subassemblies. The final assembly schedule draws the materials from the buffer for the exact configuration once the order is received from the customer. This is also known as a pull system.

3. Understand demonstrated capacity of the product family. Demonstrated means "normally executed levels," including "normally experienced" process variation (not including *unusual* process variation experienced). Don't forget that a supplier constraint is a component of the demonstrated capacity.

4. Create weekly schedules that allow for some execution variation. Schedule some buffer time above scheduled completions up to full demonstrated capacity.

5. Move future requirements into the present period to fill any unused buffer when performance is robust and no significant or out-of-the-ordinary process variation is experienced This can be accomplished automatically from the factory floor if the internal rules of engagement are specific enough to this need.

6. Allow employees to work on process improvement projects if there are no orders to pull up in the next period or there are no customer orders convertible to cash. Some suggestions include 5-S projects (housecleaning and workplace organization), setup reduction (both machine and assembly areas), or preventative maintenance. This is valuable time and must be effectively utilized. Some businesses release work ahead of schedule to make use of the time, but lean materials managers do not. It is less wasteful and much more productive to do process improvement projects during this time than to waste employee wages and material to build items that are not needed. Converted raw material loses its flexibility and is best left at the raw state when possible.

## FENCE RULES IN MASTER SCHEDULING

There are several theories and approaches to fence rules in scheduling. High-performance rules of engagement normally include specifics for each product family in terms of time fence rules. Without these rules/handshakes, it is more difficult to have high performance with the optimum efficiency of operations. In a normal process, the lead time elements might resemble figure 5.11.

The process may look different from this but usually procurement exists and at least one other conversion process exists as raw material is converted into salable product. If the process is simpler, some interpretation may have to be performed. In figure 5.12, the time fences are allied to this lead time.

As discussed in chapter 3, the "fixed" fence is sometimes referred to as the "frozen" fence. Remember, schedules are never completely locked. Because of this, most companies have abandoned the term "frozen." In figure 5.12, the inference is that more flexibility is built into the schedule. As a further reminder of the information in chapter 3, at each time fence, the rules change slightly, and all

**Figure 5.11** Accumulative Lead Time and Time Fences

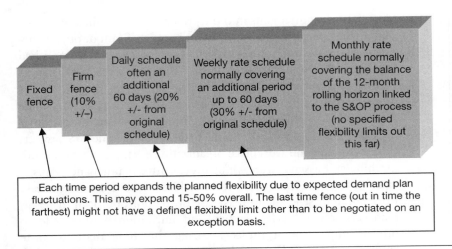

**Figure 5.12** Time Fence Norms and Flexibility Built into the Planning Horizon

the players in the supply chain are aware of the rules and the latest schedule. Flexibility is part of this handshake at each time fence break.

## MANAGEMENT SYSTEM REQUIREMENTS

Management system is a term often associated with process governance. The term is used to describe an autopilot infrastructure for management follow-up. There are several management system events required in high-performance master scheduling processes. The main one that strictly involves the weekly MPS is the clear-to-build (CTB) process. In this management system event, the master scheduler reviews the weekly schedule requirements for the upcoming week with the process owners who need to deliver it. Those players are the production managers and the procurement people. The objective of the CTB is to have clear visibility and accountability for the accuracy of each weekly plan. In high-performance organizations this is a simple and quick process but necessary nonetheless. Do not be fooled into thinking that to accomplish the CTB the schedule has to be locked for the next week. In many lean businesses next week's orders are not sold yet! The CTB process is a handshake to the levels of planned production in that environment. Since it is the objective of the master scheduler to have the highest level of accuracy possible in the MPS, it is without a doubt an important part of the master scheduling process. In chapter 14 management systems are covered in greater detail.

## THE SALES AND OPERATIONS PLANNING PROCESS

The top management planning process in all high-performance organizations includes some form of an S&OP process. It is best to begin this discussion from a platform of ERP understanding that was discussed in chapter 1. Figure 5.13 depicts the normal ERP business system with master scheduling as the centerpiece. Top management planning is at the higher points of this business system designated by process boxes within the large circle.

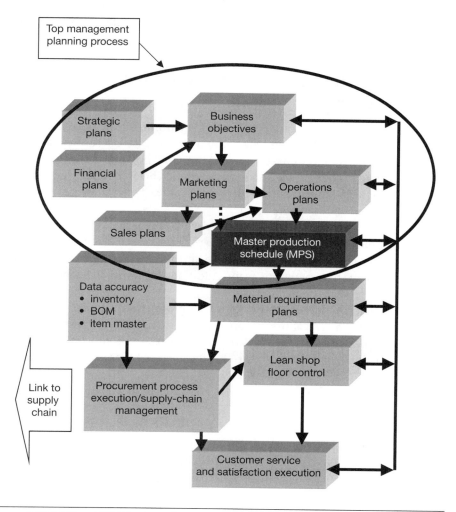

**Figure 5.13** MPS and ERP Business System Model

The S&OP process is a management system for, by, and with top management to facilitate managing the risk from the overall business process. Remember from earlier in this chapter that the S&OP is a handshake risk management process where both the demand- and supply-side managers gather once a month to review the likelihood that demand and operations plans are met.

No high-performance businesses succeed without some form of this process. Chapter 8 is dedicated to this important process. The S&OP process is the major input to the master scheduling process and without which it is difficult to effectively produce and execute an MPS. Because of this linkage, the master scheduler plays an important role in the S&OP process and is frequently the main player in prepping top management for the review.

## MASTER SCHEDULING PROCESS OWNERSHIP AND SUMMARY

Process ownership in the master scheduling environment includes making sure that the line schedules: 1) are in sync with the S&OP; 2) are accurate; 3) are communicated properly; and 4) have a 12-month rolling horizon in the business system for the supply chain to see and maximize efficiencies. In a high-performance operation, the MPS has to be updated/reviewed at least once a week and accuracy should be at least 95+% (figure 5.13).

The process owner for the master schedule is obviously the master scheduler. That individual normally documents the performance and opportunities and then reports to the weekly performance review to summarize accomplishments and progress with the operations team. Additionally, the master scheduler often facilitates the weekly CTB.

The master schedule is the driver for all production activity, including the supply chain. It is a critical process and one of the most important in any business. The handoff from the MPS is the material planning functions within the organization flow chart. In the next chapter, material planning is discussed in more detail.

## DISCUSSION QUESTIONS

1. The top management planning process performed each month to assess risk and align the demand- and supply-side activities is known as the
   a. PSI.
   b. S&OP.
   c. SIOP.
   d. all of the above

2. Most companies have one inventory strategy for several product families.
   a. true
   b. false

3. The master scheduler's job is to make sure the schedule
   a. is in sync with the S&OP.
   b. is accurate.
   c. is communicated properly to others in the organization.
   d. has a 12-month rolling horizon in the business system for the supply chain to see and maximize efficiencies.
   e. all of the above

4. The CTB process is designed to
   a. kit orders and make sure they are buildable.
   b. give schedule adherence accountability to the production supervisors and/or shop managers.
   c. determine the sequence of build by counting components.
   d. none of the above

5. Planning BOMs are used to
   a. act as a placeholder for items that might be used.
   b. give visibility to suppliers when firm orders have not been received by the customer.
   c. allow MRP to work properly.
   d. b and c
   e. all of the above

6. Planning BOMs can be used to plan both options and features. When using planning BOMs for options, the sum of parts in one BOM should be equal to 1 (one).
   a. true
   b. false

7. The MPS deals with
   a. knowns.
   b. unknowns.
   c. both knowns and unknowns.
   d. none of the above

8. When using MTO methodology, demand creates
   a. an inventory draw on finished goods.
   b. backlog.
   c. an increase in inventory.
   d. none of the above

9. When using MTS methodology, demand creates
   a. an inventory draw on finished goods.
   b. backlog.
   c. an increase in inventory.
   d. none of the above

10. A good master scheduler uses _____ to develop the master schedule.
   a. theoretical capacity
   b. demonstrated capacity
   c. planned capacity
   d. b and c
   e. all of the above

# MATERIALS PLANNING FOR EXCELLENCE IN LEAN ENVIRONMENTS

## INTRODUCTION

At the heart of nearly every material planning process within manufacturing is some form of Material Requirements Planning (MRP). MRP has received a bad rap in recent years. Between the "constraint" folks, the Six Sigma people, lean gurus, software visionaries, and the just plain inexperienced types, the word on the street is that MRP is dead. The next sentence is not considered "hip" with the latest thinking and is unexpected in a book covering lean materials management, nonetheless, it is true. In reality, nothing is further from the truth than the statement that MRP is dead. When the discussion point is strictly described as "netting of future requirements," few "experts" argue with the necessity to do material netting in manufacturing planning. The truth is that nearly every successful major manufacturing business uses some form of MRP whether they admit it or not. The software people add to the confusion, and it is understandable. Much like the term "station wagon" is out of date (these vehicles are now called SUVs or even hybrid SUVs), the MRP concept is also known by new terms. Most of these names are recognizable by hints like "advanced scheduler" or "advanced planning and scheduling module" or even "drop and drag order sequencer." These new labels are the "4-wheel-drive hybrid SUV" versions of the MRP station wagon! Some of the names are actually quite clever. At the end of the day, however, these planning

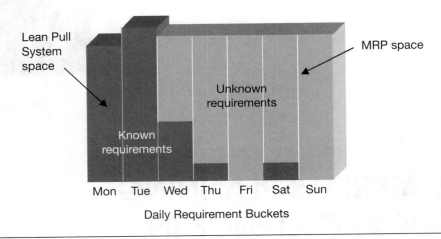

**Figure 6.1** Master Schedule and MRP

engines are basically netting requirements and time-phasing the resulting signals for either procurement or manufacturing.

Before going too much further, MRP must be fully understood in the context of lean. MRP is best when used in future planning rather than present planning. Pull systems are designed for the most effective use in the "known" space, whereas MRP or netting systems are best used in the "unknown" space (figure 6.1).

Pull systems work effectively to minimize waste on the shop floor. Pull systems do not work effectively to plan requirements out in the future for capacity and risk management. This future territory is the best place to use a material planning process that nets on-hand and anticipated on-hand against anticipated customer activity. Whatever it is called, the realities are that it is MRP!

Material planning is the process of taking the requirements handed off from the master production schedule (MPS) and determining what, if any, components need to be ordered versus those that are readily available. Availability is derived from current stock, planned in procurement, or planned in manufacturing (figure 6.2).

The MPS requirements are the real drivers of material planning. As described in chapter 5, the master schedule is massaged continuously to synchronize the supply side with customer demand. The material planning engine in the enterprise resource planning (ERP) software business system is the calculator that sorts out what to do with these MPS signals. For the rest of this discussion "MRP" is the label referred to when describing this detail planning engine in ERP.

MRP performs several activities once the MPS requirements are refreshed and fed into the planning engine. The first activity is to pick up sub-level requirements

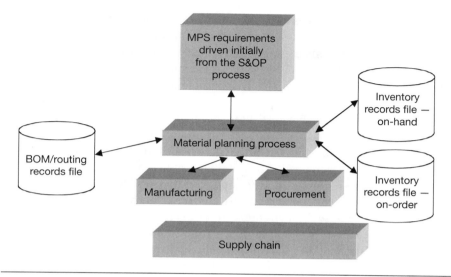

**Figure 6.2** MRP Inputs and Outputs

from the bill of material (BOM) record for each MPS requirement. Remember, the BOM record contains several pieces of important information:

a. top-level part number (parent-level number)
b. component part numbers called out in the upper level
c. usage per component in the upper-level assembly
d. unit of measure for each component
e. lead time and lead time offsets for each component

After the BOM information is accessed, the next information the MRP system requires to complete the planning job is the inventory records. There are two types of inventory records for this discussion: on-hand inventory and on-order inventory. The names are descriptive enough but for clarity there is an important performance need in this space. The importance of data accuracy becomes more critical as realization of data dependency is underlined. For this planning engine to do its job effectively, the BOM records must be impeccable and inventory records must be pristine. Minimally acceptable thresholds for this accuracy require BOM accuracy to be at 98%. This means that 98% of the BOMs are perfect. The threshold of high performance for BOMs is 99%. Inventory record accuracy has much more opportunity for process variation in most manufacturing businesses. The threshold of acceptability in the inventory accuracy space is 95%. A higher standard of 98% accuracy is required to be considered robust. In this measurement, again, the percentage represents perfect location balances. It does not mean that each balance is 98% accurate. These are important requirements to keep process variation and associated costs to a minimum.

When the accuracy of these important system elements is less than acceptable, problems can develop and will. If, for example, the master schedule is at a 90% level of accuracy, meaning that the requirements are about 90% accurate in either quantity or date, MRP is greatly affected. If the process variation exposure is increased by having less than 98% BOM accuracy and/or if the inventory record accuracy is below 95%, the accumulation of process input variation becomes an exponential problem affecting the output accuracy of MRP. This is not rocket science. It is simple, plain logic. It should be the goal of any organization to use the business system on autopilot in every opportunity possible to lower cost, especially in the planning of requirements driven from a forecast. Bad data eliminates this possibility because human horsepower is immediately and consistently required to offset this process variation caused by inaccuracies in data. Too many organizations today still do not appreciate the huge payback available from such simple efforts as process transaction disciplines (see chapter 4).

## ORDER POLICY DECISIONS

Lean-thinking materials managers understand the impact on order policy and pay close attention to both development and management of these planning directives. In many manufacturing operations, MRP is used to order components outside the firm fence. There are demand pull alternatives to this that are covered later but this option is worth discussion. MRP is used in all manufacturing applications somewhere in the horizon. MRP creates signals that the planners respond to according to the netting calculation resulting from inputs and outputs. When a requirement is determined for a particular component, the planner first has to know how many to order. Sometimes the decision is easy—only the number to exactly match the requirements; but other times it is not as simple. Take, for example, a situation in which a low-cost item is procured from a company on a continent thousands of miles away. If the requirement is for stainless steel bolts at a quantity of 17 with a price of 30 cents and the source for these bolts is China, how many is the right number to purchase? The answer, even given the data of price and source, is still "it depends," isn't it? It depends on inventory strategy of the item and the upper-level requirements, and it depends on anticipated usage beyond any known history. Order policy is a management "knob" for controlling the inventory decisions made by others lower in the organization. Order policy begins to address the issues and answer the question of "how many should be ordered." There are a few order policy types often used. One that is not often used but gets press time occasionally is economic order quantity (EOQ).

a. **One for one**—This is the JIT, lean, or kanban approach. None is ordered until there is a customer-demand requirement. If 17 are needed, only 17 are ordered. This approach is used in an engineer-to-order (ETO), make-to-order (MTO) and/or assemble-to-order (ATO) inventory strategy. In a lean environment most finished goods are made in one of these (ETO, MTO, or ATO) strategies.

b. **Lot for lot or order for order**—This policy is a deviation on one for one. In this situation, subassemblies can be requisitioned in anticipation of a customer order and required components. Items with this assigned order policy are not ordered unless there is a requirement from another parent level. In that case, the quantities are requisitioned to match the upper-level lot size. In forecasted requirements, a forecast for orders might be made on anticipated lot quantities even in an ATO or MTO environment. Lot for lot can be the right decision.

c. **Time-value or fixed period order policy**—With this order policy, parts are ordered in quantities to cover the usage for a certain period of time, often a week or more. If the assigned time value for this part is 2 weeks and the usage is expected at 3 per day, for two 5-day weeks, the order size would be 30 pieces (2 weeks times 5 days times 3 per day). This can be useful when transit times are long such as in overseas procurement.

d. **Fixed order Quantity**—This order policy dictates certain predetermined quantities. In some process flow businesses, these quantities are frequently referred to as campaigns. There can be many reasons for this practice: how many can be made from a sheet, how large the vat is in the process, or what the normal demand is for this item. In some plastics industries, for example, where demand is immediate and finished goods are made in anticipation of demand due to takt time concerns, fixed order quantity or fixed campaigns are common.

e. **EOQ**—Few high-performance organizations use EOQ. The formula is the square root of 2AS over IC (where A = cost of an order to process, S = units per year, I = inventory carrying charge, and C = unit cost). EOQ is not actually valid. The main problem with this practice is the ability to adjust all the variables and end up with whatever lot size is wanted (figure 6.3). The infamous example often related about EOQ involves machine shops. The machine shop managers, who do not focus on short setups and changeovers, do not generally like small lot orders. These managers are happy to load

$$\sqrt{\frac{2\,AS}{IC}}$$

**Figure 6.3** EOQ Formula

the EOQ equation with cost drivers that increase the lot size and artificially make their world "easier." Not good.

## ABC STRATIFICATION

Along with order policy code, stratification also plays an important role in ordering inventory from MRP signals. Inventory stratification is the segmentation of items into layers by monetary or usage values. Pareto's 80/20 rule works effectively here. Generally, the dividing layers are:

A = 75% of the monetary value of inventory, 10% of the item numbers
B = 15% of the monetary value of inventory, 10% of the item numbers
C = 10% of the monetary value of inventory, 80% of the part numbers

Some organizations also have a D category which divides the C items into two groups. D items are usually components that are very inexpensive, for example, common small washers and screws with values much less than one cent each.

Most ERP business systems can automatically calculate the inventory layers and give the user parameters that are then set as desired. Stratification is initiated to ensure that there is more emphasis on the items that have the most associated risk. Many times critical components that are difficult to get or are allocated are forced into the A item code regardless of the ABC calculation. Lean-thinking materials managers use this age-old strategy to layer inventory and allow the focus to be on the items that have the greatest cost or service risk or have some other important impact to the business.

## PROCESS OWNERSHIP AND LEAN MATERIALS PLANNING METRICS

In a high-performance manufacturing organization, the materials manager owns metrics in the materials space. Robust materials control measures include customer service, data accuracy, effective schedule maintenance, accurate purchase orders and work orders, and, in synchronization with the MPS, management of obsolete and excessive inventory and updating data fields in the item master. Lead time is a good indicator of performance in the materials world. Lead time is the critical field that drives inventory decisions and reaction time. It needs to be accurate and as short as possible but realistic.

Metrics for materials control are logical. Class A criteria for planning accuracy allow choices. This is covered more extensively in chapter 11.

Some additional common lean materials planning metrics are:

a.  percent of purchase orders let without full lead time as defined in the lead time field on the item master
b.  percent of 100% pickable assemblies released on time to assembly
c.  percent of schedule changes within the fixed period fence (usually 48 hours but can be up to 1 week)
d.  inventory turns—raw, work in process (WIP), and finished goods
e.  dollars of inventory on hand for every dollar of revenue within a product family
f.  cycle time of idea to cash (new product introduction)
g.  lead time to the customer
h.  percentage of product shipping on the original "promise" date or time
i.  percentage of product shipping on the original requested date or time
j.  inventory location balance accuracy
k.  BOM accuracy (usually belongs to engineering)
l.  time from order receipt to actual value-add in the factory
m.  time from order receipt to shipment by product family
n.  cycle time
    • idea to cash
    • new product introduction
    • order management
    • machine cycle
    • manufacturing cycle
    • customer order to action

Each metric brings some special benefit to the table. Each organization needs to determine what the greatest need is in terms of the required drivers of action. If the business is an assembly shop and currently it is common to have orders released for pick without all the components available, the percent pickable metric is valuable. If the business has myriad changes within the fixed period that create excessive cost from changeovers and material movement, then the schedule change metric is recommended. Class A requires two metrics in this area of focus and gives some leeway depending on the circumstances. There are no bad metrics in the list and implementing all of them can be a risk-free compromise.

Measuring process is useless if the information learned is not utilized. Organizations that have high performance baked into their DNA always have measures but they also always have actions tied directly to the measurements. Closing the loop on metrics is an important activity. This brings to mind problem-solving focus and effective process techniques such as lean tools and Six Sigma.

## ENTERPRISE RESOURCE PLANNING INTEGRATION WITH LEAN AND SIX SIGMA

Seemingly, the ERP integration area generates the most controversy around the appropriateness of yesterday's business system lessons when they integrate with lean and Six Sigma. Let's get Six Sigma out of the way first since it is so easily and logically justified.

Six Sigma is a process focus that formalizes effective problem-solving techniques and establishes data mining and use of facts as a prerequisite to success. Success is defined by the voice of the customer. In this case, we can define at least two customer types. The first type is the one that pays the bills through product or service purchases. The second type is top management and the stakeholders of the business that ask for a return on investment. Having ample material all the time is great for the end-item customers, but the stakeholders would rather have cash earning a return as opposed to tied up in slow-moving inventory. Using statistical tools from the Six Sigma kit does nothing but help the application of material planning. Here are some examples of Six Sigma projects that have paid back many times and connect directly to MRP effectiveness and materials planning:

a. increase forecast accuracy
b. increase accuracy of BOMs
c. decrease the lead time of major components
d. increase throughput yield
e. increase first time quality
f. decrease scrap
g. decrease cost of quality
h. decrease dependence on informal systems (lists) in the shop
i. increase accuracy of the MPS

There is an unending list of possible Six Sigma projects that can help drive lean materials planning and make the processes work more effectively. Defining lean is more involved in the ERP space but not any less helpful and easily integrated. As has been stated, lean is a strategy that focuses on waste elimination. In the early days, MRP actually was adequate in the elimination of waste; however,

**Table 6.1 Traditional Thinking MRP versus Lean**

| Topic | MRP | Lean |
|---|---|---|
| Inventory strategy | MTS | MTO |
| Inventory level | High | Low |
| WIP level | Moderate to high | One piece lots |
| Rate | To level load | To customer demand |
| Production control | Critical ratio calculation | Visible, kanban |
| Production communication | Shop work order | Kanban pull |
| Lot size | EOQ | Customer order or one piece |
| Lead time | Long (queue, move time) | Short |
| Focus | Next operation | Customer requirement |

by today's standards MRP does not come close to the best-in-class opportunities for waste elimination in the process. Waste is found in the form of excess inventory, large lot sizes, too much make-to-stock (MTS) inventory strategy, and too little concern for data integrity. All of these topics have seen major gains in the modern business environment. The "pull system" aspect of lean methodology is a good place to start the integration discussion.

MRP's traditional "push-type" system meant that orders were made in anticipation of customer demand. Sometimes this was at the lower levels and not necessarily at the finished goods level; nevertheless, too much inventory was easily generated. If this was the prevailing result, it would be easy to kill and bury MRP. However, there is more to the story than that simple explanation. Table 6.1 illustrates a simple view of an MRP and lean comparison.

One key element in modern thinking is the range of MRP use. If the planning horizon is divided into time fences (fixed, firm, and planned), the rules and techniques are clearly different in the various time fences. A hybrid MRP methodology has developed to help utilize the strengths of both MRP planning processes and lean techniques. The resulting synergy creates a high-performance planning process. Figure 6.4 helps visualize the difference and table 6.2 gives a "modern" look to the data presented in table 6.1.

When MRP and lean are integrated, the possibilities of powerful supply-chain management and the lean, efficient customer draw on inventory and process support the Class A ERP process as well as the resulting high performance. Organizations (or books) that indicate that lean replaces material netting/planning engines and processes are misinformed, inexperienced, or deceitful. This is strong language, but it is true.

**Table 6.2 21st Century Thinking Hybrid MRP Lean**

| Topic | MRP/Lean Hybrid |
| --- | --- |
| Inventory strategy | Appropriate inventory strategy with customer draw |
| Inventory level | Moderate to low |
| WIP level | Low |
| Rate | To customer demand |
| Production control | Visible, kanban, MPS |
| Production communication | Kanban pull |
| Lot size | Customer order or one piece |
| Lead time | Short |
| Focus | Customer requirement |

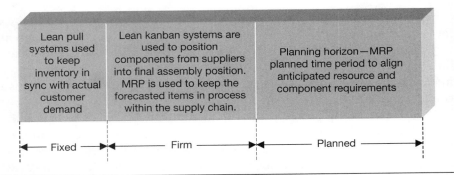

| Lean pull systems used to keep inventory in sync with actual customer demand | Lean kanban systems are used to position components from suppliers into final assembly position. MRP is used to keep the forecasted items in process within the supply chain. | Planning horizon—MRP planned time period to align anticipated resource and component requirements |
| --- | --- | --- |
| ◄— Fixed —► | ◄— Firm —► | ◄— Planned —► |

**Figure 6.4** Rules in Various Time Fences Using Hybrid MRP Methodology

## RUNNING THE MATERIAL REQUIREMENTS PLANNING NET-CHANGE CALCULATION

Since MRP was invented more than 30 years ago, significant progress has been made in both software efficiency and hardware capacity. The rule of thumb in the beginning of MRP application was to run the regenerative net-change program and calculation every weekend. The program took hours to run and often nothing else could be processed while the room-sized computer churned the data, layer by layer. Many are not even old enough to remember those days! Even more interesting was the philosophy that running it too often created a large amount of unnecessary system noise (variation) in the manufacturing process. It is actually quite humorous to think about that today. That system noise was driven from changes in customer demand and the reason it was called noise was because the manufacturing managers didn't want to change over equipment, especially in the machine shop. These shop managers wanted to run long lot orders. If MRP wasn't run too often, changes still occurred but they were not communicated to the shop, which artificially created stability in the schedule. This luxury was offset by huge amounts of inventory in finished goods. Expediting was often funded willingly and heroes were generated in the shop and in purchasing daily as companies like Federal Express became household words. It is much different today, especially in high-performance manufacturing businesses.

Customer demand is what makes organizations vital. To ignore it is foolish and costly. If the existing production process is not matched to the present customer behavior and demand, it is time to reevaluate the manufacturing strategy. That includes inventory strategy and market offerings. When these strategies are in line with market need, how frequently the MRP program is run is a non-issue. The more it is run, the more accurate the current schedule is and life is good.

Most high-performance organizations run MRP daily and many of the best ones run it several times a day. Again, if the inventory strategies and rules governing the supply chain are adequate for the markets that have been chosen, more frequent MRP runs yield gains. Most of the value comes from the supply-chain visibility. What value would come from hiding schedule updates from the suppliers? The answer is no value.

In reality MRP does not affect all inventory today. Pull systems may, at the execution level, move inventory in sync with demand and production rates. MRP netting will be re-aligning supply chains and components outside the fixed time fence. The bottom line—it does little harm to run it and it adds significant value.

## INVENTORY MANAGEMENT

Warehouse management, including transaction design and cycle count processes, are good inventory management processes, but there are still many aspects of good inventory management (see chapters 4 and 7) that should be addressed outside of data integrity. These areas fall into the lean materials management space. Robust materials management process quality focuses on predictable and repeatable processes. That includes checks and balances on manufacturing and scheduling processes to minimize unnecessary inventory. Nonetheless, inventory still exists in nearly all manufacturing companies. Inventory (planned or on-hand) is the result of a difference between the company's cumulative lead time and the lead time of market requirements. If there is a 16-week cumulative lead time but customers only want to wait 3 days, there is inventory in the system somewhere, either at the manufacturer or within the supply chain. That is not good news or bad news; it's just the news—in other words, a fact. Process variation is offset either by process flexibility or buffer. Normally, there are both somewhere in the supply chain.

Managing inventory requires a conscience even when the inventory manager doesn't directly control the ordering. Effective warehouse managers in high-performance environments have monthly routines that become a conscience for the inventory planning and forecasting people in the business. This role of conscience is sometimes overlooked due to the other "normal" demands of managing a warehouse. The sometimes overlooked routines include:

a. Evaluate all obsolete inventory each month. Investigate and analyze root cause for this obsolescence. Except for the rare operations where obsolescence is not created, each month routinely expense and remove excessive inventory. Communicate a metric of causes to appropriate management. This could include engineering, marketing, sales, and even production. This would seem like a huge waste and it is! Analysis and root cause need to be tied to the process, which results in improvements to process and, thus, a decrease of "new" obsolescence creation.

b. Monthly, list every inventoried item in the warehouse. Sort this report by current inventory days on hand. Include monetary unit value, total value, last transaction date, and ABC code in the report for each item. Items with more than a few days on hand should be suspect, especially if these items are A or B items. Investigate root cause. In many instances a Six Sigma team is a good vehicle to both gather data and propose an attack plan for use-up. Long term, eliminating the source of this obsolescence has the high impact. These sources often include a lack of total understanding of the impact that decisions made lightly in engineering or marketing have on the coordination of material use-up. Engineering changes are an opportunity in many organizations.

c. Evaluate the preventative maintenance (PM) schedule attainment for the period at the end of each month. Make sure the schedules are maintained and are kept current. This may not seem to be in the material management space but not performing PMs in a timely manner negatively affects schedule adherence and, ultimately, customer service. While the materials manager does not normally have total control over this PM execution, scheduling certainly plays a substantial part in the effectiveness of PMs. In many organizations the materials and scheduling departments do not understand the benefits and often are the source of resistance when machine time is needed for this maintenance. PMs pay back. This has been proven time and again in many studies.

d. Track the changes in unit demand volumes and material movement to ensure that the items that have the most transactions are the ones closest to the process where used, the door or docks within the warehouse.

There are many more important duties within materials management but these represent the ones most often neglected. In high-performance organizations these are not overlooked. The focus now shifts to the warehouse in which the warehouse manager reports to the materials manager.

## DISCUSSION QUESTIONS

1. Lean organizations use MRP.
   a. true
   b. false

2. In regard to ERP systems
   a. all of the most popular ERP systems have an MRP system.
   b. few ERP systems use MRP calculations anymore.
   c. lean businesses use pull systems in place of MRP for planning.
   d. b and c

3. The threshold of acceptability for BOM accuracy in high-performance organizations is normally
   a. 92%.
   b. 95%.
   c. 99%.
   d. 100%.

4. The threshold of acceptability for inventory accuracy in high-performance organizations is normally
   a. 92% location balance accuracy.
   b. 95% location balance accuracy.
   c. 99% overall quantity accuracy.
   d. 100% overall quantity accuracy.

5. EOQ using the traditional calculation is a popular order policy in high-performance organizations.
   a. true
   b. false

6. ABC stratification is initiated to
   a. make high demand visible.
   b. give more inventory to the most utilized items.
   c. layer the inventory for planning purposes.
   d. all of the above

7. Order policy in planning is
   a. sequencing the schedule.
   b. giving accountability to the floor.
   c. reporting performance.
   d. sizing the lots to be released to the floor and suppliers.

8. Materials organizations following a Six Sigma methodology
   a. strive for 95% quality and accuracy.
   b. have full time black belts.
   c. use projects to improve the performance of their area.
   d. do not use order policy.

9. Pull systems are used mostly in the current time frame and MRP is mostly used within the planning horizon.
   a. true
   b. false

10. Duties of a materials manager normally include
    a. management of obsolescence.
    b. inventory accuracy.
    c. tracking changes in demand.
    d. monitoring forecast accuracy.
    e. all of the above

# 7

# WAREHOUSE MANAGEMENT AND ORGANIZATION

## INTRODUCTION

Storage layout and design is only important if there is inventory to store. Unfortunately, few organizations have figured out processes so variation-free that no inventory is required. Organizations, for example Dell, have limited their inventory in-house but have a buffer within the supply chain to offset customer behaviors not precisely forecasted. Even Toyota, which wrote the book on lean, understands that buffer is important when there is an expectation of some process variation.

Storage layout is always changing. It is a requirement that is never-ending as process improvements are incorporated into the inventory flow model. Every time the cycle time is shortened or the product is redesigned, flow layout is affected. Linkages to process improvement as well as availability of capital to rearrange new methods all contribute to the timing. Accuracy of location balances is also important when trying to limit controllable process variation.

The main storage organization requirement in establishing accurate inventory location balances is having inventory logically stored, neat and organized. This means locations cannot be as large as entire factories and these specific geographic areas should be easily accessible but controlled. A couple of years ago a manufacturing plant in France was ready to turn on a new software system and had no locations in the system other than "plant." In effect, it meant that the locations were as *large as the plant.* While seen by some as simplification of process, in a plant like this one, without knowing the location of inventory there is no foolproof way to verify its accuracy or easily locate materials. Unfortunately, it is an all-too-frequent mistake in designing (or ignoring) material storage designs. Locations systems are not thought of as important but they *are* important.

Factories or distribution facilities that have inventory stored (by process design) for more than 24 hours and/or that want to net inventory balances against planned or actual requirements should have the capability to audit and verify inventory balance accuracy. Auditing inventory accuracy in the previous example requires searching the entire plant, every corner, aisle, rack, and cabinet drawer, to reconcile accuracy. *Bonne chance* (French for "good luck")! This is not a problem foreign to any soil. Companies trying to shortcut good processes or companies lacking a full understanding of lean manufacturing techniques often neglect the need for well-organized and accessible storage techniques linked to their planning system for the sake of simplified systems. These systems do not end up being so simple in the end.

In any facility in which inventory is resident for more than 24 hours, there should be locations sized with the process in mind. Here is the opportunity to store only enough for an hour or a day, whatever makes sense in the particular situation. This chapter defines the rules that govern good inventory organization and storage patterns.

## GOOD INVENTORY ORGANIZATION AND STORAGE PATTERNS—THE BEGINNING CHECKLIST

Experience teaches that understanding the final vision, objective, or goal helps keep the journey on track. It can also make the journey more efficient by minimizing false starts. Using this logic, the vision or short list of goals for organized storage includes the following important topics.

1. **Good housekeeping/workplace organization.** Good housekeeping is a basic rule that should be understood as a prerequisite to effective system discipline. Good housekeeping in a stores area includes having all material in its place and a place for all materials. Lines on the floor designate storage areas for specific items, racks are clearly labeled, only materials intended for the locations are present, and material is moved on a timely basis.

   In high-performance organizations pallets are in close alignment. They are not allowed to extend from racks into the aisle. While

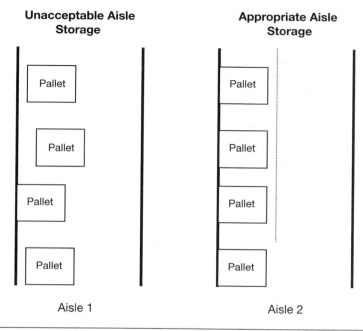

**Figure 7.1** Storage Alignment

some think that policy is unnecessary, the standard helps both safety and neatness (figure 7.1).

It is also important to have proper receptacles for waste: steel strapping or other banding materials or packaging materials including unwanted skids. These receptacles must be both sized properly and located in needed areas. Sometimes it means receptacles placed on the fork trucks. It is not acceptable to have broken banding left in the racks. It is unsightly, fosters bad habits, and is unsafe for people reaching in to order-pick customer requirements. When encountered, this packaging material must be removed from the storage area in the process.

2. **Sufficient lighting.** Lighting might seem like a fairly obvious need, but many organizations ignore it. Sometimes it is a result of racks being constructed in areas not initially designed for storage. For example, it could happen that as a business grows, storage racks are added in adjoining areas years after lighting was originally installed; there was another purpose planned for the space. The result is often heavy shadows in the spaces in which high accuracy of picks is expected. When evaluating storage patterns, it is good to take a

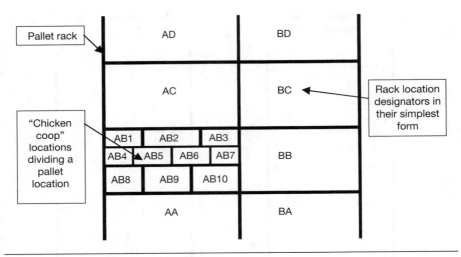

**Figure 7.2** Rack Dividers for Proper Sizing of Locations

walking tour through the storage areas with the sole purpose of evaluating proper lighting.

3. **Properly-sized locations.** Locations should be the appropriate size for the purpose and process. Mixing different parts in the same location makes pick accuracy more difficult and should be avoided if at all possible. Sometimes this "mix" is due to locations improperly sized. A common misuse of storage facilities is having multiple small parts stored in a rack within a single pallet location. In this particular example, if there are many small parts and only pallet racking in the desired storage area, it would be better to divide the pallet space up into smaller "chicken-coop"-type spaces using simple plywood dividers (figure 7.2).

These dividers are not expensive and can add percentage points to the record accuracy by eliminating unnecessary errors from picking wrong parts from common locations. This improved accuracy can quickly pay for the plywood by eliminating the waste associated with inaccurate inventory records including surprise shortages, emergency freight, and/or poor customer service.

Some organizations have large or unusual parts that have to be stored. A machine tool manufacturer in Ohio has castings that are purchased for the main frame of their large machine tools. These castings are the size of an automobile and larger. Because of variability not yet eliminated in their material flow, these castings have a one-week buffer built into the process. These castings, due to their size, cannot be stored in regular pallet racking but should not be ignored while addressing the rules for proper storage patterns. In this organization a storage area is designated with lines painted on the floor for these castings. The large components are lined up neatly and all are accessible by lift truck for the short time they are in storage. Objectives drive projects focused on maximizing velocity of flow and schedule stability and continue to reduce the quantity required for inventory. Many organizations have specific needs driven from unusual size or shape restrictions. Most of the needs can be fulfilled, and the first step is addressing the needs head-on. Solutions range from painted lines on the floor to silos for powdered or liquid materials.

4. **Clearly-labeled drop areas.** In organizations with lean manufacturing processes, inventory is sometimes pulled through the process by signals, either from location design or a message of some type that signals the next replenishment. When the location design is used, material movement is usually determined by the size of the location—if there is room for material in the location, internal or external suppliers replenish material to the location; if not, no material movement is allowed. This might be a drop area painted on the floor or, in the case of many manufacturers, a special rolling rack only large enough to carry the number of components needed for an hour. Another popular example in high-performance organizations is the two-bin system in which two bins are available for supply. When the first one is emptied, it signals the replenishment of the bin.

These concepts (restrictions on inventory storage location) are helpful in all storage applications not only for the management of material movement, but also for accuracy concerns. Most warehouses have material moving in and out regularly throughout the day. Some high-performance organizations use a "two-bin (two-location)" methodology to manage put-away. A specific area is designated for the receiving drop area with boundaries clearly defined by painted lines on the floor. A separate area is also defined as the receiving overflow area. While put-away capacity is aligned daily with requirements, sometimes peak receiving loads require periodic additional capacity. When the receiving backs up to the overflow area, the use of this designated extra space triggers additional resource to the receiving area.

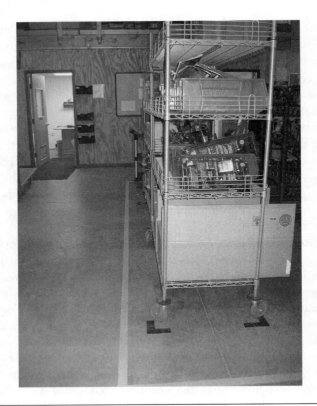

**Figure 7.3** Properly-Labeled Drop Area

This strategy allows documented procedures to easily cover capacity exception resource requirements. Therefore, supervisors are not required to inform receiving personnel each time extra capacity is required. It also helps manage the discipline of readily having parts in the proper location. Unfortunately, too many poorly-managed operations have material several layers deep in receiving and some totes are stuck in the area, inaccessible for days. No material should ever be in receiving for more than 24 hours. The norm should be same-day availability for components into the assembly operation. Drop areas should always be specifically outlined. In areas in which small parts are stored, this can be a designated, strategically located rack. In organizations where pallets are utilized, it often means lines painted on the floor (figure 7.3).

5. **Proper counting tools/methods.** There are many tools and methods that help keep counting accurate.

a. *Scales*—Scales are often utilized when small parts are frequently counted, including fasteners and small washers. This is a great application but there are others as well. Some organizations have raw material in rolls that are difficult to count or verify. One organization manufactures labels for beverage bottles. The label film is on rolls and is planned, ordered, and inventoried by the linear foot. Because there is some waste in their start-up operation when feeding film into a printing machine, the usage is not exactly predictable. Therefore, they weigh the roll each time it comes back into the warehouse, ensuring accuracy in count within the storeroom walls. This scale is not the typical small bench scale for scale counting. It is a large floor scale that the forklift and operator can drive across. The weight of the truck and operator is subtracted from the total weight and the balance is converted to feet of film. Thus record accuracy is ensured within the storeroom even if items are hard to count and process usage is somewhat unpredictable.

b. *Logically-sized or -configured packaging ("egg carton methodology")*—We do not have to count eggs when we go to the grocery store because we know that there is a dozen in the carton. Only checks for quality are sometimes necessary. The same theory works for parts in the warehouse. When items are stored randomly in a bin or on a pallet, they are especially difficult to count, both at pick time and during an audit. Often items are placed in packages of 10, 25, or some other helpful number. Computer chips are sometimes stored in static-free tubes with the same amount in each tube. Bearings are often stacked in packaging to create efficient storage patterns. Caution must be used, however, because if parts are in multiple packs, they must be clearly labeled as such on the location. The risk comes from order pickers who when instructed to pick 10 pieces of an item pick 10 packages! Some organizations even have locations painted red for multi-packed items. Eliminating the use of multi-pack packaging is not the proper way to handle problems that might arise from its use. Packing items in layers or stacks is beneficial to count accuracy.

c. *Standardized layering*—Another helpful trick for counting accuracy is to maintain standardized layering in the storage. For example, in a company that manufactures automobile components near Manchester, England, there are standard castings utilized in their process. These castings are brought in from the supplier in standardized plastic egg-carton-type containers designed to hold exactly 24 castings per layer. There are several layers (also standardized) in each container. This type of strategy makes the parts easy to count accurately. It also keeps the supplier counts accurate.

d. *Proper protection requirements*—Many components have safety issues associated with them that have to be taken into account. This would include flammables, combustibles, or even explosive materials. Additionally, protection of the component itself is important. Many parts are subject to rust and corrosion. Some materials can be affected by specifics, for example, ultra-violet light, heat, moisture, vibration, and static electricity. These conditions must be taken into consideration when designing the right storage pattern.

e. *Material handling equipment*—Having the right equipment to access inventory when needed ensures proper handling and timeliness of material movement. This often means dedicated equipment in high-activity areas. Forklift trucks are not the only consideration. Often pushcarts and/or pallet jack-type equipment is all that is needed. Carousels (discussed later in this chapter), which are moving racks, are efficient and effective and eliminate the need for picking vehicles and associated travel time. Putting the right equipment in the area not only makes the job more pleasant and efficient, it also helps ensure timeliness, an important factor in customer service, schedule accountability, and, ultimately, record accuracy.

f. *All material is accessible*—Material should be accessible by authorized personnel. Inventory is not piled behind other material in an aisle or location. High-performance organizations do not locate inventory in areas that would require other inventory to be moved prior to availability. This inconvenience discourages proper housekeeping and workplace organization and ultimately accuracy of schedules and data. Everything should have a specific location and be accessible by the people responsible to pick it.

g. *Access is limited to authorized personnel*—There is an old manufacturing saying: "You can't keep inventory away from people who need it to meet their customer's need." Not only is that statement true, but it also illustrates the irony of locking up inventory. Companies that have accurate inventories do not necessarily lock up the material or limit access. What they do have is a shared understanding and well-established organizational discipline that

**Figure 7.4** Clearly-Labeled Aisles

ensures a timely transaction for each inventory movement. All people must understand the processes and reasons for procedural discipline or they will naturally shortcut the system and corrupt data integrity.

h. *Every physical location has a specific/unique location identification*—Simply stated, everywhere in the plant should have a recognizable address for reference. Storage aisles should be labeled and easily understood (figure 7.4). Racks should have separate location addresses for each pallet opening on each level. The only exception is when there is a bulk storage area for one item and that is the only item stored in the entire rack. In that case, the rack would have just one location. In some older Enterprise Resource Planning (ERP) business systems there is no multiple location capability. In other organizations, backflushing (automatic transactions triggered from an action such as a job completion) is used and the business computer system is not advanced enough to recognize from which location the parts are to be transacted. These cases sometimes force organizations to abandon location management. In some rare cases, it is acceptable (and desirable) to have an off-line spreadsheet-type inventory tracking system until better integrated systems can be installed. In the case of limits due to backflushing, alternatives should be explored including the elimination of the limits. Backflushing is frequently used in high-performance organizations, but when considering all operations, it is more frequently misused.

i. *Adequate availability of system access*—Lack of proper access to system tools can become a deterrent to accuracy. High-performance organizations have system access in all areas that require it. Make it easy for employees to be timely and accurate. Lean materials managers know that it is easier to do transactions in this manner.

## POINT-OF-USE STORAGE

Many high-performance organizations are eliminating or at least minimizing their main centralized storage areas and opting for storage at point of use. For example, inventory is stored in assembly at the work cell where it is consumed. The rules for storage do not change for point-of-use storage. Regardless of where the inventory is kept, it has to be neat and organized for proper accuracy disciplines (figure 7.5).

## STORAGE PATTERNS

There are various storage patterns that are used in storing inventory: dedicated storage, random storage, zone storage, and golden zoning. Each has its place in manufacturing and each has advantages and disadvantages.

### Dedicated Storage

In the dedicated or primary location storage, inventory is stored in the same place each time it is received. In a grocery store, typically the milk is always stored in the same location. Dedicated storage methodology employs the same behaviors. "A place for everything and everything in its place."

**Advantages of Dedicated Storage (or Primary Storage)**—Employees know where to look for certain inventory. Occasionally, as in the case of silos for powder and resins, there is little choice but to have dedicated storage because of contamination issues that would be caused by changing the contents of a location periodically.

**Disadvantages of Dedicated Storage (or Primary Storage)**—This system is inflexible. When schedules are increased or decreased on certain products, storage

**Figure 7.5** Point-of-Use Storage

space requirements change. This is especially ineffective when numerical sequencing is used. In that case, engineering changes can become a nightmare for the warehouse. Using dedicated locations can create wasted and/or inadequate space utilization.

**Application of Dedicated Storage (or Primary Storage)**—Most point-of-use storage is an appropriate application for dedicated storage. Also, some components are large or of high volume and require dedicated storage, including silo storage or odd-shaped large components. Companies that employ this storage concept at point of use typically have more frequent deliveries, which negates the problem of physical location capacity tied to the schedule.

## Random Storage

Random storage is a popular and proven method of inventory control in high-performance warehouses. In this methodology, as it arrives, inventory is put away in the first available slot. Inventory from different shipments is not generally consolidated with prior stock.

**Advantages of Random Storage**—There are several advantages to random storage: 1) empty locations are always utilized; 2) no restriction on how much or how little material is stored, so the locations always match the need as long as the warehouse itself is not capacity restricted; and 3) each time a location is emptied, it is zeroed out, allowing for stock balance checks at zero quantity. There is no easier time or faster way to count inventory than when it is at a zero balance. In some applications a card is attached to the location each time it is utilized. When the picker empties the last part, he/she pulls the ticket, verifying the zero balance and placing the location on the "empties" list. In applications that utilize barcode readers at the location, pickers are taught to automatically cycle count balances when the last part is picked in the location. While this does not take the place of good inventory control or even cycle counting procedures, it is a good cleansing process for the location balances that adds little cost.

**Disadvantage of Random Storage**—The random storage methodology requires a locator system. It also can require more space unless inventory is controlled in small quantity flows (just-in-time [JIT] or lean principles are utilized). This space inefficiency results simply because all locations are emptied as the material is used up before new inventory is put into the location. At any one time, there can be more than one location for the same part in storage as the re-order process flows through the replenishment cycles.

**Application of Random Storage**—Most general warehouses can use this system. Random storage is generally accepted as the method of choice in high-performance inventory control associated with central storage. It is often mixed with other methodologies such as zone storage.

## Zone Storage

When using zone storage methodology, inventory is randomly stored within location "zones." This sometimes makes picking of materials more efficient and/or certain types of inventory need to be in a specific area because of their characteristics. Frozen food in a grocery warehouse is only stored in the freezer, for example. In a warehouse storing steel, flat plate might be stored in an area configured differently from where bar stock would be stored. One client stocked diamond chips for use as an aggregate. This material was stored in a locked vault prior to need.

**Advantages of Zone Storage**—Picking can be more efficient as parts common to one assembly can be in the same area. For example, kit components all stored in one area create an efficient picking area to replenish items for assembly. Storage patterns match the size, shape, and special needs of specific parts. Consigned inventory is normally stored in a zone separated from other inventory.

**Disadvantages of Zone Storage**—As production plans fluctuate, these specific zones need to also expand and contract or the result is forced process deviation.

**Application of Zone Storage**—Electronics components that need to have a static-free environment, specialized components, grocery, retail sales, and other high-volume picking operations are applications for a zone storage methodology.

## Golden Zoning

Golden zoning is a great method in many applications. Like zone storage, golden zoning limits the areas within which specific items are randomly stored. The difference comes from the fact that within these zones there is an acknowledgment of the frequency of pick requirements. The most ergonomically-friendly locations and the locations most easily and efficiently picked are where the most picks are concentrated. In the grocery warehouse application, all canned vegetables are in the same area but the "fast movers" are stored at the most accessible locations within the canned vegetable zone. In assembly operations, it often makes sense to have assembly components stored in the same area for pick efficiency and accessibility. Carousel storage can work effectively because carousels are available in both vertical and horizontal applications. By design, carousels are zones affected by the size and volume of the parts stored. Within the carousel one might put high-moving parts in the storage bins located (height-wise) from the chest to just below the waist. This minimizes the amount of stooping and bending as well as stretching upward, thus minimizing costly and otherwise unfavorable injuries.

**Advantages of Golden Zoning**—Random locations within golden zoning have all the advantages of random storage plus much more efficient picking. Because ergonomics is considered in the planning of golden zones, there can also be benefits in employee and equipment efficiencies due to wear and tear on humans and equipment alike.

**Disadvantages of Golden Zoning**—As production plans fluctuate, these specific zones need to also expand and contract or the result is forced process deviation.

**Application of Golden Zoning**—Grocery, retail sales, high-volume picking operations, carousel storage, point-of-use storage, and/or work cell storage all make good applications for the golden zoning storage methodology. Point-of-use storage can be a perfect application of golden zoning.

## STORAGE LAYOUT

Several methods of storing material have been described. These methods support various processes within the order fulfillment stage of a manufacturing or service organization. Decisions regarding the storage of material take some consideration.

    a. Does the material storage area force or require backtracking in the process flow? Obviously this should be minimized.

    b. Are there limiting factors such as availability of material handling equipment? Overhead cranes, floor scales, and other devices are sometimes critical in the flow.

    c. Business plans, including forecasted growth and product line fluctuations, play a part in the design of material storage.

    d. Safety is the most important consideration in any process design. Some components (e.g., flammables or explosives) have regulations requiring certain storage containers or methods of handling.

    e. Accessibility for the users is important. Are all stock keeping units (SKUs) or part numbers available at the location face or are some inaccessible without first moving other items?

## CAROUSELS FOR STORAGE

Carousels are moving racks that store components and finished parts for order-specific picking. Most people are familiar with the carousels used at dry cleaners to store cleaned clothing. The manufacturing application of carousels is similar except the equipment is much more heavy-duty, allowing for part storage. The location bins move to the picker rather than the picker going to the storage locations. When tied to a location system, this saves the storekeeper time in finding the component or finished good. It also eliminates travel time required in traditional rack storage (figure 7.6).

    Industrial carousels have been in existence for years. Initially, they were used most widely in distribution applications such as wholesale consumer goods. In the early 1980s, they received renewed attention and are now utilized much more in non-distribution applications such as manufacturing. Carousels offer an easy method of quick access especially with today's software linkages to demand signals. If an organization is involved with customer order picking or kitting of small materials or components, and has not yet improved processes to the point of eliminating buffer inventory, carousel storage is helpful and offers efficient picking capability. Many retail distribution operations (e.g., TV shopping networks or Internet sales distribution) have found carousels to be effective. The ease of access,

**Figure 7.6** Carousels

worker efficiency in picks-per-hour, and the space utilization advantages make this an idea worth pursuing in certain applications.

One forklift manufacturer has most of its service distribution requirements stored in carousels that are stacked two high utilizing pick platforms. It eliminates the need for material handling equipment and the transporting of pickers—interesting given the fact they are a world leader in the manufacturing of forklift equipment.

## LOCATION SYSTEMS

The location label or identifier is the record that resides in the warehouse management system that tells the storekeeper or stock picker where to find the item needed. Location labels are most convenient if the fields or characters are "intelligent." Each additional digit or alpha character in the location should give another clue to the location of the needed item. A U.S. zip code is an example of a location label. Each digit gets the user closer to the detailed location. It works the same way in naming locations in a manufacturing or distribution facility.

All racks and bins areas should be clearly labeled and readable from 25 feet away. High-performance organizations have these location signs professionally painted in block letters at least 6 inches in height and hang them at the ends of each rack. One organization that uses man-up order-picking vehicles equipped with spotlights has the location markers on the racks in reflective labels so they

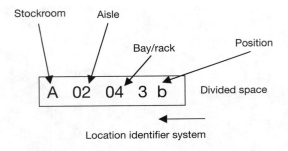

**Figure 7.7** Location Label Design

are not missed or misread. Time and effort taken to make the location system easy to see and understand pay back in training costs saved and/or improved accuracy (figure 7.7).

Having an easy-to-use and easy-to-understand location system added to a well-organized storage area with locations properly fitted to the product stored facilitates the maintenance of accurate inventory records.

## STOCK DETERMINATION

Inventory strategy is a critical management decision in high-performance businesses. Inventory strategy, also sometimes referred to as manufacturing or business strategy, determines where in the bill of material (BOM) stock is held. Lean-thinking materials managers know that inventory is most flexible prior to raw material being converted into the next level in the BOM. Inventory strategy was reviewed in chapter 5 during the master scheduling discussion. Inventory stocking is not the major decision that many managers think. It actually is dictated by a couple of factors: 1) the amount of lead time it actually takes to make or procure the SKU and 2) how long the market allows for it. In manufacturing operations, the minimum inventory is no inventory providing the market allows time for full procurement and material conversion. This gives substantial power to the efforts to shorten lead time and cycle time within the process. This is understood within the manufacturing process. Many companies have aftermarket requirements which are often a different market driver.

## AFTERMARKET STOCKING

Manufacturing firms that make assemblies with wearable components and mean time between failures (MTBF) less than the product life cycle must provide aftermarket components to the market. This would include automobiles, appliances, machinery, and equipment. Consumers who have purchased these end items generally expect to receive service parts quickly when the product breaks down. Aftermarket need is one of the highest pressures on quick response. Since customer service is often a measurement, the warehouse manager reports can apply pressure to stock more and more items. Rules of engagement between the demand and supply sides of the business can again be helpful. In many high-performance operations, an agreeable formula is developed between sales and materials. The following is an example of rules for an aftermarket handshake:

1. All wearables as identified by engineering are stocked initially as the products are introduced.
2. As experience develops on MTBF, it becomes more and more apparent which items need to be stocked. History of demand should be captured and documented.
3. Many times items specific to one particular customer order (unique configurations not widely available) are not so quick to be stocked at the original equipment manufacturer. It can be communicated to the customer or local distributor and left up to them whether to stock these items. Such policy must be a handshake between sales and production. It obviously cannot be made solely by the warehouse manager or materials manager.
4. Stocking service parts is important. Monitoring historical demand for items not identified initially as wearable items is necessary for keeping current with the aftermarket need. For example, some organizations allow a couple "hits" of demand a year (on non-wearable items) before considering a stock position on the part in question. Others businesses restock the shelf as soon as the first item is sold. There are no foolproof rules that work for every company, but it is important to have a practice and a handshake between demand and supply as it applies to the aftermarket offering and expectations. In the business that I grew up in, the expectation was that we would service any product ever sold by our company. This did not mean we stocked everything, however!

Lean-thinking materials/inventory managers insist on the handshake agreement. Additionally, the demand part of the organization should review these decisions frequently. These stocking decisions change as new models replace older ones and the market fluctuates. Without continuous monitoring, it is easy to lose control of the inventory level. The warehouse manager, while not the main process owner in this handshake, must take the challenging responsibility for the tracking of this monitoring process. The warehouse manager is the conscience for the sales organization that needs to be reminded of the importance of this requirement.

The warehouse is often not given the attention it deserves because of the belief that inventory is a bad thing. In fact, inventory is a great thing when there is someone that wants to buy it. This moves the thought process toward the demand planning process in high-performance organizations. This top management planning process is generally known as the Sales and Operations Planning (S&OP) process in which inventory plans and forecasts are reviewed and finalized.

## DISCUSSION QUESTIONS

1. Large inventory locations are good because they tend to make location balance accuracy easier because fewer locations are needed.
   a. true
   b. false

2. Egg carton methodology is appropriate in efficient warehousing.
   a. true
   b. false

3. Topics of concern to the warehouse manager include
   a. ultra-violet light.
   b. fire protection.
   c. pilferage.
   d. a and c
   e. all of the above

4. Re-using pallets even when the dimensions are smaller than the rack location size saves money in efficient warehouse practice.
   a. true
   b. false

5. Carousels are especially efficient for order picking small items.
   a. true
   b. false

6. Random storage of locations is dangerous because of the possibility of lost inventory.
   a. true
   b. false

7. Fences surrounding the warehouse material inside a building are helpful in keeping inventory balances accurate.
   a. true
   b. false

8. Dedicated storage (primary location system) in some specific inventory situations is the only logical method of storage pattern.
    a. true
    b. false

9. Golden zones are
    a. areas in which the housekeeping is excellent.
    b. accident-free areas in the warehouse.
    c. locations in which ergonomics and frequency of pick are best suited for storage of specific inventory.
    d. drop areas.

10. Stocking service parts is dangerous because aftermarket demand is tough to predict. Only the top-moving items should be stocked.
    a. true
    b. false

# 8

# TOP MANAGEMENT SALES AND OPERATIONS PLANNING

## INTRODUCTION

Sales and Operations Planning (S&OP) has been used in well-managed businesses for years. Also referred to as Sales, Inventory and Operations Planning (SIOP) in many circles, this top management planning process is the directional management system that sets the monthly cycle and calibrates the execution with the strategic plans of a business. The flexibility and effectiveness of this process are obvious when executed competently. Businesses that enjoy benefits from this planning tool and methodology include manufacturing businesses, banking institutions, distribution companies, and even consulting companies. In fact, any business that manages demand and synchronizes resources, including capital, manpower, machinery, or brick and mortar, to that demand has a need for a robust S&OP process.

The S&OP process is an effective, inexpensive improvement mechanism recognized for its benefits by more and more companies. Managers around the world are focusing on improvements in this important area of business control. The S&OP methodology is, in fact, one of the hottest topics in business today. It is not a new process; in fact, some might agree, it is an old process. It has attracted a renewed interest and for good reason—it pays off. Freudenberg-NOK, a well-respected auto manufacturing first-tier supplier known for its "lean" approach, is an example of this focus, is Electrolux Home Products

(Frigidaire), a market leader in kitchen appliances. Many other organizations honed their S&OP processes years ago, for example, Honeywell and Nestlés.

## WHAT IS THE SALES AND OPERATIONS PLANNING PROCESS?

The S&OP is a popular top management planning process used in many high-performance businesses. Stated in simple terms, the S&OP is a monthly planning cycle during which plans for both customer expectations and internal operations are reviewed for accuracy, process accountability, lessons learned, and future risk management. Plans are monitored, updated at specific times, and reviewed systematically. Process owners are defined with clarity, top management expectations and roles are clearly understood, and measurements are not only reviewed but are visible to the organization for communications and synchronization purposes.

As the monthly cycle progresses, process owners throughout the business are monitoring plans and updating the go-forward proposals. The forecast for demand is revised during the month, with demand reviews facilitating these discussions weekly. On the first week of the month, top managers are presented with options for approvals to forecasts and operations commitments. Inventory and backlog plans are either approved or revised by top management at this meeting.

The benefits of this top management planning process are obvious and include improved communications and shared goals, decreased costs, decreased inventory, and increases in customer service. There is no magic to this planning process; it is simply discipline administered in a top-management application, a discipline difficult to accomplish in many organizations without a formal process. Materials managers are often in the middle of the process, especially those who have master scheduling reporting to them.

Virtually all high-performance organizations do some form of an S&OP process regularly. In these organizations, the S&OP is a monthly top management planning meeting in which metrics and performance are reviewed and adjustments made based on recommendations developed from data collection and analysis prepared for this review. The key to success is preparation, data streams, and good data mining in advance of the decision process. Managing the data into workable product families is a prerequisite for success. Historical data is always anticipated to be a major factor and it can be but, in reality, data collected from history is only a part of this data stream. New influences from the marketplace and actions from the sales and marketing team also must be plugged into the forecast. Data collection is followed by analysis and risk assessment. It is at this point that the forecasts influence operational commitments. Once these plans are all on the table, an analysis of the 12-month rolling horizon is completed.

## History

The history of S&OP probably started in many companies through lessons learned and process testing and experimentation. It is likely that some credit has to go to the father of Material Requirements Planning (MRP). The late Oliver Wight developed the formula in the 1980s and perhaps as early as the late 1970s, although by the time Oli knew he had a winning formula, many businesses were sharing experiences through organizations like the American Production and Inventory Control Society (APICS) and were evolving the process. A lot of water has gone over the dam since those early S&OP days. The first book to document the Oli Wight organization's widely-recognized process was published in 1988 (*Orchestrating Success*, Richard Ling and Walt Goddard, Oliver Wight Publications, Inc., 1988). About the same time, both the Oliver Wight organizations and the David W. Buker organizations were selling video tools that helped businesses accomplish this top management planning process. That's how long this process has been evolving. Of course, as expected, there have been many lessons learned and resulting improvements in the methodology since the 1980s.

S&OP has grown into a strategic weapon in a competitive world and should be part of the tools used by a high-performance organization for advantage in its market. Companies of all sizes, from $1 million to $10 billion, find this process helpful in managing risks and getting everyone to the table in the handshake decisions, thereby resulting in better decisions overall.

To describe the process briefly, the S&OP process is like top management's "knobs" on the business. When (or if) the top management team in an organization wants to turn up the marketing effort in some specific area, dial back inventory, or if they want to change direction entirely and still keep the entire organization in synchronization with any of these changes, the S&OP process is an important management system to ensure the decisions are implemented as top management requires. This is accomplished through a common plan for the next 12 rolling months shared with all of the management team, including sales, engineering, materials, and production.

## Balancing the Needs of Business

Markets are changing every minute of every hour. High-performance organizations have skilled executives who understand this and either forecast these changes and allow pre-planning or adjust to surprises by changing course quickly and nimbly. This is the case with successful companies in nearly every market today. Once, while working in the supply chain in the young adult sneaker (what used to be called the tennis shoe) market it became excruciatingly obvious that demand could shift almost at the speed of light as one sneaker style would go out of favor and be replaced by another merely by the introduction of some favorite advertisement on Friday night television. The problems that had to be faced were numerous. If demand grew rapidly for one particular style, the supply chain had to react as quickly. Not to react quickly enough could easily mean getting to market just as the next favorite sneaker was moving to the top spot in demand. This could only result in missed opportunity and inventory that would end up on the discount rack. Fashion, like many markets, tends to be a fickle one. Businesses that operate in this space or similar ones need to minimize risk and keep the organization, both demand and supply sides of the business, headed in the same direction, even when the direction is changing constantly and quickly. This, of course, means lean thinking. The more a market changes like this, the more a robust S&OP process can help minimize risk and manage the change throughout the entire business. No small task, but one that is valuable indeed!

Slower markets can be just as difficult. Kitchen appliances, for example, are products that in many cases, except for electronic controls, haven't changed that much over the years. Most consumers do not buy a refrigerator simply to get the latest style. Refrigerators tend to serve a reasonably long service life. This does not stop the need for robust planning. In this market the competitive pressures are enormous. When a business is making thousands of units a day, just a couple cents per unit can make a significant difference in the profitability of the business unit. The S&OP in the kitchen appliance market serves to help with demand changes as the market shifts.

The S&OP process is the forced event that requires inspection of these issues and decisions made by top management as to how the business will react to these changes, if it reacts at all. The S&OP does not take the place of good judgment or provide easy answers. The process simply forces the right people to talk about the right areas of focus in a timely manner. This often increases the chances of making the right decisions in the right time frames. It is all about supply and demand synchronization (figure 8.1). The better the job of balancing these two elements of business is performed, the more likely the business will succeed.

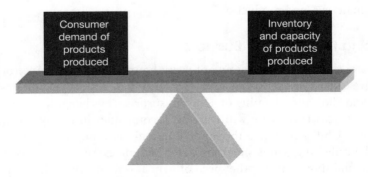

**Figure 8.1** The Balancing Act between Demand and Supply

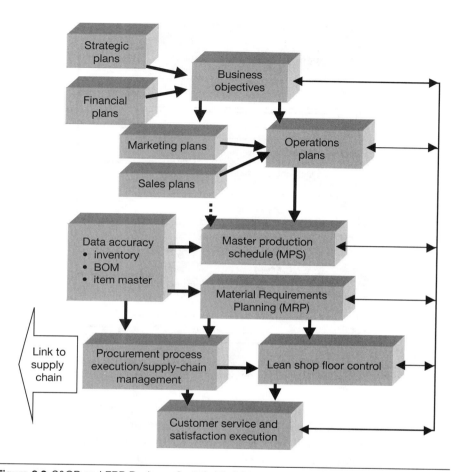

**Figure 8.2** S&OP and ERP Business System Model

## Enterprise Resource Planning Process at the Center

At the center of the S&OP need is the business system. In most manufacturing businesses today, the term "business system" refers to the Enterprise Resource Planning (ERP) business systems. At the top end of this system is the strategic planning process that includes long-term strategy as well as shorter-term business imperatives. Intertwined into the strategy and tactical planning process is the market need with supporting decisions on how to deal with the market variation (figure 8.2). Within the ERP model, the top management processes must link with the operations planning and execution processes if the strategy is to be implemented effectively.

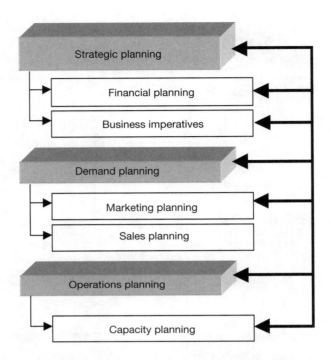

**Figure 8.3** Top Management Planning Component of ERP

To clarify, the acronym ERP when mentioned in this book is not referring to the software system also known as ERP; they are often confused. This would be the same as referring to a toolbox as a carpenter. ERP system tools are just that: the tools that allow efficiency in an ERP process. The S&OP methodology makes up the top end of the ERP business model. The S&OP process allows the once-a-month approved plan to be communicated on an expected and regular basis. Management receives regular feedback from the organization and meets at the same time every month to access the data and either approve or alter plans for the next 12 rolling months. There is no substitute for this regular and predictable (in terms of schedule) management direction. Lean-focused organizations are not immune to the need. These businesses are just as reliant on robust planning processes and top-end management direction (figure 8.3).

There are few arguments that support the absence of top management planning. In one baking company with four major baking factories in the United States, the S&OP planning allowed the frequent shifting of product from one plant to another, saving thousands of dollars in freight in a market in which moving product across the country rapidly added unnecessary cost to the product. In another example, a first-tier European auto-manufacturing supplier found that the S&OP process allowed much lower inventory to be engaged without negatively affecting customer service. Yet another plastics company has its S&OP process directly linked to its customers in a monthly sharing of top management planning data. All of these companies share little in terms of market needs and customer requirements, but in every case the S&OP process is a powerful part of their strategic competitive advantage.

How does this process affect the lean-thinking materials manager? Material planning is in the middle of all of these processes and is often the one that benefits most from the working process. There are several important roles in the S&OP process.

## SUMMARY OF THE ROLES OF PLAYERS IN SALES AND OPERATIONS PLANNING

The S&OP process belongs to the top manager active in the business. Normally this is the president or chief executive officer (CEO). In some companies it can be, by design, executed at a lower level in the organization. The chief operations officer (COO) position is commonly chosen, but it is rarely effective unless the COO is the power base within the organization or has complete support and faith of the top manager. This may sound amazing but the kinds of decisions made at the S&OP process can affect millions of dollars of resource, inventory and, most importantly, profit. The right people need to be plugged in and attuned to the S&OP cycle and the opportunities. The materials manager alone cannot run the process, although I have been involved in a few that were initiated by this manager. Again, it took a top management sponsor for full success.

These are some of the more important roles:

- **President or CEO**—The top manager in the business or organization
  - reviews plan spreadsheets in preparation for the S&OP
  - discusses risks with key employees, including the master scheduler, before the S&OP meeting to be as fully prepared as possible
  - leads the S&OP monthly meeting by asking the tough questions
  - keeps the meeting at the same time each month and insists on attendance from key players
  - owns the process for the performance plan called business plan in the S&OP process
  - understands and evaluates root cause for process variation in the business plan accuracy and drives change accordingly

- ensures that clear objectives are communicated and documented (In a lean-thinking environment this can often include objectives focused on waste elimination, flexibility, and responsiveness.)
- **Vice President of Sales and/or Vice President of Marketing—** Depending on the organizational structure and size of a company, the S&OP roles of the demand-side leader are to:
    - communicate frequently with the supply side of the organization
    - attend the weekly demand reviews or at least send valid authorized representation
    - review and approve the final demand plan (forecast) and updates to same
    - distribute the demand plan to the supply side of the organization by the end of the month, every month
    - measure the demand plan accuracy and post visibly to enable the organization to observe performance
    - serve as the process owner for the demand plan
    - understand and evaluate root cause for process variation in the demand plan accuracy and drive change accordingly
    - answer the demand-side questions in the S&OP meeting
- **VP of Operations—**The top supply-side manager also has an important role in the S&OP process. His/her role includes:
    - preparing the operations plan by product family for review at the S&OP meeting
    - measuring the operations plan accuracy and posting same
    - serving as the process owner for the operations plan
    - understanding and evaluating root cause for process variation in the operations plan accuracy and driving change accordingly
    - answering the supply-side questions in the S&OP meeting, especially as these questions apply to the build plan rate or capacity
    - supporting the master scheduler in the full role of providing an accurate master production schedule
    - evaluating/monitoring an operation's objectives
- **Chief Financial Officer (CFO)—**The CFO is involved in the currency impact of plan accuracy. This top manager's role includes:
    - preparing the financial plan accuracy by product family
    - providing the performance measurement for the business plan
    - providing a review of root cause for any process variation within the business plan accuracy

- **Materials Manager or Master Scheduler**—The S&OP role for the "master of schedules" within operations is extremely important. The master scheduler is responsible to the organization in the S&OP role to:
  - lead the demand review sessions each week with the demand side of the organization
  - facilitate the pre-S&OP meeting at the end of the month in preparation for the S&OP
  - develop and document the schedule changes in the monthly operations plan
  - prepare the spreadsheets for the S&OP process (usually with the exception of the financial business plan performance which is completed by the CFO)
  - prepare the CEO with areas of plan accuracy risks prior to the S&OP meeting
  - communicate directly with the sales or demand-side team regarding capacity issues, lead time, inventory, and customer service levels
  - serve as process owner for the weekly schedule accuracy (not normally reviewed at the S&OP)

As is clearly shown in the roles, one main focus at the risk management event is to understand and learn from process variation experienced in previous and recent history (figure 8.4). These lessons are helpful in eliminating this variation in the 12-month rolling horizon.

## TIMETABLE FOR SALES AND OPERATIONS PLANNING

In high-performance organizations, the S&OP process is a top management meeting that is scheduled at the same time each month. In many companies that schedule would be the 2nd or possibly the 3rd or 4th workday of the month. In these high-performance companies, this schedule does not get pre-empted. People who need to attend put it on the calendar months in advance and schedule other required plans around this top management priority. Having the right decision makers at the meeting every month keeps the meetings not only effective but also efficient. It should be considered a "must" by all of the top staff.

A preparatory meeting is normally scheduled for the week prior to the S&OP and is attended by the master scheduler and demand people to ensure the risks are made visible and questions are anticipated and answers prepared (figure 8.5). The demand plan is at the center of this scrutiny as this is the driver of decisions and

**Figure 8.4** S&OP Hierarchy

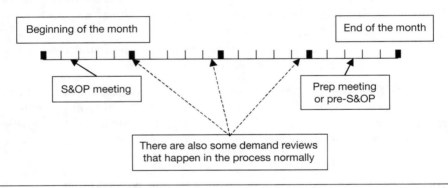

**Figure 8.5** Timeline of the S&OP Process

activity. That is not to say the demand plan accuracy is the only decision to be reviewed. It is not. What is important is how much confidence the company's management team has in the demand plan and, accordingly, what investments the company is willing to make to support that confidence. There is no perfect forecast and probably never will be.

## DECISIONS IN THE SALES AND OPERATIONS PLANNING PROCESS

In a robust S&OP process, there are several decisions that are made at the monthly meeting. Here are a few examples of the types of determinations that might be routinely executed at this management system. Keep in mind that these are only examples and may not be the exact decisions required at every business. The management, markets, and resources determine those specifics. The following list should be helpful, however, in understanding the general idea of the value of this powerful management system.

- Does management need to put more resources on a new product introduction to ensure schedule adherence?
- Is the increase in customer demand expressed in the demand plan appropriately supported by evidence and, accordingly, top management confidence?
- Does the risk in the demand plan outweigh the costs of increasing capacity for the anticipated increase in orders?
- Is there enough capacity in the fourth quarter of the year?
- Will there need to be shift changes in the next 12 months for the manufacturing process?
- Is the marketing plan that was implemented earlier actually paying off in incremental demand as planned?
- Is the business effective in a new market recently entered?
- Is there an adequate supply chain for the growing needs of the business in the near future and in the 12-month future requirements?
- What lessons were learned by the misses in demand forecasting in the last month?
- What was the root cause of the operations misses this month?

Of course there are a number of other questions that might be discussed at the S&OP. The advantage of the forum is to have measures discussed, lessons learned, and decisions made regarding risks and opportunities. How does the management team, given the data required, continue to steer the business in the proper direction for success? Indeed, this is worthy of a regular process.

## SALES AND OPERATIONS PLANNING AGENDA

The meeting structure should be consistent at each S&OP meeting. This allows all process owners to know exactly what to expect and to come prepared with their homework completed, ready to reconcile gaps in performance and to share learning (figure 8.6). This top management gathering which occurs every month should include the following agenda:

1. **Review of last 30 days**—The accuracy metrics by product family are reviewed.
   a. *Financial plan accuracy by product family*—The top management financial manager (usually the CFO) communicates root cause

**S&OP Agenda**
- Review last 30 days
  - Review financials
  - Review demand plan accuracy by product family
  - Review operations plan accuracy by product family
- Review 30 to 60-day risks in detail as required by product family
  - Review financial risks
  - Review demand plan risks
  - Review operations plan risks
- Review 90 to 120-day risks as required
  - Review financial risks
  - Review demand plan risks
  - Review operations plan risks
- Review balance of 12-month horizon (exception only)
  - Review financial risks
  - Review demand plan risks
  - Review operations plan risks

**Figure 8.6** S&OP Agenda

analysis of any process variation and actions to improve upcoming accuracy. Because in many businesses the "books" are not yet closed for the month at the time of the S&OP, the numbers are often built from averages—average cost of units per product family and average revenue per unit from the same product families. These estimates can be compared to forecast margin or gross profit. This is another reason to make sure the product families are the right ones. If there are substantial swings in cost or price within the family, it might make sense to reevaluate the family groupings.

By defining the families correctly and having the spreadsheets available for analysis during the SIOP, better decisions are made regarding capacity changes or inventory investments. After all, profit is why everybody is at the meeting! When and if the actual numbers available later after the closing do not match, again, great lessons can be learned as a result. It is always good to know that estimating is not accurate and why it was not.

b. *Review demand plan accuracy by product family*—The top management demand-side manager (usually either the VP of Sales or the VP of Marketing) shares the performance measurement of the demand plan accuracy prior to communicating root cause analysis from process variation affecting the performance. This plan is especially interesting to the organization for several reasons. Not only does the forecast tell what inventory and capacity to position but also time-phases the plan over the next 12 months. The demand plan does not stop there.

Regardless of inventory strategy, the revenue plans are always tied to the demand plan. MTS demand plans suggest the demand from stock. In an MTO environment, the demand plan lays out the expectations of increases to backlog that drive the operations plan. This operations plan in an MTO environment or product family is the revenue plan. In MTO, the plant builds what the customer ordered and it normally ships soon with consolidation of orders or ships as soon as it is built. It becomes easy to understand the interest in this plan!

c. *Review production or operations plan accuracy by product family*—The top operations management manager (usually the VP of Operations) communicates the performance measure of the capacity fulfillment plan and the root cause analysis of process variation made visible through the measurements. Actions are the resulting report aimed at improving upcoming accuracy for any shortfalls. As stated previously, the operations plan is the revenue plan in any MTO product families. Obviously, the revenue plan is of high interest.

Nearly as important is the risk management associated with the operations plan. This includes new product introduction, the implementation of new suppliers or plants, or even new machine lines. All of these projects represent significant risks to the business if not managed properly. This agenda item in the S&OP welcomes the scrutiny of these risk opportunities with the hope that with the right attention fewer mistakes or oversights occur (figure 8.7).

2. **Review of the 30 to 60-day plan expectations (figure 8.7)**—During this agenda item, risks and/or changes since the last monthly meeting are reviewed in detail.

a. *Financial plan risks*—Of course there can be financial risks on the radar screen as well as new changes in financial plans since the last review. The close-in, one- to three-month horizon normally involves risk. This time frame often overlays promises made by the

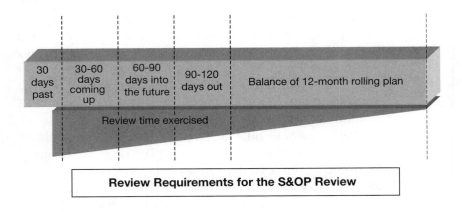

Figure 8.7 Review Expectations for the S&OP

top management team to outside stakeholders and customers. This, along with the short lead time to fix any issues, leaves this span in time a critical execution horizon and one that needs to have identified logjams removed quickly.

b. *Demand plan forecast risks*—With demand so closely associated with revenue, there should be little question about the importance of looking out 30-90 days with a high level of scrutiny. Most companies that are focused on growth realize that increases in demand require one of two actions to occur: 1) get existing customers to buy more or 2) get new customers. If growth is predicted, corresponding actions regarding new or existing customers should be reviewed. The importance of these actions in the next 30-90 days is obvious to all. The S&OP format does not provide the answers, but it does provide the opportunity to ask the questions and ultimately to find the answers.

c. *Production risks*—In many companies there are probably no more obvious risks than ones in operations planning and execution. With the obvious risk comes the not-so-obvious risks that can slip through the cracks (and seemingly too often). These risk opportunities include new product introductions, new machine line implementations, additional shifts, product transfers from one plant to another, and new suppliers coming on-board. It is probably unnecessary to explain these risks in this chapter; the risks should be obvious. It can be said that any time a manufacturing facility has a large project that requires several coordinated support activities and there is a financial impact if the dates, quality, or details are not met, it becomes fairly obvious that a management system is of value. The S&OP process is exactly that. Scott, one of the best plant managers with whom I have worked, and a friend, recently asked why plant managers shouldn't be expected to take care of this follow-up. "Why does top management need to be involved all the time?" he asks. The answer is simple. Each plant manager has a defined world and his/her own priorities and objectives. These do not always perfectly correspond with other plant managers, and top management can best see this quickly. When working with AlliedSignal in Europe a few years ago (pre-Honeywell), Bill Amelio, the president of the Transportation and Power Systems (Garrett) division at the time, wanted product to be produced by the most cost-effective plants. This often created situations in which product manufacturing was shifted from one European plant to another because of differences in plant efficiency. This created a healthy competitive situation, but the receiving plant manager always had a much different perspective than the sending plant manager even though all parties were mature, experienced managers. When top management asked a few appropriate questions as the project approached, the quality of transfer seemed to improve. The S&OP (they called it SIOP at AlliedSignal) created the forum to make sure the right measures were in place to make smooth transitions. Simply knowing there was a reporting structure at the highest level facilitated smoother transitions.

3. **The 90 to 120-day plan expectations**—On an exception-only basis, this time frame is detailed in figure 8.8.

   a. *New product introduction discussed for risks of plan accuracy*—This was briefly mentioned in the shorter term view earlier in the chapter but new products do not normally cover merely the horizon of 30-60-90 days. In fact, often from the point of justification there can be several weeks, or in some businesses months, before the increase in volume and required capacity is scheduled. There are several important gates that need to be reviewed and quality of actions ensured. When this is completed correctly, companies have a much greater chance of high performance. After all, it is these new products that allow growth from either new customers or additional purchases from existing ones.

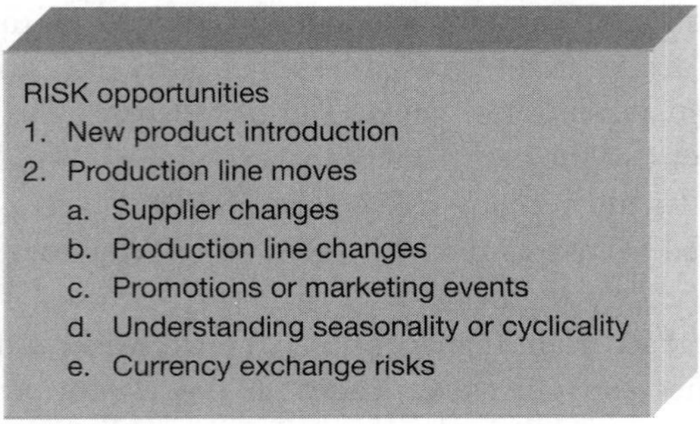

RISK opportunities
1. New product introduction
2. Production line moves
   a. Supplier changes
   b. Production line changes
   c. Promotions or marketing events
   d. Understanding seasonality or cyclicality
   e. Currency exchange risks

**Figure 8.8** Common Future Risk Possibilities

b. *Production shifts to alternative sources*—Shifts include moving product lines to off-shore sites, supply-chain changes, and risks. The list can be infinite on this topic. All risks should be fair game for the S&OP review.

c. *Promotions, shows, and customer actions, for example, are reviewed on an exception-only basis*—Many businesses do not hold planned marketing impact with the same high level of expectation that planned engineering innovation or operations success is held. Marketing events are planned from time to time in most businesses. If these are justified then an expected outcome is assumed. This impact on demand should be visible and identified on the horizon. The business gets full benefit of the learning that can occur from each of these with the visibility created in a well-managed S&OP process.

d. *Review/verification of normal cyclicality/seasonality is completed*— This usually does not take long when everyone is aware of the normal cycles. In one business that makes dance costumes, the seasonality was severe. Dance recitals are only held in the May/June time frame, making up the bulk of their annual sales. As new products were introduced, the seasonality began to change. Halloween, for example, was an opportunity on the other end of the calendar. Making sure everyone is on the same page is helpful. The S&OP process review forces this aspect.

e. *Anticipated currency exchange issues affecting the plan accuracy are discussed*—Here is an impact that too often is not monitored until too late and an unfavorable surprise. The top financial manager, along with the CEO, is normally the risk manager in this high-risk category. It is nearly impossible to be correct on currency futures every time but since it affects the bottom line in most global businesses, it should be a topic of review at the S&OP. Although it might not help improve the accuracy, regularly asking the right questions can remind top management of the risks—exactly the reason the S&OP process exists in high-performance businesses.

4. The balance of the 12-month rolling schedule is quickly reviewed for anomalies or expected changes. This agenda item is designed to review exceptions only, making sure there are no unforeseen high-stakes risks in the 12-month rolling plan.

a. *Any new information is communicated*—In most businesses there are anticipated projects linked to either the strategic planning process or the business imperatives. Either can provide opportunities to trip over risk in the future months. By maintaining a short list and reviewing it for new information each month at the S&OP meeting, the chances for success are enhanced. These possible review topics might include:

i. New plants being built.

ii. New machines or lines being added to existing plants.

iii. Changes in volumes requiring an additional shift.

iv. Large customer coming on or going away.

v. New market being targeted.

vi. Numerous other risk opportunities.

b. *Changes from the previous plan are reviewed*—Maybe the most efficient way to structure the agenda in the 12-month rolling time frame is to work from an exception-only basis. With efficiency, however, comes danger. Organizations that only discuss the exceptions and do not perform due diligence to the opportunities for trip wires in the future do not get full value from their efforts. If it is easy to miss important risks because of negligence, there can be a steep cost. While there is no magic formula for keeping this future 12-month rolling review at a high quality, probably one of the best approaches is to have the functional manager from each area review all risks in their space going out through the 12-month window. This review simply means the question is asked of each functional VP concerning upcoming risks. Honesty brings the right topics to the floor. In many organizations an ongoing list reminds the organization of specifics, for example, large projects. This project list is a good follow-up list.

## WHAT BUSINESSES NEED A SALES AND OPERATIONS PLANNING PROCESS?

In my many years of helping companies achieve performance improvements through the implementation of an S&OP process, the products and organizations vary as much as manufacturing businesses vary. Here are just a few involved in my experience:

- first-tier automotive manufacturer/supplier
- business-to-business packaging materials manufacturer
- sporting goods manufacturing sold through distribution
- molded consumer goods sold through stores like Target, Kmart, and Wal*Mart
- baked products sold through distribution
- shampoo manufacturing sold to all markets
- forklift truck manufacturing sold through distribution
- kitchen appliance manufacturer sold to retail stores
- business-to-business urethane film manufacturer
- business-to-business engineering services company
- furniture manufacturing sold through retail outlets
- nail manufacturing sold in several market outlets
- pharmaceuticals sold through normal health provider channels
- printing sold through numerous channels
- consulting services (e.g., DHSheldon & Associates!)
- business-to-business aerospace manufacturing
- electronics manufacturing sold through retail outlets

The number of different businesses can be continued through several pages but the diversity should be apparent. From baked goods and pharmaceuticals to automotive supply chain and engineering services, the S&OP process adds value. Businesses with varied stocking or inventory strategies (MTO, MTS, ATO) are all impacted equally by the value-add of the S&OP process.

## WHO DRIVES THE SALES AND OPERATIONS PLANNING PROCESS?

The question of S&OP leadership is dealt with on several levels. The meeting leadership or process owner is easily determined. It is the CEO or president at the corporate level, the vice president if executed at the division level, or plant manager at the plant level. At this point it only needs to be remembered that the highest-ranking manager in the facility in which the S&OP process is exercised is the process owner for that level within the S&OP (figure 8.9).

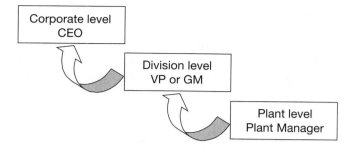

**Figure 8.9** Levels of S&OP Ownership

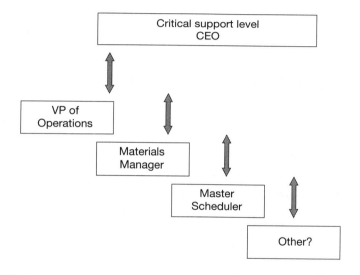

**Figure 8.10** Who in the Business Normally Drives the S&OP Implementation?

A multilevel S&OP process is simply the application of the monthly management system at each level to make sure the detail supporting the corporate S&OP is as accurate and thorough as possible. In many small businesses there is only a corporate S&OP.

On another level is the question of process driver or initiator if the business does not have an S&OP process currently. This answer is not as consistent business to business. Some of the more common drivers/initiators of the process are the VP of Operations, the materials manager, the master scheduler or, the most effective, the CEO. There have been many successes driven from grassroots passion supported by top management insightfulness (figure 8.10).

Many times the one who leads this process, once the internal marketing is complete and the CEO is on board, ends up positively influencing his/her career substantially through the exposure and impact to the organization. The S&OP process only works with proper supporting processes in place. In the next chapter one of the most important of the processes to S&OP, demand planning, is covered in detail.

## DISCUSSION QUESTIONS

1. The materials manager owns the S&OP process.
   a. true
   b. false

2. The S&OP event should take place
   a. once a year.
   b. once a quarter.
   c. once a month.
   d. twice a month.

3. The rules of engagement between sales and operations are determined by materials.
   a. true
   b. false

4. Product family designations play a key role in the S&OP process.
   a. true
   b. false

5. An adequate S&OP horizon is at least 18 months.
   a. true
   b. false

6. Forecasting accuracy is expected to be in the 98%-100% range in high-performance organizations.
   a. true
   b. false

7. The S&OP is about
   a. risk management.
   b. performance assessment.
   c. root cause of variation.
   d. a and b
   e. a, b, and c

8. The S&OP event is the president's, COO's, or CEO's meeting. This person chairs it.
   a. true
   b. false

9. The S&OP process is separate from an overall ERP planning process.
   a. true
   b. false

10. The process ownership for demand generally is delegated from the VP of Sales.
    a. true
    b. false

# DEMAND PLANNING

## INTRODUCTION

Probably no single process within the Enterprise Resource Planning (ERP) business model gets any more attention than demand planning. Demand planning is normally a popular topic with materials managers! After all, if there was full understanding of what the customers wanted before they wanted it, then it would be easy to have the right inventory at the right time. It hasn't happened in any business I have worked in. In lean-focused materials departments there is occasionally an unrealistic viewpoint that the forecast is not needed in a pull system, lean-driven environment. In most businesses there is not an overabundance of capacity waiting for the signal to come. It is usually too costly to have this kind of waste. Any time a manufacturing firm can have a window into the future requirements, there is a better chance of containing costs.

The popularity of the demand plan comes from the frequently observed broadband process variation introduced into nearly every business by customers. All businesses have unruly customers! Sadly, in many businesses the demand plan or forecast is actually developed by the materials department because the demand side has not willingly come to the planning table with a forecast. In high-performance businesses, it is necessary to have a solid handshake between the demand process and the operations side of the business. This handshake culminates in the Sales and Operations Planning process as described in the previous chapter. Not only is this partnership attitude important for minimizing risk, but it also creates an environment in which everybody has shared goals and understands how variation from their part of the business affects other parts of the operation.

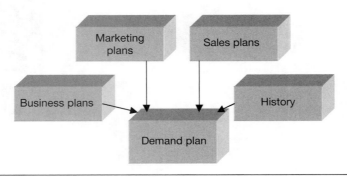

**Figure 9.1** Class A ERP Demand Plan Inputs

**Figure 9.2** Class A ERP Demand Planning Inputs and Business Plans

The quality of the inputs makes the quality of the demand plan (figure 9.1). If the emphasis is on the right tasks and these tasks are linked to the business plan properly, the results are fun indeed! For this to occur, there has to be effectively communicated, well-understood objectives with shared ownership in the outcomes.

## BUSINESS PLANNING AS AN INPUT TO DEMAND PLANNING

In businesses that are focused and continually developing competitive advantage, it is important to have the plans and actions tightly linked. As management direction influences new product development, new markets, and service offerings, it is extremely helpful if everyone is on the same page. The business plan inputs (figure 9.2) are most important to the company's success. It is this input that directs specific resource assignment in marketing and sales and redirects goals. *It is not about following the customers' desires; it is about leading them when possible.*

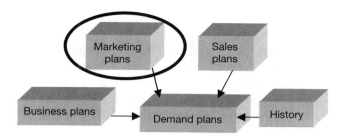

**Figure 9.3** Class A ERP Demand Planning Inputs and Marketing Plans

If management has prioritized a new service offering to potential customers, then actions need to result that affect this outcome. Metrics also need to be implemented to gauge results to monitor effectiveness in implementing this strategy and to create the feedback loop for management. One packaging manufacturer I work with is a first-tier supplier to the food industry. They have decided to focus on just-in-time (JIT) deliveries for a competitive advantage with their best customers. The corporate business plan established the objective of building new plants across the street from their best customers but not until there was a partnership agreement from these customers. Longer-term agreements, in this case, mean less inventory requirements for the customer to hold and shorter lead time. Shorter term it requires the sales force to sell the idea and get the signature. This could not have been the sales plan without the business plan input. There are many more examples of business plan input requiring a shift in resource and effort. Some might include: a new service offering to customers who already buy product, new markets being entered, selling to Asia as a new venture, or raising prices in a tight market for strategic purposes. All of these activities affect customer behavior and, accordingly, the demand planning process. When the demand planner develops the 12-month rolling forecast, for example, the known goal of a new product offering must affect the demand numbers somewhere in the future of that product family. Top management should expect to see it in the demand plan as soon as the idea is approved. The next major input to the demand plan is the marketing input (figure 9.3).

## MARKETING PLANS AS AN INPUT TO DEMAND PLANNING

When operations people think about forecasts, too often they focus on wanting a perfect forecast. It is not a healthy expectation to have—"improving" is reasonable; "perfect" is not. It is common to hear statements like, "If we could just know ahead of time what customers were going to want, we could run very effectively and with very little inventory." This kind of thinking is only half right. As stated previously, when planning input in high-performance businesses, the correct thought process for demand planning is not to *guess* what customers are going to do, but instead *affect* what they are going to do. Think about it: this strategy makes much more sense when linked to the business planning strategy. Most businesses today are not trying to repeat yesterday; they are trying to do things differently to continuously improve position in the marketplace. This means that the marketing team needs to estimate what impact each of its strategies will have on customer behavior. That requires commitment from the marketing folks. This commitment is referred to as process ownership.

In many of the best manufacturing companies dealing within fast-moving markets, new products are being introduced constantly. For discussion, let's say that the business plan has outlined two new products for design and introduction. One is in a totally new market; the other is a new design in an existing market. Marketing usually aligns with the new product introduction teams and has marketing team members assigned to each new product. In this fictional example, the products are also in a new market. Adding more reality to this example, the company has three marketing ideas to implement to "teach" the customers to buy this new offering. Marketing, at this point, needs to link its plan to some sort of expectation. As a former boss of mine used to say about *everything*, "There's always math behind it." This company in the example needs to get to the math. Let's say that the company's three ideas include one trade show, one customer event, and one advertising campaign. If the marketing group puts a value on each, some effect would be calculable on expected demand. Let's say that there was an estimate of 30,000 units if they did nothing except introduce the new product through existing markets. Splash from the planned trade show might add another 10,000 units. The estimate is more valuable if the potential new customers are listed with anticipated buy quantities. The customer event designed to create excitement for a few of the largest potential customers for this product could add another 50,000 units and the advertising campaign might have an effect of 25,000 incremental units. Doing the math, this marketing team could add 30,000 (pre-existing potential) plus 10,000 (trade show), plus 50,000 (customer event), plus 25,000 (advertising campaign) and get a total of 115,000. Many may be thinking that it would be a miracle if the 115,000 was accurate and they would probably be right. Marketing needs to estimate process variation just like operations has to. As uncomfortable as this idea is to the operations group, it needs to be stated that it is better to be slightly off on the low side of the forecast than to have too much inventory and nobody buying it. Marketing needs to factor the estimates. What makes this process powerful is process ownership. The factoring has some risks and the marketing people need to know they are measured on their accuracy. High-performance organizations should expect 85-90% average accuracy per

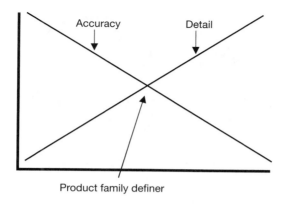

**Figure 9.4** Accuracy versus Detail Comparison and SKU

product family in demand forecasting once accountability and ownership have been established. This accuracy is measured at the product family level, not stock keeping unit (SKU) level. There is a proven reason for this logic (figure 9.4).

At the product family, companies can experience the highest level of detail at the highest level of accuracy. This optimum level of detail takes some experimenting. If both marketing and operations have the shared goal of accuracy in this metric, the job can actually be fun. There are three simple rules that work effectively. They are so important and yet so simple that hanging them on the wall in the main conference room could be helpful. If organizations can secure an agreement between the two key groups (demand and supply), mountains can be moved.

1. Operations needs to have a greater appreciation for the difficulty of developing accurate forecasts and needs to help the sales force succeed. As hard as it is for operations to hear this, it is true; forecasting accurately is much more difficult than accurately scheduling products. There are often simply more uncontrollable variables in the process.
2. The marketing people need to step up to the bar and understand and acknowledge that the farther the forecast is off, the more cost potential and/or service degradation is generated for the company's products and services.
3. In areas in which forecasts are unstable or consistently inaccurate, there needs to be an agreement on how much cost in terms of flexible capacity and/or inventory will be endured to offset this process variation. This must be a joint decision.

**Figure 9.5** Class A ERP Demand Planning Inputs and Sales Plans

The next input to the demand plan is the sales process. This one is good because there is math behind it naturally.

## SALES PLANNING AS AN INPUT TO DEMAND PLANNING

The next input area within a robust demand planning process is the sales plan (figure 9.5). This plan is more calculable than the marketing plans. In many businesses there are experiences to work from or historical knowledge and data within the business in terms of closure rates and sales cycle times. In capital equipment, for example, there is normally a relatively long sales cycle, but it is known and can be reasonably predictable over a broad customer base. Other consumer product sales cycles require little time. In either case, the customer reaction is somewhat statistically predictable.

Sales are also often linked to seasonality or some sort of cyclicality. One clothing manufacturer I worked with that specialized in dance costumes had 80% of sales in 3 weeks of the year (dance recitals are always in the May time frame). Another multiple-site ice cream cone bakery client did the lion's share of business in 4 months of the summer. (I found it interesting that in hot climates ice cream cones still only sell briskly in the summer months.) Still another client, a kitchen appliance manufacturer, found sales seasonal as well. The most familiar saying I hear in businesses is "You don't understand, our business is different." The truth is there are more similarities than differences in most businesses.

Getting the math behind the numbers in the sales function is critical. This can mean requirements predictability in terms of: numbers of customer calls needed to hit plan, frequency of visits to hit plan, follow-up on late orders required, and/or number of cold calls needed to make the objective. While the business plan is the major driver of demand activity, marketing and sales plans are what make these objectives and, ultimately, the forecast happen. It's all about *affecting* customer behavior.

## HISTORICAL INPUTS TO THE DEMAND PLANNING PROCESS

The last input to the demand planning process is the one that is most often thought of first, historical data (figure 9.6). The reason it is thought of first is most likely because, unfortunately, in many businesses it has been the role of operations to do forecasting. Since the operations personnel know little about what is happening in the marketplace because they are not out in it, the only useful data is history. In many businesses, history projected forward is interestingly accurate. That is not always a good sign, however. In the early 1990s, I was a division manager within The Raymond Corporation. The CEO at that time was Ross Colquhoun. He was a professional businessman who had been successful long before he came to lead Raymond. He made it clear in the monthly divisional reviews that he did not want to hear about history. He had good reason. Businesses that can accurately predict the future using the past are often not changing the landscape enough in what, for many businesses, are changing markets. This comes back to haunt an organization in lost market share. In this case he was absolutely right in his thinking. The Raymond Corporation grew into a successful original equipment manufacturer of material handling equipment supplying well-known companies.

That is not to say history isn't valuable. Quite the contrary, it is valuable. Within the data are the seasonal stories and the normal cyclicality that are so necessary to understand. The leaner a company's objectives are in terms of low inventory, little unutilized capacity, or short lead time, the more a little bit of market visibility can be helpful.

Today there are also many good software tools that can organize data and historical information to statistically predict future events. Some are built into the ERP business system but many more are add-ons. These system tools can be helpful in organizing historical customer data. These tools have progressed in the last few years and should be considered in a business that has predictable trends.

**Figure 9.6** Class A ERP Demand Planning Inputs and History

The message on the topic of forecasting from history is this: History is the most difficult input to use accurately for the demand planning in businesses that are making waves in their markets. If the business is shaking things up with new products and services, history becomes less likely to be accurate or even as valuable. Historical data can be manipulated in many ways as well. Software forecasting equations that allow weighting in any period desired actually allow for whatever result that is wanted. That is good and bad. Keeping history in perspective is helpful. Use it wisely!

## UNDERSTANDING THE OUTPUTS OF DEMAND PLANNING

The demand planning process is performed so that the business understands profit potential (figure 9.7). Indirectly it sets the stage for capacity, financing, and stakeholder confidence. The forecast is one of the most valuable inputs to the risk management of the business. At the Sales and Operations Planning (S&OP) process meeting (chapter 8), top management evaluates the likelihood of the demand plan being accurately executed and, accordingly, commits resources and cash to allow for it to occur. Demand planning is not a one-way communication or plan that gets thrown over the wall to manufacturing. Instead, it is a handshake agreement between all of the top managers in the business, especially demand and operations. From another perspective, it is also about each top manager delivering part of the requirements. When everybody does the job and the agreement and risk assessment is performed accurately, the result is a lean and successful operation.

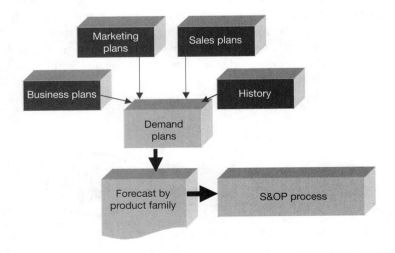

**Figure 9.7** Class A ERP Demand Planning Outputs

**Table 9.1 Forecast for Company XYZ**

| Date 2 February 20-- | | | | | | All numbers in thousands | | | | | | | |
|---|---|---|---|---|---|---|---|---|---|---|---|---|---|
| **Product family** | **Jan*** | **Feb** | **Mar** | **Apr** | **May** | **Jun** | **Jul** | **Aug** | **Sep** | **Oct** | **Nov** | **Dec** | **Jan** |
| **Line one** | 30 | 30 | 20 | 25 | 34 | 35 | 45 | 78 | 67 | 50 | 35 | 35 | 30 |
| Actual | 30 | | | | | | | | | | | | |
| **Line two** | 30 | 27 | 22 | 21 | 20 | 25 | 15 | 20 | 19 | 16 | 15 | 12 | 10 |
| Actual | 29 | | | | | | | | | | | | |
| **Line three existing** | 60 | 80 | 86 | 90 | 88 | 89 | 90 | 78 | 65 | 50 | 35 | 30 | 32 |
| **Line three new**** | | | | | | | | 20 | 25 | 50 | 75 | 80 | 90 |
| Actual | 66 | | | | | | | | | | | | |
| **Line four** | 50 | 51 | 55 | 65 | 64 | 66 | 73 | 78 | 67 | 55 | 56 | 55 | 50 |
| Actual | 54 | | | | | | | | | | | | |
| **Line five** | 5 | 8 | 6 | 7 | 7 | 7 | 8 | 9 | 10 | 9 | 7 | 6 | 6 |
| Actual | 5 | | | | | | | | | | | | |

*The January column in this example has both planned and actual numbers from the month's performance; the balance of the months are planned quantities.

**New products are generally reviewed separately from existing products due to the high risk opportunity.

The output of the demand plan is the forecast. The final demand document should be divided into product families and have a horizon of 12 rolling months. This document is the basis for the S&OP review and drives the drumbeat for inventory flow and capacity availability. It must be in product family configuration (table 9.1).

## THE WEEKLY DEMAND REVIEW

The demand plan is a moving document due to the simple fact that customers are generally ill-behaved. Each week we are (hopefully) smarter than we were a week ago and it is foolish to ignore that fact. For that reason, each Friday there should be a demand review held with all product managers, plant managers, materials and master scheduling. In most businesses, this allows changes in the current week to be quickly implemented and baked into the schedule changes for the upcoming week. In some lean supply chains, that might mean changes to the supplier signals (make to order or engineer to order), or this might drive changes in the manufacturing schedule (make to order or assemble to order), or it could drive changes in distribution (make to stock). It just depends on the inventory

**Table 9.2 Monthly Demand Review**

**Sample Month – January where the first day of the month happens to be a Monday**

|         | Mon  | Tue | Wed | Thu | Fri             |
|---------|------|-----|-----|-----|-----------------|
| Week 1  | S&OP |     |     |     | Demand review   |
| Week 2  |      |     |     |     | Demand review   |
| Week 3  |      |     |     |     | Demand review   |
| Week 4  |      |     |     |     | Pre-S&OP review |

strategy—if inventory is kept in finished goods, in components, or at the supplier's facility. In many lean businesses the move is to eliminate most finished goods and to keep the inventory as low in the supply chain as lead times facilitate. All of this adds up to the need for reasonably clear visibility into the market requirements. The weekly demand review is simply a forum to ensure that the demand and supply sides of the business are talking regularly and about the right topics. The following agenda reflects a robust process. In most businesses, the meeting should not take more than 5-10 minutes per product family.

### AGENDA FOR THE WEEKLY DEMAND REVIEW MEETING
1. Review current week accuracy of forecast for each product family.
2. Review upcoming week forecast and any changes necessary.
3. Agree on any required adjustments to the production plan.
4. Determine any effect on monthly revenue or profit.
5. Review actions and agreements left from last week and new ones for this week.

The schedule for the demand review should correspond with the S&OP review. To make this the most effective, the last demand review of the month should focus on preparation for the top management S&OP meeting following soon, in addition to the normal updates. See table 9.2 for a typical schedule.

The agenda for the pre-S&OP meeting is not unlike the weekly demand review. The biggest difference is two-fold: 1) in the pre-S&OP, the discussion around demand and production plan variation is more of a summary for the month rather than just last week's variation, and 2) there is a full acknowledgement that the S&OP meeting is only a few days away and questions need to have both answers and proposals for improvement. That includes risk analysis on the 12-month rolling horizon by product family. This acknowledgement makes the meeting more productive knowing that there is a deadline pending. With everybody in the room to make important decisions, the process can be quite efficient.

## Process Ownership in the Weekly Demand Review

Process ownership in demand planning can differ from business to business because of differences in organizational structure and job titles. In The Raymond Corporation, the business in which I started, the VP of Marketing had all the product managers reporting to her. Product managers had a huge influence on the business and were aligned by product family—the same divisors that are used in the S&OP process and demand planning. Product managers determined marketing plans and helped manage the sales force policy at the distributors, which were independent dealerships. The product managers were responsible for gathering information from the dealers and for massaging it to their liking, including marketing plans and sales influences, and then for delivering forecasts to the VP of Marketing. She would, in turn, deliver these estimates to the S&OP process, where the records would be reviewed and "blessed" accordingly. She was ultimately the process owner for demand planning although she received ample help from the VP of Sales and detail support from the product managers. All of the team attended the demand reviews, both the end-of-month demand review (pre-S&OP) and the S&OP.

In many businesses, especially smaller firms, the VP of Sales is also responsible for marketing. In these businesses, everybody from the demand side reports to the VP of Sales. There is little question who is the process owner in these organizations—the VP of Sales. If possible, one approach to avoid is having the process ownership for demand planning accuracy delegated too far down the organization. It is the president's or CEO's job to ask the tough questions. The vice president level is normally the appropriate level for process ownership to reside for the demand plan accuracy and this person should answer to that accountability. It takes substantial help from in and outside the organization to get the forecast right, and the more handshakes there are, the more likely there will be a successful process.

## MEASURING THE DEMAND PLAN

The metric for demand planning accuracy is simple. The calculation is always from the product-family-level data and normally has an acceptability threshold of 90%. The measurement is the average accuracy by product family. Some get a little uncomfortable with "average" accuracy because accuracy itself is depicted as an average. The examples in tables 9.3 and 9.4 illustrate demand accuracy calculation for Class A ERP. The average product family accuracy is the reporting objective.

One frequent question about demand planning accuracy measurements concerns the interpretation of measurement rules. The forecast and the actual are not always what they seem. For example, most companies have blanket order agreements with the best customers in some form or another. This just makes good sense. It eliminates unnecessary documentation and paperwork flow. Many

## Table 9.3 Demand Plan by Product Family

| Date 2 February 20-- | | | | | | All numbers in thousands | | | | | | | |
|---|---|---|---|---|---|---|---|---|---|---|---|---|---|
| **Product family** | **Jan*** | **Feb** | **Mar** | **Apr** | **May** | **Jun** | **Jul** | **Aug** | **Sep** | **Oct** | **Nov** | **Dec** | **Jan** |
| **Line one** | 30 | 30 | 20 | 25 | 34 | 35 | 45 | 78 | 67 | 50 | 35 | 35 | 30 |
| Actual | 30 | | | | | | | | | | | | |
| Performance | **100%** | | | | | | | | | | | | |
| **Line two** | 30 | 27 | 22 | 21 | 20 | 25 | 15 | 20 | 19 | 16 | 15 | 12 | 10 |
| Actual | 29 | | | | | | | | | | | | |
| Performance | **97%** | | | | | | | | | | | | |
| **Line three existing** | 60 | 80 | 86 | 90 | 88 | 89 | 90 | 78 | 65 | 50 | 35 | 30 | 32 |
| **Line three new**** | | | | | | | | 20 | 25 | 50 | 75 | 80 | 90 |
| Actual | 66 | | | | | | | | | | | | |
| Performance | **90%** | | | | | | | | | | | | |
| **Line four** | 50 | 51 | 55 | 65 | 64 | 66 | 73 | 78 | 67 | 55 | 56 | 55 | 50 |
| Actual | 54 | | | | | | | | | | | | |
| Performance | **92%** | | | | | | | | | | | | |
| **Line five** | 5 | 8 | 6 | 7 | 7 | 7 | 8 | 9 | 10 | 9 | 7 | 6 | 6 |
| Actual | 5 | | | | | | | | | | | | |
| Performance | **100%** | | | | | | | | | | | | |
| **Perf. Total** | **95.8%** | | | | | | | | | | | | |

*The January column in this example has both planned and actual numbers from the month's performance; the balance of the months are planned quantities.

**New products are generally reviewed separately from existing products due to the high risk opportunity.

companies make the mistake of using the blanket order as the "actual order" in the demand planning metric. This often does not make sense because most customers normally commit to a blanket order and then change the quantities or schedule just prior to the ship date. These last minute schedules are often referred to as "releases from the blanket order." In reality, blanket orders are just forecasts even though in some rare cases these forecast signals are pretty firm.

Demand planning is more effective if initiated as a monthly metric. The demand plan is updated as required throughout the month, obviously, but for measurement purposes only; the "plan of record" remains locked. The forecast should be locked (for measurement purposes only) at the S&OP each month and is measured for monthly accuracy. The focus should not be on accuracy alone, but also what can be learned from the inaccuracies experienced. Demand planning in a high-performance organization is about shared goals and process ownership

**Table 9.4 Calculating the Average Accuracy of Demand Planning**

|  | Accuracy |
| --- | --- |
| Product family 1 | 100 |
| Product family 2 | 97 |
| Product family 3 | 90 |
| Product family 4 | 92 |
| Product family 5 | 100 |

Total performance = (100 + 97 + 90 + 92 + 100) / 5 families or 95.8%

clearly defined. Management systems such as the S&OP and the weekly demand review should be in place to keep everyone communicating properly and predictably. In the next chapter, the direction shifts back to the topics of lean and Six Sigma and how the integration should come naturally in high-performance organizations.

## DISCUSSION QUESTIONS

1. Demand planning is generally made up of the following input(s):
   a. history
   b. marketing plans
   c. business strategy
   d. a and b
   e. all of the above

2. A demand review should occur frequently—at least once a week.
   a. true
   b. false

3. Demand planning is generally at the part number level and mainly functions to develop a forecast based on history.
   a. true
   b. talse

4. History is always the most important aspect of demand planning.
   a. true
   b. false

5. The last weekly demand review of the month is often referred to as the pre-S&OP.
   a. true
   b. false

6. Demand planning is
   a. a one-way communication from sales to operations.
   b. mapped from marketing plans.
   c. a major component of an ERP process.
   d. none of the above

7. Demand planning is calculated by
   a. the accuracy of the cumulative product family unit plan.
   b. the average of the product family accuracy.
   c. part number accuracy.
   d. looking out 3 months and measuring accuracy.

8. Product family choice normally is looking at
   a. the highest level of detail with the highest level of accuracy.
   b. color as a commonality.
   c. price as a consideration.
   d. all of the above
   e. none of the above

9. If marketing is planning a booth at a convention and justified the expense with the expectation that sales would increase 15% in one product family as a result, what would the demand plan include?
   a. A 15% increase in sales of that product family following the convention.
   b. A factor of "convention influence" built into that product family demand plan.
   c. No influence until the demand starts coming and they have a better feel for it.
   d. none of the above

10. The following can be inputs to or have an effect on the demand plan:
    a. price
    b. cost
    c. cyclicality
    d. seasonality
    e. capacity
    f. c and d
    g. all the above

# INTEGRATING LEAN AND SIX SIGMA WITH ENTERPRISE RESOURCE PLANNING

## INTRODUCTION

Materials managers are usually the first people in the organization to embrace lean concepts. After all, they are usually the ones on the front line limiting any inventory exposure they can control. Nonetheless, there are still a few people in the world who are convinced that there is an integration issue with the three elements: Enterprise Resource Planning (ERP), lean, and Six Sigma. I visited a large company recently in which lean audits were performed. In the audit there was a criterion disallowing Material Requirements Planning (MRP) to be used. This is a perfect example of misunderstanding. None of their plants, if honest concerning the criteria, will pass that audit. Nearly all high-performance organizations start with a basic foundation of discipline and build upon it with good tools and techniques from both the lean toolbox and Six Sigma technique. This performance improvement track has different names; however, the names I ascribe to are shown in figure 10.1.

## CONTINUOUS IMPROVEMENT

Some argue that process design must link to customer needs and that elimination of waste is only defined after the customer requirements are thoroughly understood. In many of the best organizations, process mapping, especially in the form

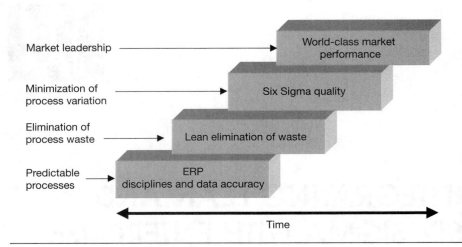

**Figure 10.1** Journey to World-Class Performance

of value stream mapping, is a major element in the continuous improvement process. Process mapping makes no differentiations between organizational buzzwords or acronyms such as ERP, lean, or Six Sigma. Each is a different topic when comparing these improvement or business models. If we think of lean and Six Sigma as tools, we could accordingly think of ERP as a schematic. For example, ERP might be comparable to the electrical infrastructure in a new house. It defines where the flow of information or, in this case, electricity travels. In this example, lean might be the set of tools that are required to build the house in the least amount of time. Six Sigma could be compared to the method used to assure quality and customer specifications were maintained. There are many more similarities between the tools lean and Six Sigma than there are between the business model ERP and the tools. This is a topic of confusion for many, especially with the "lean-only" crowd. The realities are that continuous improvement finds many forms. Frequently, I am sitting in the front of airplanes simply because of the amount of travel I do. The other people sitting around me are often also in the consulting business. It is never surprising when we compare notes that we all use the same tools but have different names for them. The names do not matter, only the focus on good process and continuous improvement. In most successful businesses, when the facts are really exposed there are some levels of proficiency that must be achieved. Materials people are involved in all of them. These levels are:

1. **Becoming predictable—making promises.** Accountability and associated management systems really are "business 101"! Promises when meeting market requirements can make a substantial difference in competitive advantage but they are not the whole picture. By

focusing on process capability first, specifically repeatability, processes often get reinvented or redesigned or made repeatable through the use of metrics, management systems driving root cause analysis, and barrier elimination. The deliverables from this element of process improvement are the management system and cultural shift to measurements and analysis. It is known as process ownership. With disciplined ERP-driven emphasis on sales and operations planning and supply-chain management there is little need to do prioritization of projects. Because the methodology is defined, the process becomes an efficient cultural-shifting strategy. It is not the complete answer, however; it is just the beginning.

2. **Lean tools help improve processes by eliminating waste.** Lean focus works effectively for the second step in the journey to excellence as the emphasis naturally shifts from process design and capability to process improvement. There are many examples in which major processes get redesigned a second time in this space. In successful businesses it can occur repeatedly. There is never an end to process improvement. However, the focus is complementary although different when looked at through the lean glasses. The emphasis in this space shifts from only process capability to process flexibility, speed, and responsiveness to customer need, a step above the foundation-level ERP emphasis. The ERP prerequisite deliverables of the daily/weekly/monthly management systems and habits of measurement also make lean efficient as the emphasis moves to speed.

3. **Lowering costs further by minimizing process variation.** All the steps to world-class excellence share a common thread—continuous improvement driven from understanding and eliminating root causes to achieve increased levels of performance. The third step in some businesses is the step that never ends, Six Sigma. Process variation in all organizations is unavoidable, but in high-performance organizations, *decreasing* process variation is also unavoidable. One sigma is equal to one standard deviation. Remember from college statistics that as process variation is decreased so is the standard deviation. Customer requirements are the limits of acceptability in any process, and as the standard deviation is decreased, the likelihood of missing customer requirements is also decreased. This is the theory behind the Six Sigma measurement. The likelihood of a customer requirement being missed is rare; the quality level of Six Sigma is limited to 3.4 defects within a million opportunities!

## UNNECESSARY WORKER MOVEMENT REVISTED

A few years ago at a client site in Kodama, Japan, the plant manager wanted to show me the improvements they had made to their material flow since my last visit. When we reached the second floor on which the assembly operation was stationed, I could see no difference from the last visit. He then proceeded to show me how they had moved a machine approximately 6 inches! It was not even noticeable to the outside observer but they had discovered that this movement affected their ability to meet the tight schedule requirements. The driver for this change, along with safety requirements, was wasted space and cycle time. A kaizen had led to the machine layout change which eliminated a physical movement (of one step) that the operator had to take between operations in the work cell.

## LEAN AND PROCESS MAPPING TOOLS

Lean is the next step after ERP process capability in high performance (figure 10.2). To be a successful lean material manager, one must know and use the proper tools. The emphasis of the first step, Class A ERP, is on process capability and process discipline. The next steps are leveraging this process capability into waste-free lean processes that are flexible and responsive. This requires new skills and knowledge, not the least of which is an understanding of the proper tools. There are other books that focus on that topic specifically, but it is good to be introduced to or reminded of the most important ones.

In the lean space there is ample opportunity to use various process mapping tools including:

- **Value Organization Alignment Mapping (VOAM)**—A VOAM is a mapping exercise to track information or decision making through an organization chart. Lean materials managers might use this to track

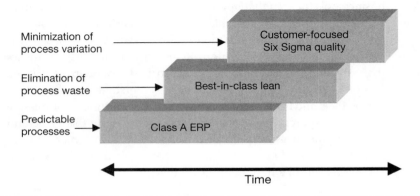

Figure 10.2 Steps to World-Class Performance

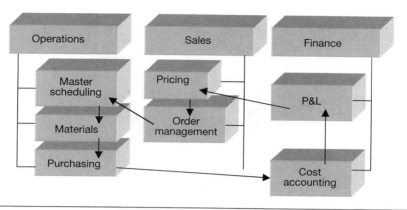

**Figure 10.3** Value Organization Alignment Map

decisions through the organization, for example, establishing rules of engagement for order management (figure 10.3).

- **Time Value Mapping (TVM)**—TVM is a methodology used to map both activity and duration of a process. This is a unique approach in that time value becomes visible in the diagram for each step. Also, by placing value-add process elements below the time line and cost-add activities above the line, visibility becomes a driver for change. This can be an effective tool for reducing process cycle time (figure 10.4).
- **Swim Lane Flow Charts**—Swim lane flow charts show activities separated by "lanes" of functions in the process map. These are helpful in tracking information or material movement through the organization (figure 10.5).

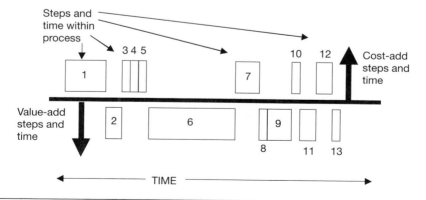

**Figure 10.4** Time Value Map

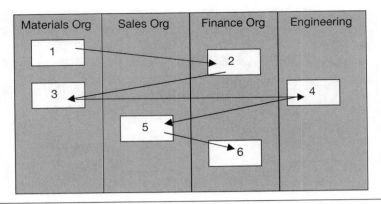

**Figure 10.5** Swim Lane Flow Chart

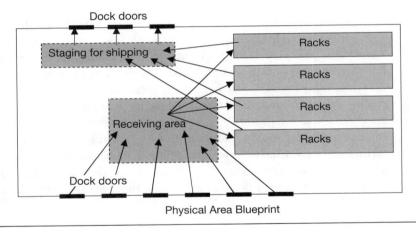

**Figure 10.6** Physical Process Map

- **Physical Process Maps**—Process maps of building layouts that show material flow, people movement, or information flow-mapped on the blueprint. Materials managers typically own storage areas and this tool can be helpful for material movement and storage patterning (figure 10.6).
- **Logical Process Flow Map**—The most common logical process flow maps are simple process maps depicting all activities in a line with decision points and various alternative routes shown with specific shapes (figure 10.7).

Lean tools certainly overlap ERP, lean, and Six Sigma project management. It is really unnecessary to differentiate the project management methodology title as

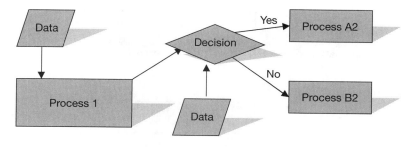

**Figure 10.7** Logical Process Flow

long as a robust process is in place. This occurs when the priorities are understood, people are empowered, and they know how to use the tools properly. Root cause analysis and actions close the loop on performance measurements. Without good disciplines and problem-solving tools, the metrics may not result in needed actions. It is the analysis that leads the way, and lean tools are at the center of this analysis. These various mapping tools include several important methods to identify waste in a process.

## FUNCTIONAL MANUFACTURING VERSUS PROCESS FLOW

Not so long ago manufacturing areas were always arranged by function. Welders were all together, lathes were all in the same department, and milling machines were set side-by-side. It just made sense. This was prior to lean thinking, which increased the awareness of waste. In today's high-performance organizations, there is a more educated view of material flow.

In the 1970s, in the company in which I grew up, there was what we considered good process flow. I gave tours through this plant and explained that material started in the steel shop and progressed through to shipping in a logical layout (figure 10.8).

While the factory flow in figure 10.8 might seem like a logical path for process flow, and during tours it was even described in that way, in reality it was not. It took an exercise of tracking actual material flow through the process to understand the opportunity. On a factory layout drawing we tracked the flow and marked the path on paper. What we found was similar to figure 10.9. Material actually flowed around and around the shop. If we dropped a string on the path, we probably would have needed miles. We did not measure it. This was an eye-opening experience. We immediately took action to solve this cost-added opportunity.

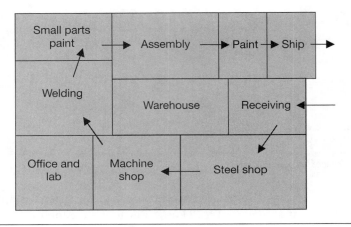

**Figure 10.8** Functional Manufacturing Flow Layout

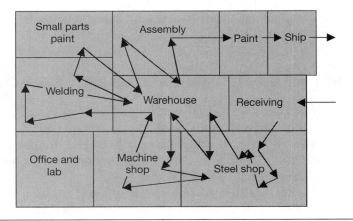

**Figure 10.9** Functional Manufacturing Flow Layout Showing Additional Movement

At first the group had some concern about the unwieldy task. Many of the machines in the factory had deep foundations made of solid concrete. To move these machines would be costly, and if they weren't moved to the right spot, the move might not provide results. It seemed risky. The answer was to devour this formidable project one bit at a time. We started with forks. This seemed simple enough and a manageable place to begin.

Prior to this project launch, it took several weeks to get forks from raw steel to assembly. There were several operations that required a long string of travel and waste. The result was a horseshoe work cell that took the lead time to 4 hours. All forks for a particular assembly line were made in 4 hours the day prior to the

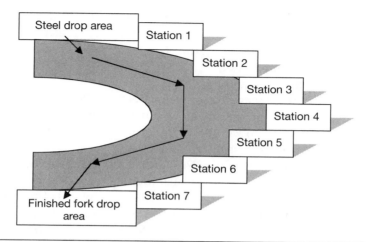

**Figure 10.10** Fork Work Cell

master production schedule (MPS) requirement in assembly. Daily, a nearby distributor delivered the steel necessary for the day's production. These requirements were driven from the MPS shared with the supplier—several weeks to 4 days! Once the project was successfully completed, it was actually more surprising that it could last weeks than the fact that it could be completed in 4 hours. Figure 10.10 is an illustration of the work cell implemented.

## CUSTOMER-FOCUSED QUALITY (SIX SIGMA)

The next performance-level goal is extremely ambitious and one that is seldom, if ever, totally reached—the Six Sigma objective and methodology. With only 3.4 defects allowed in a million opportunities, the standards are higher than most objectives. Class A ERP with lean concepts built into the recipe creates the right foundation for this third level of performance criteria and tool set. In my experience, there is substantial value in ratcheting the steps. It is also apparent as one understands all three methodologies (ERP, lean, and Six Sigma) that there are no conflicts between these approaches. The integration is a natural, logical one.

Six Sigma is actually a definition of the levels of defects found in a certain process. Allowing only 3.4 defects for every million opportunities in a given process, Six Sigma has also become a label for a specific methodology of problem solving and project management. Six Sigma, the methodology label, is believed by many to have been started by Motorola and made famous by the former CEO of General Electric Jack Welch, who was one of the major advocates for this methodology and helped popularize it at several companies. Most large companies have some form of Six Sigma process improvement methodology. Hundreds of successful companies utilize Six Sigma somewhere in their strategy, including the more successful Dell, Lockheed Martin, GE, Honeywell (former AlliedSignal), Motorola, and NCR Corporation.

All processes have variation but few are better for it, so a methodology to minimize it would make sense to most people. Setting allowable defects at 3.4 in a million opportunities appears ambitious and it is. Class A, remember, is a celebration point on the way to world-class performance. Class A 95% acceptability or 3.2 sigma is more difficult than you think.

I work for the State University of New York's Empire State College in my spare time. My role there is to verify experiential learning for college credit. I recently interviewed a finance student with several years at a reputable U.S. defense contractor. She has a finance background and was working on her black belt certification. It is beneficial for finance people to become involved in process improvement and change, especially given the fact that, in my opinion, the accounting profession has been locked into a specific approach for many years. Accounting standards have created a culture in some organizations that can make change difficult. It is refreshing to hear a finance professional talk about the need for change.

In most companies, Six Sigma is built around the DMAIC (define, measure, analyze, improve, control) methodology (figure 10.11). Some Deming fans see the similarities between the DMAIC process and Deming's plan-do-check-act wheel; the approaches are based in the same learning.

## DMAIC PROCESS

It is beneficial to look at the DMAIC process and the activity in each step of problem solving.

### D—Define the Problem and the Tools to Use

The first step in DMAIC is to define the problem. There are a few tools that can be helpful in this defining effort. An effective tool to use in defining a problem or opportunity is called a SIPOC (suppliers, inputs, process, outputs, and customers). The SIPOC is a step to view a process effectively and to discover the potential for improvements to the process (figure 10.12).

It is important to know the details behind a process as the project is launched. By asking about suppliers and sources of input to the process, opportunities are revealed for solution sources that might otherwise be ignored. This is the spirit of Six Sigma, opening up all the possibilities to ensure that the best solutions are found. Outputs are just as important. When mapping the process, many times it is discovered that data from the process are used by people unknown to the

D — Define the problem
M — Measure and collect data
A — Analyze opportunities from the data
I — Improve the process by implementing solutions
C — Control the process to the new standards

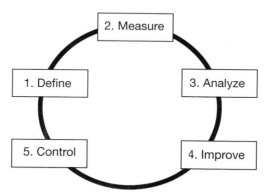

**Figure 10.11** Six Sigma DMAIC Approach

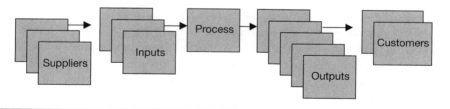

**Figure 10.12** SIPOC

process owners. The reverse is also true; people supply data or outputs only to find that they are not used or needed. Asking the questions posed by the SIPOC is a good exercise. Other tools used during the "defining" stage include brainstorming, process mapping, and stakeholder analysis.

Stakeholder analysis can be fun for most teams. In this exercise, team members are asked to define the people who have the most influence on the process as change is introduced. That can mean, for example, if one of the leadership team is interested in this particular process and has specific inputs and expectations, that person is defined as a major stakeholder even if not officially assigned to the team. Stakeholder analysis includes not only defining the level of interest but also both negative and positive influence factors. A client recently had to replace the VP of Operations because he had become so rigid that change as determined by a continuous improvement process within the operations group was being dragged down by the lack of engagement and enthusiasm. He was not necessarily opposing the implementation of continuous improvement; he just was not promoting it, which sent a powerful message. This influence is good to get out on the table in the beginning of the project. Define who the team needs from a support standpoint and who they have. It is not always the same list of people. Ranking influence can be helpful in determining actions. Sometimes education and marketing of ideas are part of the solution.

The deliverable from the "define" stage is an approved project scope document that includes the objective, length of time the team has to finish the project, participating team members, and even what is *not* included in or is out of the scope of the project.

### M—Measure and Collect Data

This stage is easily understood but not performed thoroughly. There are tools that make this stage easier and more effective. One of the most widely used is process mapping, which is the documentation of a process by visibly depicting the components or actions of the process. This can be helpful in determining the opportunities and possible solutions as detailed previously in this chapter.

Another valuable tool in the "measurement and collection of data" stage is the fishbone or cause-and-effect diagram, which reminds the user to look in all the corners for opportunities. The reminder is normally the 4-M memory jogger of manpower (people involved), materials (both materials used in the process and chemicals used in the periphery), methods (or process approach), and machinery (tools or equipment used in the process). Additionally, "environment" has been added to the 4-M list even though it does not start with "M." Environmental factors include barometric pressure, altitude above sea level, humidity, and temperature. Obviously these factors can cause process variation.

Common tools used in this stage are frequency charts, Pareto charts, run charts, and metrics. The deliverables for this stage include a data collection plan, actual data collected, and, frequently, a project goal validation. This stage does not necessarily end as the next stage begins. Collection of data often continues well into and even after the project is completed.

### A—Analyze the Data for Possible Solutions

Analysis is a key component of Six Sigma. Many times I see teams that jump to solutions too quickly. They are in the "let's try this" mode. Six Sigma requires deeper thinking and understanding in terms of the causes and effects within the process in question. Some of the tools normally used in this stage are similar to the "M" (measure) stage including fishbone analysis, process mapping, and cause and effect with the addition of cards (CEDAC). Another important point in this stage is to have the organization's finance people involved in the analysis. It is especially important for the Six Sigma process to have the savings or impact verified by the financial experts. The finance people should be involved in each project to the level that they understand the potential financial impact of that project.

There are different types of financial impact. The most beneficial is obviously a project that results in direct benefits, which decrease existing costs and improve cash flow. There are also benefits that would be categorized as cost avoidance. These savings do not reduce budgets or improve cash flow but can be an improvement to planned cash flow. The analyze stage deliverables include process maps, proposed solutions, and financial analysis reports.

### I—Improve the Process

"Improve" focuses on implementing the solutions determined in the analyze stage. This doesn't mean that the solutions always work. A testing process that determines the best solutions is appropriate and is documented for future reference. The deliverables from this stage are the solutions proven and financial results verified. Celebrations are often finished after the "improve" stage. Measurements need to be continued well into the "improve" stage to ensure that improvements have had the planned process impact. At this stage the solutions normally have high confidence levels and are becoming the standard process, replacing prior versions.

Probably the most common tool in the "improve" stage is the Gantt chart. The Gantt chart shows the actions of each expectation and the times for starting and completing various actions. A Gantt chart simply details the time-phasing of specific actions required to complete the project solution. It includes what, who, and when. In most cases there are critical path elements that include prerequisites to some important steps. Software such as Microsoft Project can be helpful in tracking these steps.

### C—Control the Process and the Solution

The last step in the DMAIC process is the step to ensure sustainability. This step is normally focused on fool proofing, mistake-proofing, and documentation, which is especially important. Many people do not want to take time to document. Most of us hate paperwork, but through experience I have found that if a process is to be enforced, the rules must be documented. It is impossible to enforce disciplines that do not exist except within people's minds. Deliverables in this space include policies, standard operating procedures, and work instructions. It is empowering to have strong documentation expectations and audits to ensure that the documented process is followed. The result is documentation that is in sync with the performance expectations of the business. Deliverables from this stage in the problem-solving methodology can also include celebrations as well as documented savings and controlled process improvements.

## OTHER SIX SIGMA TOOLS

An additional Six Sigma tool probably is variation-based metrics. Nothing is more important in any process improvement methodology than measurements and within Six Sigma that is no exception. Variation-based metrics are not written as percentages. Some Six Sigma training actually makes a case against using percentages in any application. Variation-based measurements are always visibly shown with limits calculated (figure 10.13).

### Six Sigma Belt Recognition

Many of you have heard or read about green belts and black belts earned through Six Sigma efforts. Although there is variation from one implementation to another, the General Electric standard is the one most often referenced. Most green belt recognition standards include:

- 1-2 weeks (40-80 hours) of training and education on Six Sigma methodology and tools
- one project as a team member with a minimum savings threshold
- one project as the project leader using proper Six Sigma tools
- presenting the project results to a Six Sigma council for certification

Black belt minimums frequently include additional requirements:

- an additional week (40 hours) of education and training
- facilitating a minimum of 6 successful projects
- presenting the project in front of the Six Sigma council for certification

Six Sigma "belt" certification is a clever way to promote the culture shift and get people on board for the new standards of process improvement. People are motivated by receiving recognition. In most successful organizations using Six

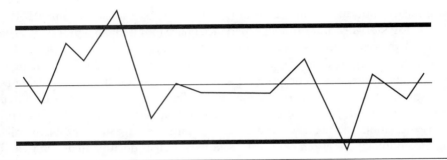

**Figure 10.13** Variation-Based Metrics

Sigma, top management follows the pattern by becoming certified. It clearly sends the right signal to the organization.

Six Sigma is a logical and rigorous methodology to help an organization reach the highest levels of process proficiency. There is no conflict with ERP methodology or lean; in fact, the processes complement each other. Six Sigma is a high standard and one that can become a great motivational process. In chapter 11 the measures that are often found in robust lean material management are discussed.

## DISCUSSION QUESTIONS

1. Six Sigma is another definition of 98% quality.
   a. true
   b. false

2. 95% defect free is equivalent to 3.2 Six Sigma.
   a. true
   b. false

3. ERP and lean conflict in basic principles.
   a. true
   b. false

4. Lean companies do not generally use MRP.
   a. true
   b. false

5. Lean is a focus on the elimination of waste. ERP is a focus on computer functionality.
   a. true
   b. false

6. Which statement is most true?
   a. ERP is a process, and lean and Six Sigma are methodologies.
   b. Lean is most effective in a factory environment.
   c. Six Sigma requires full-time black belts to be most effective.
   d. ERP, Six Sigma, and lean do not actually overlap.

7. The "S" in SIPOC stands for
   a. sales.
   b. selective.
   c. suppliers.
   d. simple.

8. A Gantt chart would be found only in a Six Sigma application and is not strictly used in an ERP implementation.
   a. true
   b. false

9. The "I" in DMAIC stands for
   a. implement.
   b. integrate.
   c. imagination.
   d. improve.

10. A CEDAC is
    a. a project tracking system.
    b. a variation on cause-and-effect process.
    c. a process improvement exercise usually completed in 24 hours.
    d. an acronym used in a supplier certification process.

# 11

# METRICS IN LEAN
# MATERIALS MANAGEMENT

## INTRODUCTION

Metrics are the window into process. They monitor inputs, process elements, and outputs. Each view is helpful in specific process requirements. Materials managers are usually well-versed in measurements and take quickly to lean concept measures. Metrics are the drivers and source of needed information. High-performance companies do not operate without them. On the other hand, poorly-managed and poor-performing companies either have the wrong metrics in place, have them but do not drive action from them, or have no measures at all. Performance measurements are a necessary part of the feedback loop in businesses that are serious about improvement. Metrics, in many ways, are the keys to the palace. Class A ERP, lean materials management, and Six Sigma are built around metrics and management systems to keep the metrics changing and fresh.

## TWO BASIC TYPES OF METRICS

There are at least two types of metrics. Bob Shearer of The Raymond Corporation, one of the first and best master schedulers with whom I have worked and a good friend, determined that the normal Class A metrics always appropriate in every business are "barometric" measures—they tell if a storm front is coming. These metrics do not necessarily relate the cause, but rather point in the right direction. The barometric measures should be maintained even when the performance level is sustained for many months. The reason these metrics

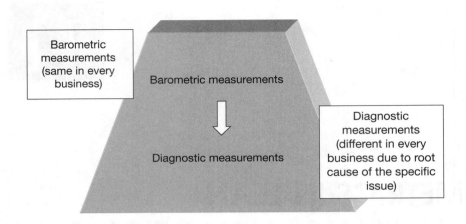

**Figure 11.1** Barometric Measures versus Diagnostic Measures

continue to exist is for audit purposes—understanding things are still in control from that perspective.

Another required level of metrics is the "diagnostic" measures. These measurements can change from business to business and should. These metrics are driven from root cause and focus on areas of weakness in a specific situation. Environment, skills, and process variation are different in different companies and therefore require different metrics, which is why they are referred to as diagnostic measures (figure 11.1).

In Class A ERP the measures correspond with the ERP business model plus quality and safety. There is a barometric-type metric for each of the darkened boxes in the business model in figure 11.2. This is an excellent place to start with serious performance measurement to achieve lean materials management.

## MAJOR CLASS A ENTERPRISE RESOURCE PLANNING MEASURES

1. **Business Plan**—Accuracy of the monthly profit plan of the business by product family. (If the facility is a cost center, the accuracy of the budget becomes the measure for accuracy.)
2. **Demand Plan (Forecast)**—Average accuracy of the monthly demand forecast by product family.
3. **Operations Plan**—Average accuracy of the monthly capacity plan by product family.

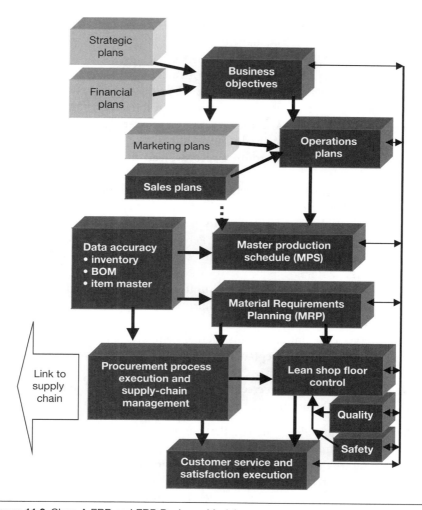

**Figure 11.2** Class A ERP and ERP Business Model

4. **Master Schedule**—Accuracy of the weekly detailed schedule of each product line or major cell.
5. **Material Plan**—Percent of orders that are released with full lead time to suppliers. This is measured to the current lead time field value in the item master.
6. **Schedule Stability**—Percent of orders that have completion dates revised within the fixed period time fence. Frequently, each product family has a separate fixed fence time value.

7. **Inventory Location Balance Accuracy**—Percent of location balances that are perfect, allowing minimal tolerances (A = ±0%, B = ±2%, C = ±3%).

8. **Bill of Material (BOM) Accuracy**—Percent of BOMs that are perfect, matching three data points: 1) the print or spec, 2) the ERP system record, and 3) actual performance on the factory floor.

9. **Item Master File Accuracy**—Accuracy percentage of other item master fields that appear during the initial assessment of ERP weaknesses. This includes routing records, lead time records, and cost standards.

10. **Procurement Process Accuracy**—Percent of complete orders that are received from suppliers on the day (or hour) currently scheduled in the ERP business system. This is matched the day of receipt.

11. **Shop Floor Control Accuracy**—Percent of complete orders that are completed on the day (or hour) currently scheduled in the ERP business system.

12. **First Time Quality**—Percent of units that make it through a process without exception handling, adjustments, exception movement, or rework.

13. **Safety**—Lost-time accidents "actual compared to plan." The company's minimum acceptability is the objective, along with continued improvement.

14. **Customer Service**—Percent of complete orders that ship to the customer on the original promise date.

There are a multitude of metrics that can be found in a high-performance, Class A business (figure 11.2). The preceding list represents the barometric measures only. These are the same in every business, from plastics molding to automobiles and from paint processing to capital equipment manufacturing. Class A requires these metrics to be at minimum levels of proficiency. These levels should not be misconstrued with high performance. Table 11.1 compares Class A minimums with high performance.

The key to getting the value from metrics is not the metric itself or even the collection of data. The real value comes from the action driven from the data that makes it all worth the effort and time. This closes the loop on measurement and continuous improvement. One of my clients is a plastics business with four plants and a fifth being planned. The CEO is intuitive about where the focus needs to be. He initially started a continuous improvement process using the four-step journey (figure 11.3).

When we met to discuss his organization's needs, his first comment was that he believed in metrics. He imparted that the business was full of measurements

**Table 11.1 Minimums for High-Performance ERP Metric Performance**

| Metric | Minimum Class A | High Performance |
|---|---|---|
| 1. Business plan | 95% | 98% |
| 2. Demand plan (forecast) | 85% | 90% |
| 3. Operations plan | 95% | 98% |
| 4. Master schedule | 95% | 98% |
| 5. Material plan | 95% | 95% |
| 6. Schedule stability | 95% | 95% |
| 7. Inv. location balance accuracy | 95% | 98% |
| 8. BOM accuracy | 98% | 99% |
| 9. Item master file accuracy | 95% | 98% |
| 10. Procurement process accuracy | 95% | 98% |
| 11. Shop floor control accuracy | 95% | 98% |
| 12. First time quality | 95% | 99% |
| 13. Safety | plan plus improving | zero accidents |
| 14. Customer service | 95% | 98% |

and performance was even good but one problem still existed—the performance had stopped improving a couple years prior. Their profits were acceptable and customer service was adequate but the numbers were not growing at a rate that satisfied his high standards for improvement. This is exactly the attitude that makes change easy and fun—top management recognizes the need for continuous improvement and is never fully satisfied. Class A ERP, the first step in the journey, establishes the management systems necessary to progress. It creates the expectation of improvement day after day.

### OTHER VALUABLE ENTERPRISE RESOURCE PLANNING METRICS

1. percent of purchase orders let without full lead time as defined in the lead time field on the item master
2. percent of 100% pickable assemblies released on time to assembly
3. inventory turns—raw, work in process, and finished goods
4. dollars of inventory on hand for every dollar of revenue within a product family
5. percentage of product shipping on the original requested date or time
6. time from order receipt to actual value-add in the factory
7. time from order receipt to shipment by product family

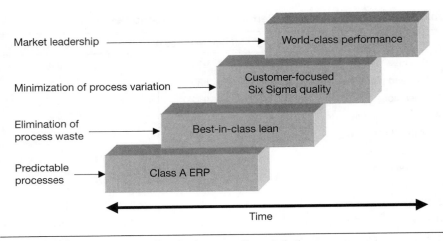

**Figure 11.3** Journey to World-Class Performance through Action

8. 24-hour maximums of material, dock to stock
9. linearity of schedules (units averaged first week versus last weeks of a normal month)
10. bandwidth from adjustments from cycle counts

## STARTING THE MEASUREMENT PROCESS

Some businesses measure every process and the expected action has become part of the culture. In other businesses, as metrics are added to the deck, resistance is apparent. Performance measurement in high-performance organizations is not "something they do" it's "the way they think."

Typically, in the beginning stages of process improvement implementation, people are not receptive to measuring performance throughout the business. They frequently view the change as a threat to their security or even a violation of their honor or trust. "Why do you want to measure my performance anyway?" is the question in their mind, or "Do you not trust me or do you think I am not doing appropriate work?" In my experience there are stages that people go through when first introduced to performance metrics:

- Stage 1—"It's not me you need to measure, it's him/her" (points finger at another employee). This is the denial stage.
- Stage 2—"Okay, I guess you (management) are not going to forget this new idea (with sort of a disgusted slant). What was it you wanted measured anyway?" This is the acknowledgement stage—it is real. "It's

going to happen; there isn't much we (the employees) are going to do about it."

- Stage 3—"I have been measuring this and I found that there are some other diagnostic indicators that help in the elimination of the root cause of the variation." This is the exciting stage—the stage of discovery.

Obviously education plays a part in this transition, as does practice. Management must send a clear and consistent message that the measures are about process and not people. This is accomplished through both actions and words. Management's signal on this point cannot be delegated to their staff. The employees watch and know what management thinks is important! People always attain the norm of expectation provided there is some feedback—either good or bad.

The most successful metric process start-ups involve education and communication. Normally management starts the process, and once the metrics are confirmed from a standpoint of data and process ownership, the metrics are made visible. The first educational session can be basic communication with the employees.

## LEAN MEASURES

Some of the more advanced measures would fit into the lean category. Regardless of the category we apply to these measures, what is important is the action to close the loop on performance and improvement. There are measures that are thought of as more lean metrics also. Some of these include:

1. Waste dollars eliminated per month as compared to plan:
   a. waste from movement
   b. waste from inventory
   c. waste from delays and waiting
   d. waste from overproduction
   e. waste from unnecessary transport
   f. waste from scrap and rework
   g. waste from unnecessary transactions
   h. waste from untapped creativity
   i. waste from unnecessary process steps
2. Percent of projects from engineering released and correct to plan.
3. Cycle time of idea to cash determined (new product introduction).
4. Upside capacity flexibility is equal to 20% out 30 days.
5. Cycle times equal 50% of previous year.
6. 100% gain in inventory turns from previous year.

7. 100% of supplier lead times are equal to or less than the internal fixed time fence.
8. Labor productivity has improved at least 15% from previous year.
9. Lead times to customers are equal to or less than sales has identified as needed for competitive advantage lead times per product family.
10. Material review board area has average disposition time of less than 8 hours.
11. 98% of material is available, on the ERP system, within the same shift that it is unloaded in receiving.
12. Percent of material held at point of use with no additional storage within the business.
13. Percent of material that is not handled until it is put into the assembly (moved to point of use by supplier).
14. Length of travel the average part moves through the facility.
15. Accuracy of the new product introduction gate adherence to schedule.
16. Changeover improvements:
    a. decrease in time spent in changeovers
    b. increase in number of changeovers
17. Run size is decreasing.
18. Visible controls are in place throughout the plant.
19. Preventative/productive maintenance:
    a. schedule adherence
    b. quality of process
    c. uptime
20. Pull systems engaged.
21. Priority freight decreases.

Of course, these represent only a portion of the possibilities. There are less barometric measures in the lean space. The measures are mostly focused on flexibility and speed. The source of these gains in speed and flexibility can vary from business to business and therefore become more diagnostic in nature. The preceding list should initiate ideas that might make sense in your business. Although the list is mostly made up of result or output measures, there are also process measures that reflect the lean materials management spirit. Some of these include:

1. 24-hour or week-long kaizen events
   a. number launched
   b. number completed
   c. impact per kaizen
   d. number of departments actively using kaizen events

2. 5-S engaged
    a. number of departments showing improvement
    b. number of cells meeting goal
    c. average scores

Lean focus has a huge impact on the business. It can also come from many areas and involve everyone from the CEO to the line workers. The topic of measurement just introduces one important aspect of this complex subject. In chapter 14 management systems are covered in detail. Management systems must be tightly tied to measures for the value to show on the bottom line.

## CUSTOMER-DRIVEN QUALITY

As we continue to ratchet the topic of measures, the next area is at the top of the excellence chain—quality. Although this is labeled by many names, we call this level of focus customer-driven quality and Six Sigma is a component of this focus. The measures in this space are more focused on problem solving and process improvement. When a good job is performed through measuring, process predictability in the ERP baseline, and measuring the lean focus areas of speed and flexibility, many opportunities are identified, feeding the project funnel with an unending amount of process improvement fodder. The measurements in this final (at least as far as we know) frontier of improvement include:

1. Projects launched compared to plan.
2. Projects completed compared to plan.
3. Return from projects compared to plan:
    a. direct incremental currency gains
    b. indirect gains
        i. time saved
        ii. planned spending reduced
4. Monetary impact per project leader.
5. Duration of projects (project start to finish).
6. Number of green, black, and master black belts certified:
    a. office
    b. factory
    c. management
7. Project ideas introduced into the funnel.
8. Customer complaints eliminated (reduction of incidents—normally called defects in Six Sigma).
9. Out of box quality (OBQ) improved (reduction in incidents).
10. First time quality or yield determined.

11. Benchmarking to other businesses/industries:
    a. time from idea to cash
    b. dollars shipped per employee
    c. velocity of changes including new product introduction or improvements
    d. flexibility to meet a specific voice of the customer
12. Return customer percentage/experience.
13. Customer satisfaction calculated.
14. Dollars per customer sold.

In this higher level of quality focus, the sophistication of the problem solving ratchets. There are often process improvement experts versed in statistical problem-solving tools and characteristics of data at this point in a mature organization. Differentiations that were not obvious such as discrete versus continuous data become more important than in the earlier phases of improvement. My experience is that process improvement comes in phases and, accordingly, the level of expertise and skill that any business has dictates where it is on the path.

When followed, the levels of focus make sense and provide a solid foundation that allows steady improvement and less opportunity to aggressively move forward and burn out quickly like a first stage rocket. I have worked with many organizations that, prior to my involvement, had kicked off Six Sigma but did not successfully make it through the early stages of excitement. In many of those companies, Six Sigma seemed to take on a life of its own and the goals became more focused on numbers of projects than incremental gains to the business.

World-class performance is the last level of focus. To think that the existing knowledge base takes us as far as we need to go to be competitive in the future is probably flawed thinking. On the same hand, knowing what the focus will look like is currently a bit transparent. It will undoubtedly have to do with the customer and will include value. Fill in the rest for now.

Measures are of much less value without the corresponding management systems to close the loop on improvement properly. Measures must drive action. The management systems are the vehicles to help that happen.

## DISCUSSION QUESTIONS

1. Lean measures should focus on
   a. 5-S.
   b. cycle time.
   c. waste elimination.
   d. delivery fidelity.
   e. all of the above
   f. b and c

2. A kaizen is limited to a 24-hour fast-paced improvement event.
   a. true
   b. false

3. The following are common lean metrics:
   a. number of green, black, and master black belts certified
   b. project ideas in the funnel
   c. customer complaint elimination
   d. reduction of defects
   e. all of the above
   f. b and c

4. OBQ improvements are not normally a lean metric.
   a. true
   b. false

5. High-performance organizations often utilize 24-hour kaizen events. Measurements should include
   a. number launched.
   b. number completed.
   c. impact experienced per kaizen.
   d. number of departments actively using kaizen events.
   e. all of the above

6. The measurement "percent of orders that are released with full lead time to suppliers measured to the current lead time field value in the item master" is generally considered a
   a. Class A ERP measurement.
   b. lean measurement
   c. Six Sigma measurement.
   d. none of the above

7. When 5-S is fully engaged, measures often include
   a. number of departments showing improvement in 5-S.
   b. number of cells meeting goal in 5-S.
   c. average scores.
   d. all of the above

8. Typically, in the beginning stages of process improvement implementation, people are not receptive to measuring performance throughout the business. They frequently view the change as a threat to their security or even a violation of their honor or trust.
   a. true
   b. false

9. The key to getting the value from metrics is not the metric itself. The real value comes from the measurement process.
   a. true
   b. false

10. Which of the following are measurements within the preventative/productive maintenance arena?
   a. schedule adherence
   b. quality of process
   c. uptime
   d. all of the above
   e. b and c

# 12

# HIGH-PERFORMANCE MANAGEMENT SYSTEMS

## INTRODUCTION

The term "management system" was used several times in chapter 11. This chapter describes the methods that top businesses use to keep the processes moving and people engaged. There is no magic; it comes down to accountability, plain and simple. That is the single reason why some process improvement efforts fail. We blame it on the lack of top management involvement but the involvement that is needed is accountability. Not bloodletting, just accountability. Without management systems, measures would be no more than a window into process. Metrics do not drive change. High-performance companies, in every case—no exceptions—(how many times can something like that be said?), have robust management systems.

Effective management systems have several elements. They range in frequency from minutes to months and even years. Some of the more common ones, up to semi-monthly and excluding the strategic and longer-term management systems, are listed in figure 12.1.

## MONTHLY SALES AND OPERATIONS PLANNING MANAGEMENT SYSTEM

The Sales and Operations Planning (S&OP) process was detailed in chapter 8. This monthly management system is one of the most important and beneficial to any business. In this review the top management team comes to an agreement on

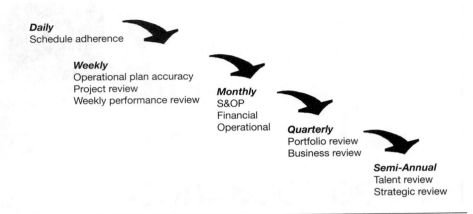

**Figure 12.1** Monthly Management System Elements in Class A ERP

the course of action, including inventory, production rates, and anticipated demand by product family. This sets the direction for the current month and allows risk management to take place for the next 12 rolling months.

A prerequisite to the S&OP is the development of the business plan. In this management process the long-term objectives—12 months and beyond—are determined. These objectives, in turn, drive projects.

## MONTHLY PROJECT MANAGEMENT REVIEW SYSTEM

There are several layers to project review in medium to large companies. Reviews can occur daily, weekly, or less frequently. Project scope can range from business acquisition to moving equipment inside an existing plant. Probably the most important projects, however, are the ones that line up with the business impera-tives. These are the objectives that *will* be completed in the next 12 months for competitive advantage. These are top management's highest priorities for the organization in the short term (figure 12.2).

Of course it makes sense to have a robust project management system to ensure that the proper amount of prioritization and resource is actively pursuing the objective. Too many of the businesses I visit do not have this robust system ini-tially. Instead, projects are left to the project managers and when "the spirit moves" they are asked to report, often without being prepared. This ensures slower project progress.

High-performance organizations have regular project reviews. The form varies and depends on the number and complexity of the projects on the table. If there are only a few assignments, and the projects are not complex, a monthly

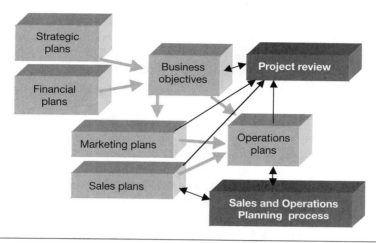

**Figure 12.2** Two Management Systems: Project Review and S&OP

project review is enough. If there are many complex, multi-level projects, it is often necessary to meet weekly to review components of the major tasks. The following lists a few highlights worth mentioning from one business with a successful review process:

1. Managers had the business imperatives listed, framed, and hung on their office walls where they could read them from their desks.
2. In the cafeteria there was a large white board with several communication components:
   a. A folder contained all of the proposed projects written individually on index cards. These were all approved by the staff prior to inclusion.
   b. A bulletin board with the index cards of all projects in process tacked in place for visibility included:
      i. owner
      ii. team members
      iii. objective and scope of project
      iv. time frame to completion
      v. sponsor
   c. Pictures of teams that had successfully completed their projects in the past few weeks are part of a short story that includes accomplishments and contributions to the organization.

The board served dual purposes. It was a visible reminder that projects were an ongoing and important aspect of this organization's culture, and it helped give credit where credit was due. In this environment it was common for people to be on several teams per year. Some were quite complex while others were simply 30-day improvement focus activities. Other companies have success simply holding a monthly review.

In the *monthly* management system in most high-performance organizations there is always an appreciation for overall accountability and follow-up. It is in this space that management defines the priorities and makes sure these objectives are accomplished. This is achieved through follow-up according to the business imperatives that were established earlier in the year. This monthly review is simply the opportunity for management to observe progress on these important projects and to provide support when needed. It can take many forms. The one just described was a more evolved process. In the beginning it is beneficial to have all top projects scheduled with the top management staff for a 15- to 20-minute description of where they are on their Gantt chart and where they expect to be in the next 30 days. It should not be a place to work the project, only to listen to progress. One plant manager in Boston liked to have lunch with his top project managers once a month to listen to the updates. It made it less formal—more relaxed and normal—and the plant manager liked that. This did not mean the project owners did not have to report progress and effort, however. These were the organization's top projects after all! His message was that it was a regular part of operations and that is what he wanted.

The monthly management systems, S&OP and project management review, are the ones that the materials manager in a high-performance organization is most frequently involved in. As the time frame gets smaller, the involvement from materials increases quickly. The monthly management systems are about setting policy and making decisions about the direction and tactics month to month. Top management owns the monthly space.

## WEEKLY MANAGEMENT SYSTEM PERFORMANCE REVIEW

The weekly management system is more detailed and incorporates the majority of the organization. It includes all measurement process owners, middle and line managers, and supervisors. For solid, predictable performance there are three elements that must be included:

**Weekly Management System Elements**
- weekly performance review
- clear-to-build
- weekly project review

The weekly performance review is one of the most powerful elements of a high-performance management system. With the exception of the S&OP process, there is no process more influential in a well-run and -led business. Implemented correctly, within a short time, this meeting makes management into converts, and in every case in which I have been involved, there is nothing that stops the weekly review. The weekly performance review has top priority for time management, and the rule to follow is that it is never pre-empted. In my experience the meeting to review the performance of the preceding week is most effective when held on Tuesday afternoon. Since process owners report the performance and actions driven from this process to the rest of the operations management staff, Monday is too early in the week for them to be fully prepared with analysis of last week's performance and misses; therefore, Tuesday is the best day for the review. The week is still young but there is adequate time to prepare. To come to the meeting unprepared must be considered unacceptable or the reviews lose their effectiveness. High-performance Enterprise Resource Planning (ERP) criteria require that this meeting be held consistently each week, but do not dictate the specific day that the meeting be held. Holding to a set day and time each week ensures a successful meeting, thus eliminating the possibility of issues such as "I did not get the email and didn't know when the meeting was."

At a minimum, the starting metrics normally reported in this format include but are not limited to:

- schedule adherence
- schedule stability
- first time quality
- bill of material accuracy
- inventory record accuracy
- item master accuracy (this can be more than one metric)
- procurement process accuracy
- shop floor accuracy
- customer service

Note that the list is mostly ERP measures. Lean metrics should be added as soon as the process is in place and effective.

The weekly performance review process is an integral part of a robust management system that allows management to be involved in the follow-up of process control on a regular and predictable schedule. It helps establish accountability for process ownership. Without it, process ownership has little or no real meaning to the organization and is not effective. In a high-performance organization, as metrics are added to the deck, they are included in the weekly performance review. It becomes "how the business operates" in terms of process ownership and follow-up.

By using this type of format for reporting progress and performance, the organization becomes consistent and effective at problem solving and continuous improvement. It should be used consistently for all performance metrics; therefore, as metrics are included in data analysis, it makes sense to have these metrics reported at the weekly performance review meeting.

## Agenda for the Weekly Performance Review

The weekly performance review meeting should be predictable. As stated, the meeting should be the same time every week unless there is a holiday. The agenda should be simple. Each process owner reports progress from the previous week. Progress includes all elements on a quad chart (figure 12.3). It is appropriate for other team members to question the process owner if the reporting performance is not at acceptable levels. The objective is not to "pile on" problems for the process owners but rather to offer help. Help can be in the form of resources, ideas, or a change in handoffs.

### Weekly Performance Review Reporting Format—Top Left of Quad Chart

In this example, the process owner for inventory accuracy is reporting the process performance, but the same format is used by all process owners. In the top left-hand quadrant, the daily performance is reported along with the weekly overall performance summary. Most Class A metrics are expressed in percentage points, reported as a daily performance and as a weekly total performance number.

### Weekly Performance Review Reporting Format—Top Right of Quad Chart

The trend chart is displayed in the top right-hand quadrant. This visualization of data is important in determining if the process is having a positive effect on the performance. If only the performance for the current period is reported, it is not clear if progress is being made. The trend should be a minimum of 5-6 weeks of performance data. The trend graph reported in this quadrant is typically weekly data points. This creates a smoothing effect that gives a more effective and truer trend summary.

### Weekly Performance Review Reporting Format—Bottom Left of Quad Chart

A Pareto chart showing the reasons for misses allows the organization to focus energy and resource on the most important barriers to successful accuracy and

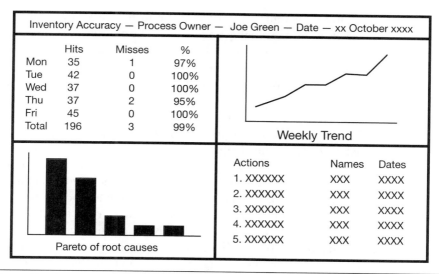

| Inventory Accuracy — Process Owner — Joe Green — Date — xx October xxxx |

| | Hits | Misses | % |
|---|---|---|---|
| Mon | 35 | 1 | 97% |
| Tue | 42 | 0 | 100% |
| Wed | 37 | 0 | 100% |
| Thu | 37 | 2 | 95% |
| Fri | 45 | 0 | 100% |
| Total | 196 | 3 | 99% |

Weekly Trend

Pareto of root causes

| Actions | Names | Dates |
|---|---|---|
| 1. XXXXXX | XXX | XXXX |
| 2. XXXXXX | XXX | XXXX |
| 3. XXXXXX | XXX | XXXX |
| 4. XXXXXX | XXX | XXXX |
| 5. XXXXXX | XXX | XXXX |

**Figure 12.3** Quad Chart Performance Reporting Format

performance. This is especially important early in process focus and measurement when process is affected by the most sources. The best-performing organizations focus resource on the worst root causes, allowing the biggest return for their investment. It is this quadrant that reveals the greatest challenges as the culture migrates.

Process owners frequently struggle with the definition of root cause. Management normally has to combat "categories" versus real root cause. Without root cause, it is impossible to eliminate the variation causing performance below goals. It is common for newly-assigned process owners to come to the meeting with "root causes" such as "missed operation" or "operator error." The actual root cause must be sought. Operator error might be caused by a lack of training because there is no defined and documented way of instructing new operators. The resulting actions might include (for this example) assigning a small team to determine the correct procedure, to prepare documentation followed by training of existing operators, and to implement a training policy for new hires. The most effective materials managers pay attention to this quadrant in the reporting. It is critical!

### Weekly Performance Review Reporting Format—Bottom Right of Quad Chart

Process improvement comes only by driving change through actions as illustrated in figure 12.3. Actions close the loop on the management system. By institutionalizing and reporting the action process, follow-up is much more systematic and predictable. The root cause bar at the left side of the Pareto chart should have actions easily linked on the right side of the chart.

It is common in the beginning of the weekly performance review implementation that root cause is not thoroughly understood. The old rule of asking "why" five times facilitates understanding. Another simple root cause rule is to ask why until the answer is actionable. During the weekly performance review meeting, process owners need to stay focused on root cause and avoid excuses. The focus drives proper corrective actions and reduces the cost of eliminating the barriers to high performance. Management has to play a role in this if it is to become a required behavior and a predictable component of the management system.

Actions need to have all the elements of a normal Gantt chart including defining the action, assigning the action, and stating a completion date. It is also important to remember that this is a *weekly* review and the actions should be designed accordingly. The actions reported at this meeting are not to be out a month or two; they are actions expected to be completed in the next few *days*! Management must insist on it. I think of the weekly review focus as one to "keep the train from coming off the tracks." In other words, this management system is not at the execution stage of simply making sure the "train is on the tracks" or that the "train is getting back on the tracks" quickly. The emphasis for the process is: "Of the problems we have encountered, which ones can we stop from *ever* happening again?"

## Weekly Clear-to-Build

The clear-to-build (CTB) process has been discussed in chapter 5 but is so important that is needs to be reiterated here. The CTB process mainly consists of a commitment from production and procurement managers to the master production schedule (MPS) for the coming week. The master scheduler distributes the new MPS late in the week. In most businesses this is on either Thursday evening or Friday morning. On Friday the key players are expected to either confirm their commitment and confidence at a gathering or, in more experienced and thoroughly mastered scheduling environments, no meeting is held. The process owners report back only if they require adjustments prior to providing commitment. Please note that the schedule does not have to be firm to determine the weekly schedule. In some businesses this is simply an agreement on how high the capacity bar is stationed for the week. The CTB is about getting a handshake between purchasing, production, and scheduling. When everybody is on the same page, it is easier to maintain stability and superior customer service (figure 12.4).

In a home appliance manufacturer the CTB was held with the specific schedule complete for the week. Often changes occurred during the week (stuff happens) but the plan of record effectively highlighted the factors that contributed to the needed schedule changes and lessons were learned. The objective was to keep the schedule as stable as possible and still keep the customers happy.

**Figure 12.4** Handshake

## Weekly Project Review

The format at the weekly level of project review is not appreciably different from the monthly review that has been discussed previously. In many organizations high-level management reviews projects at least once a week. It depends on how many projects there are, how important the outcomes are to management (high-profile projects are reviewed more frequently), or what the impact or risks are. In other organizations there are top management monthly reviews but there are also more detailed reviews that occur at the middle management level. Materials managers might, for example, have weekly reviews on projects such as lead time reduction, data accuracy projects, or schedule adherence projects. Some of these might be important but not make the "business imperative" list from top management.

While the monthly review tends to be more of a "reporting up" process, this weekly review is normally a two-way communication. The materials manager is often directly involved in the projects and is frequently a sponsor of many of the projects.

## DAILY CLASS A ENTERPRISE RESOURCE PLANNING MANAGEMENT SYSTEM EVENTS

It has been said many times that if we get the day right, the week will go well. If the week goes well, we don't think about the month. It is oversimplified in terms of the real world but the spirit of the statement is correct. Since many businesses have an "end of the month crunch" there is something to be learned from a daily management system. I like to refer to the Class A ERP criteria for robust daily management system requirements. This list is proven to be effective. In Class A ERP the criteria include:

### Daily Class A ERP Management System Elements
- daily schedule alignment
- daily walk-around
- visible factory boards
- shift change communication

## Daily Schedule Alignment

In Class A ERP it is expected that all information in the system is as current as possible. Every time a situation changes, the system should reflect that change. Therefore, there are rarely any past-due requirements in the ERP business system. There is plenty of process variation in the world because all processes have variation. Given the importance of keeping the system up to date and the frequency of process variation, alignment needs to occur daily.

The alignment is as simple as an assessment of production schedule adherence from the previous day and adjusting accordingly. In some businesses there is no extra capacity. That is especially the case in high-volume, repetitive manufacturing. When the schedule is missed, it is lost. The schedule needs to reflect that change. By the same token, if the business has some flexibility, misses from the prior day might be made up by working overtime or doubling up on resource. Either way, the schedule should reflect the latest expectations. When the MPS is updated, Material Requirements Planning (MRP) can align signals to the supply chain accordingly and both inventory and shortages are minimized.

The alignment in the system should occur at *least* once a week but in most high-performance businesses it is completed daily. When schedules are accurate and realistic, the result is minimal system noise. The schedule is reviewed daily by the production managers and materials as well as master scheduling, frequently in a daily communication first thing each morning. Some organizations implement this communication with phone calls; others have a short update meeting. During this meeting the focus is on alignment—how many were completed yesterday on the line and how many in the sequence do we expect to finish today? This is discussed on each line, agreement is reached, and the master schedule is updated accordingly. In high-performance organizations the communication is completed quickly. If there are many problems, the process is slower. In many manufacturing plants the daily schedule white boards are bolted to the machine lines. In the daily schedule alignment process, the boards—simply referred to as visible factory boards—are updated daily with yesterday's performance and changes to the schedule. The boards should be large enough to be easily read when walking by. The master scheduler collects and confirms changes and the new schedule is updated into the system.

## Daily Walk-Around

The daily walk-around is exactly that. Management reviews schedule adherence daily by walking around the facility to each line supervisor to ascertain the progress made the previous day and to learn the expectations for the current day. This visibility helps in several ways:

- Establishes that schedules need to be accurate.
- Keeps management in the loop for variation development.
- Allows management to acknowledge good problem-solving behavior.
- Keeps management in the loop to help with more difficult issues when appropriate.

One example always comes to mind when talking about the daily walk-around. While working in a plant in Shanghai, China, I was completing the final Class A audit. The daily walk-around consisted of four people—the plant manager, the production manager, the master scheduler, and the engineering manager—who met each morning to review the schedules in the facility. These four managers would meet in the factory every morning at the same time to tour the facility and talk to each line supervisor. In this particular facility there were no middle managers. All of the line supervisors reported to the production manager. Line supervisors were team leaders who worked on the line as a team member most of the time.

I met the other daily walk-around attendees in the designated aisle at 8 a.m.; they meet every day in this facility. We walked to the first work cell. The supervisor stopped his work and greeted us. The visible factory board showed no misses from the previous day and the supervisor informed us that he did not expect to miss any schedules in the current day—all good, but admittedly not too exciting. The same thing was reported on the second line; however, when we reached line three I realized there was going to be some discussion on this line. Line three had missed several units the night before. Performance was posted at 92%, which is unacceptable in a Class A ERP organization. It was reported that the third shift had trouble with a machining center. A motor had burned up on the machine and production was halted. The third-shift supervisor went into maintenance, obtained a new motor, and assembled it himself. This was quite impressive from my experience, but it didn't stop there.

The machine was restarted and production was able to minimize loss to the schedule. After production was back on track, the supervisor went back into maintenance to fix the problem. He pulled the records for the machine and found that the scheduled preventative maintenance (PM) was to take place in about 2 weeks. This PM would have included taking the motor apart, checking and cleaning it. All of this would have likely prevented the unscheduled machine-down situation experienced that night. During the same shift the supervisor changed the PM schedule to a shorter interval and left communication for the maintenance manager.

I don't see many supervisors who are trained and empowered to fix their own equipment and, further, to understand that this was not the actual fix of the problem. This operator had been trained to ask the question "How do I stop this from ever happening again?" This is clearly the spirit of high performance and certainly in the spirit of lean materials and operations management! The walk-around is designed to keep management in the loop and to keep accountability at the line level. It is not expected that, given safety and training concerns, every team would be able to do their own machine repairs, but understanding root cause can be a substantial help to a process owner.

Several processes can be reviewed during the daily walk-around: schedule adherence, inventory accuracy, and housekeeping. Additionally management can observe progress on recent projects. With the meeting schedules of plant managers, this is a favorite time for many. When things are running as they should, it also gives the plant manager another opportunity to show appreciation by thanking individuals and acknowledging acceptable performance in public.

## Visible Factory Boards

To keep the schedule effectively communicated and understood, most high-performance factories are not relying on paper schedules hung by the machines. Instead, these well-managed companies are using large, easily-read white boards with the daily schedule information. Toyota made this practice popular and coined the name visible factory boards (figure 12.5).

Of course, variations to the visible factory board layout are acceptable. Many organizations also put safety and first time quality performance on the board, which can be helpful. Some organizations choose to do schedule checks more than once a day. A client with whom I am currently working chooses to have schedules checked twice a shift or four times a day. On the day shift the schedule check is at 10 a.m. and 2 p.m. The communication is beneficial and ensures that everyone is on the same sheet of music when they start the day. It also helps underline the importance of making schedules as planned.

## Shift Change Communication

Each shift change affords an opportunity to lose continuity in production because different people come in to replace the people who are presently working on the schedule. In some businesses it means that the processes and speeds vary. In high-performance businesses this is not the case. Substantial effort is made to educate and train operators to understand machine operation and capability and to provide standard procedures to be followed by all operators. In one client organization, manufacturing measures all changes to process. Every time there is a change from the standard process settings required to bring product into spec, a miss is reported on the line. The metric is reported at the weekly performance review meeting and receives intense focus. It facilitates operator awareness to the root cause. The client has learned a great deal from the metric. I recommend it.

| Schedule __/__/__ | | Schedule __/__/__ | | Perf MTD |
|---|---|---|---|---|
| Product | Quantity Plan | Product | Quantity Plan | |
| Act | | Act | | |
| XX | 23 | XX | 78 | |
| XX | 111 | XX | 99 | |
| XX | 5 | XX | 455 | |
| XX | 589 | XX | 4 | |
| XX | 45 | XX | 135 | |
| Total | 773 | Total | 771 | |
| Performance XX% Open issues | | Performance XX% Open issues | | |

**Figure 12.5** Visible Factory Board for One Production Line

Shift communication is difficult because the departing shift's crew is ready to go home. Hanging around to answer questions is rarely the most effective means of communication. Instead, many high-performance companies have communication processes established in which formal, visible communication boards are used. Having a diary-type log in the cell is also helpful.

## OTHER MANAGEMENT SYSTEMS IN HIGH-PERFORMANCE BUSINESSES

Management systems are about accountability in organizations and, thus, are everywhere in high-performance businesses. When these elements are second nature and weaved into the fiber of the organization, there is no discussion about management systems. They just happen. Whenever there is a process change, the documentation is automatically changed because it just makes sense. If a metric is changed or a new metric is born out of need, the first, natural action is to include it in the weekly performance review system once it is documented. All projects are naturally included in some form of project review. In these companies there is no decision to do this; it is obvious. It is the way these businesses *think*. This also describes a waste-conscious, lean-thinking environment. Predictable process comes from a combination of two things: an effective plan and successful execution. One without the other spells failure at one level or another. There are no exceptions. Thought and planning on management system elements can foster a culture where high-performance thinking happens naturally. I have met many people years after we first worked together who are still following the basics of this thinking born of the Class A ERP process, even if their current mission is strictly in the Six Sigma space. It is simply good process.

Tools are helpful in the process of drilling down for facts and for initial visibility. Although the process elements and management system are probably the most critical, nonetheless tools are important. In chapter 13, the discussion around tools and, specifically, the requirements for software aids is detailed. The right tools can make the management systems more effective.

## DISCUSSION QUESTIONS

1.  Management systems within manufacturing are
    a.  management training processes usually offered by human resources.
    b.  computer systems used by human resources to compile training information for employees.
    c.  disciplined accountability infrastructure elements.
    d.  PC training in Microsoft Office.

2.  What interval do management systems normally influence?
    a.  hourly
    b.  daily
    c.  weekly
    d.  monthly
    e.  all of the above

3.  Who are the process owners in management systems?
    a.  employees
    b.  supervisors
    c.  line managers
    d.  top management
    e.  any or all of the above

4.  Knowing you are fully to root cause is when
    a.  there is no cause found to the level investigated.
    b.  the cause seems to be actionable.
    c.  time is running out to do more research.
    d.  it is impossible to understand actual root cause.

5.  A visible factory board can be a management system.
    a.  true
    b.  false

6.  The S&OP process is a management event, not a management system.
    a.  true
    b.  false

7. The daily walk-around is exactly that. Management reviews schedule adherence daily by walking around the facility to each line supervisor to ascertain the progress made the previous day and to learn the expectations for the current day. This visibility helps in several ways:
   a. Establishes that schedules need to be accurate.
   b. Keeps management in the loop for variation developing.
   c. Allows management to acknowledge good problem-solving behavior.
   d. Keeps management in the loop to help with more difficult issues when appropriate.
   e. a, b, and d
   f. all of the above

8. Many projects in a manufacturing organization are driven from the top management business planning process.
   a. true
   b. false

9. The weekly performance review is one of the most powerful elements of a high-performance management system. With the exception of the S&OP process, there is no process more influential in a well-run and -led business.
   a. true
   b. false

10. In the following quad chart, the bottom left quadrant is for
    a. Pareto of root causes.
    b. number of incidents.
    c. performance in last 5 weeks.
    d. misses in last 5 time frames.

Inventory Accuracy — Process Owner — Joe Green — Date — xx October xxxx

| | Hits | Misses | % |
|------|------|--------|------|
| Mon | 35 | 1 | 97% |
| Tue | 42 | 0 | 100% |
| Wed | 37 | 0 | 100% |
| Thu | 37 | 2 | 95% |
| Fri | 45 | 0 | 100% |
| Total | 196 | 3 | 99% |

Weekly Trend

| Actions | Names | Dates |
|---------|-------|-------|
| 1. XXXXXX | XXX | XXXX |
| 2. XXXXXX | XXX | XXXX |
| 3. XXXXXX | XXX | XXXX |
| 4. XXXXXX | XXX | XXXX |
| 5. XXXXXX | XXX | XXXX |

# 13

# SOFTWARE TOOLS

## INTRODUCTION

Some might wonder why there is a software discussion centered around Enterprise Resource Planning (ERP) included in a book about lean materials management. All manufacturing organizations use some form of an ERP system. In fact, manufacturing businesses nearly always start the software discussion with the ERP business system. The business system is the nervous system of the manufacturing body. However, although software is a major topic in most ERP discussions, it is not the only focus (figure 13.1).

APICS, the Associaton for Operations Management presently has two definitions for ERP, which includes the software as one version. ERP without software is impossible to accomplish in today's complex and competitive world. Software is much like the tools in a carpenter's or cabinetmaker's bag. Elaborate cabinets can be made with a hammer and a chisel but the time needed and the inefficiency of this approach make it an undesirable process. Additionally, the skill level requirements would be exponentially above that of the cabinetmaker utilizing modern tools. Instead, today's competitive carpenters and cabinetmakers use elaborate fixtures and powerful tools. Intricate designs can be copied and duplicated quickly. The quality actually can be enhanced as a result.

ERP business systems today are similar to the power tools. The new systems can make changes to schedules quickly and easily through "drop and drag" capabilities. As soon as the change is updated in the system, modern systems can quickly renet the changes and recalculate them to requirements and connect directly to supplier signals communicated through the Internet. Try that without software! In our ERP classes we try that manually. It gives the materials professionals an appreciation for the process of requirement netting. In a short time they gain an understanding of the efficiency of modern ERP systems support.

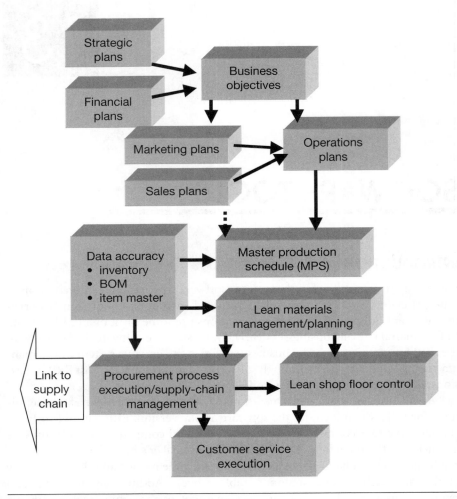

**Figure 13.1** Software ERP Business System Model

Along with gaining an understanding of the importance of software, it is equally important to emphasize the need for effective process. Without solid and robust process design, the tools do not work. Just as undisciplined and unknowledgeable people cannot make cabinets even with modern tools, neither can undisciplined and unknowledgeable people succeed at high-performance ERP. This is the spirit of Class A ERP, which was designed, developed, and has evolved for this reason—applied discipline makes ERP techniques and efficient supply-chain management both possible and probable. As Tim Frank, former CEO of Grafco PET Packaging, once stated, "Why wouldn't everybody want to do this?" I agree, why not?

Selecting software is not unlike buying a car or making another important investment. Books have been written about the basics of choosing a business system but most were written when business systems were evolving quickly and there was little expertise in the marketplace. Today, although systems are still evolving and will continue to do so, technology is more the driver now than functionality. From a functionality standpoint, most systems can do much more than is required or even desired by high-performance businesses. In a well-managed and -executed software implementation, estimates suggest that less than 30% of a system's total capabilities are used regularly. This is good, by the way! Software companies have to design packages to work in many environments including poorly-managed ones. I have been a speaker at ERP user group meetings and have been surprised by questions addressed to the system providers. Some of the more popular ERP systems available today have over 5000 system switches on the front end of the software that give users variation to use the system. It is doubtful that many people, if any, understand the function of all 5000 switches or how they affect other switch decisions. Technology, on the other hand, is helpful. The ability to drop and drag within the master schedule saves steps. The ability to simulate a change to the schedule without affecting the present schedule is helpful. These aren't new concepts in functionality; they are merely easier thanks to new technology. Like the essence of lean, flexibility and speed are on the path of continuous improvement.

I have the best result with *simple* software even in complex applications. The truth is that there are few "extremely complex" applications. Nearly every business person I have met expresses the complexity of their business. They usually begin with "Mr. Sheldon, you do not understand, our business is different." Nevertheless, these businesses are all the same. The simpler the software the better for these businesses, providing the software has all the *necessary* functionality. I do not endorse any specific software. I have seen all of the more popular tools used successfully and effectively—even the ones with the 5000 switches! The message, then, is that if you like the people with whom you are dealing, believe they are trustworthy, and they are a stable provider who is going to be there in the future to continue their support, the decision is probably low risk. The risks are further minimized if the process disciplines, skills, and knowledge in your business maintain high standards. I highly recommend using the Class A ERP standards in this space. By following the principles and implementing the Class A ERP standards, software is the tool that enables effective process and positive, continuing results.

When I began speaking publicly about Class A ERP in the 1980s, I frequently used the "golf story" to make my point. The origin is unknown, but the story has circulated around the Class A world for several years. If I went golfing with a professional golfer and we swapped clubs, who would probably have the best round? After all, I would have his high-value set of signature clubs and he would have my garage sale set. The answer is not rocket science. We all understand that the professional's disciplines and knowledge of the game would easily overshadow the fancy clubs used by someone who only plays a couple times a year. Software provides exactly the same story.

## ROLE OF ENTERPRISE RESOURCE PLANNING SOFTWARE IN LEAN MATERIALS MANAGEMENT

Lean concepts are centered on the execution of process with speed, flexibility, and minimized waste. While the planning process itself needs to be lean in nature, planning is complementary to the execution process. It is the means through which robust execution can occur. It is in this planning space that ERP systems shine when used properly. That is not to say that ERP systems are not helpful in the lean execution phases; the shop floor components are helpful but the bulk of ERP system value frequently comes prior to the execution. I think of it as dividing the "knowns" and the "unknowns." The "knowns" drive the finalized sets of actions that occur through lean execution, for example, firm replenishment orders through kanban or actual customer orders pulling activity through the manufacturing process. The "unknowns" are exactly that, planned orders that can change. The planning system can facilitate organizing the capacity plans and point out deficiencies when forecasts are different from demonstrated capacity. Even lean environments have to have adequate capacity to be lean (figure 13.2).

The plans must drive the supply chain to prepare for the customer-driven pull signal that inevitably comes. To respond effectively to customer behaviors, it is necessary to have planning and inventory control systems. These fall under the umbrella of ERP systems. In this chapter we explore the requirements for choosing a software system for a manufacturing or distribution organization. Understand that, in a service organization, ERP systems are helpful and frequently used. Larger service organizations, like their manufacturing equivalents, have no choice.

## SIMPLE ENTERPRISE RESOURCE PLANNING SOFTWARE SYSTEM CRITERIA

A reminder begins our discussion. Simple is better when it comes to ERP systems. The more complex the system is, the more costly, and, accordingly, bad decisions are easily made, especially during the system setup. The system designers of the software accommodate ineffective leadership in their customer base as well as those with effective leadership. By offering all the possibilities in their system setup, they have their customer base covered and all the choices available, both good and bad. That creates dangerous software swamps that are easy to enter.

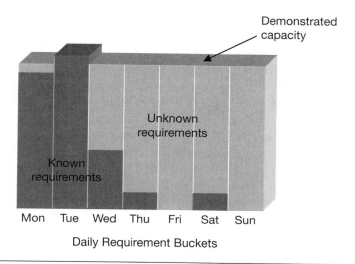

**Figure 13.2** Daily Requirement Buckets

Following is a starting list to utilize during the search for software:

- **Company reputation**—This is perhaps the most important. Knowing the software supplier is no different than making an important consumer purchase. There are times when help is needed after implementation and certainly during. People buy from people. I was looking at cars recently at a local high-end dealer. I was interested in a used sports car and I asked about the warranty. He replied, "My personal phone number is the warranty. Call me if you have a problem and we will come and get it." With this commitment to the customer, we do not hesitate paying a little more for the security that is offered. This is extremely important with software. No matter how simple the product, some issues inevitably arise that require outside expertise.

- **Software used in other similar businesses successfully**—Successful software purchases often come from seeing and talking to another company using the system in a similar environment. We may not be able to go to our competitors' facilities to watch and learn but we can normally find other industries that have similar inventory strategies (e.g., make to stock, assemble to order, make to order) or similar bill of material (BOM) complexity or simplicity. It provides a significant advantage. We can also confirm the service provided by the software supplier by asking for the users' experience concerning support. These contacts can be made through the supplier but, as we would expect, only the best examples surface; therefore, other contacts are beneficial as well. Professional societies (APICS is one of the better organizations for this) can help in this endeavor. If the system has no users within a reasonable radius, it might not be wise to be the first.

- **Capabilities around a short list of specifics that seem important to management**—The search team needs to develop the short list of requirements for the business. Many suitable systems can be located if the search is implemented properly and the system chosen will be capable of supporting the needs of the business. If the proper system is not found, it might imply that processes need to be reviewed before the software is selected. For example, I was involved in a situation in which necessary changes were made in the process, which resulted in the decision not to buy software. The needed benefits occurred without initiating any business system enhancements. Their opportunities were centered in process deficiencies even though they were convinced it was poor software tools.

- **Query ease and flexibility**—Process improvement only occurs with access to effective root cause analysis. Data mining aids this effort immensely. Good systems have robust drill-down capabilities. Make sure that these system features are easy to use and do not require IT to develop all the reports. Systems with numerous already-developed reports are rarely the easiest systems on which to do drill-downs. Some of these systems require high code-writing skills to develop flexible reports; thus the high number of reports already written by the system supplier. In fact, some of the most flexible systems have few reports already developed and, instead, have easy report-writer capability built into the system. This is one of the most important points about a new system choice. Have a comfort level for the report-writing capability. Develop one while testing the system to see how it works before the purchase order is signed.

- **Price does matter**—There are some inexpensive packages available that work quite well. Unlike some items, the more spent in this market does not ensure getting the best match for the needs. Cost-effective systems can have a surprising amount of functionality yet adhere to the simplicity requirement. Shop around. The system sellers want to emphasized the bells and whistles that are available in their package. Do not be drawn in by their allure! Remember that the more functions there are in the software, and especially the more software switches on the front end, the more complex the system is to use. Simple (within reason) is good when it comes to ERP systems.

# THE NEXT LEVEL OF DETAIL: SOFTWARE SPECS

This book does not include a detailed discussion regarding software, but if you are interested in more specific characteristics a few are listed below:

- effective master scheduling capabilities
  - drop and drag master production schedule capability is a "nice-to-have"
  - order entry available-to-promise capabilities
  - forward and backward scheduling capability
- efficient supply-chain management capabilities
  - Internet communications capabilities for supply-chain management
  - supplier performance capability
    - supplier promise accuracy
    - accuracy of the required date as compared to the receipt date (shouldn't be but can be different from the promise date)
  - web portal integration capability for supply-chain management
- user friendly menus
  - quick shortcuts to other screens, shared drives, and Internet
  - part number (or order number) carried screen to screen
  - easy links to spreadsheet uploads and downloads
- query/drill-down capabilities
  - easy-to-use report-writing capability (this is better than most existing hard-coded reports—be wary of those systems)
  - drill-down and screen-to-screen capability without having to re-key data such as a part number
  - several user-defined fields available in the item master
- metrics capabilities
  - frozen date field for original customer promise
  - performance measurement capability such as schedule adherence and schedule stability
- warehouse capabilities
  - real-time balances
  - location balance capability
  - multiple location capability for the same part
  - ability to backflush from designated locations at chosen operations within a routing
  - cycle counting tools

- o barcode interface capability and RF capability for factory and warehouse
- materials management functionality
  - o multiple BOM-level capability
  - o ABC inventory stratification and associated reporting capability
  - o pegging capability to discover who drives requirements (forecasted or customer orders)
  - o real-time transactions—no batch
  - o ability to have expensed items on the BOM along with inventory and non-stocked items
  - o bills of resource (BORs) or BOMs with routing capability in which components are linked to the point of use within the BOM
  - o ability to create schedule printouts for each work center
  - o ability to allocate inventory with options to affect the inventory availability or not, depending on the situation
  - o ability to have some inventory locations (such as quality-hold) as non-nettable locations
  - o bucketless MRP (any time frames needed—i.e., hours, days, or months)
- robust accounting functionality
  - o standard cost system with product line profit and loss capability
  - o multiple cost standard fields (standard, actual, other?)
- shop floor control
  - o efficiency reporting along with labor and material variance reporting
  - o capacity planning—Sales and Operations Planning (S&OP) database

Obviously there are many functions within an ERP software business system. The ones listed are a representation; however, they are also the ones that I encounter that are frequently shortfalls of installed systems. Although it is a beneficial short list to check against, it is not representative of a complete request for quote list.

## WHAT ABOUT THE "CORPORATE STANDARD" SYSTEM VIEW?

I go into numerous large organizations that are in the process of converting to the corporate standard for the ERP system. Usually the business has several of the plants on one software system and a few (usually acquisitions) on various other systems. Invariably, some of these "foreign system users" are doing fine with the existing software system and see the conversion as a death sentence. (I am working with one of those situations presently.) These people don't want to read the next few lines! The reality is that software does not make a plant or distribution center successful; people and processes do. There are benefits in having the entire company on one piece of software. They include:

1. capability of corporate drill-down into the plants
2. ease of financial information integration—this is even more important with the strict laws on accounting compliance post-Enron
3. commonality of processes and procedures such as rules of engagement, master scheduling, and preparation for the S&OP process
4. common standard operating procedures documents can also be much more common throughout the organization, making International Organization for Standardization (ISO) and QS certifications easier to accomplish
5. ease of worker flexibility when moving employees around the world when needed

The organizations cursed with the need to change perfectly good working systems for the sake of the entire organization need to gain comfort in knowing that the change is never fun, but organizations with good processes and discipline never, I repeat never, experience more than minor blips on the performance screen. Once everyone knows the new system, life goes on as normal, sometimes even better than before because of the ease of communications between facilities.

*Note to "corporate" people reading this:* For those organizations on "other systems" that are not successful prior to the corporate software conversion edict, be aware that the conversion does not make them well. It takes more than just the tools, as discussed several times in this chapter.

## FINAL THOUGHT ON SOFTWARE

If you take nothing from this chapter except one thing, it should be the understanding that all of the popular ERP systems work. Use the checklists to remind yourself to look carefully during selection.

- There is always some emotion in the purchase, similar to purchasing a car, so be wary just as with that purchase.
- Buy the system that has the most internal support and anticipate the best service externally.

- Most importantly, implement the Class A ERP disciplines and the new tool will facilitate success. Software does not create the payback; disciplines in the business utilizing it do. Before the conversion, not during, be sure the disciplines and processes are thoroughly understood. Otherwise, how do you look for the right capabilities for application?

When that much money is being spent, ensure the purchase is effective and functional in the business and nothing less. Many material managers have battle scars from system implementations. For nearly any question asked, including "Will the software do [fill in the blank]?" the answer should always be a reasonably truthful "yes." This eliminates cost and distress. Bottom line—software is a beautiful thing when used properly and respected! Keep any unnecessary, self-inflicted pain in that regard to a minimum!

## DISCUSSION QUESTIONS

1. Which of the following statements is true?
   a. ERP is a computer software system.
   b. ERP is a planning process linking business planning with execution.
   c. ERP is a business model.
   d. all of the above
   e. none of the above

2. Supply-chain management should have which of the following software support capabilities?
   a. Internet communications capabilities for supply-chain management
   b. supplier performance capability
      i. supplier-promised accuracy
      ii. accuracy of the required date as compared to the receipt date (shouldn't be but can be different than the promise date)
   c. web portal integration capability for supply-chain management
   d. all of the above
   e. a and b

3. The bulk of ERP system value often comes prior to the execution phase.
   a. true
   b. false

4. Data mining is helped best through
   a. Six Sigma.
   b. the more popular ERP systems available.
   c. robust query capabilities.
   d. lean focus.

5. Service industries have no need for MRP.
   a. true
   b. false

6. Software is a tool to the materials manager as a hammer is to a carpenter.
   a. true
   b. false

7. People are one of the most important aspects of purchasing software, especially the relationship between the buying company and the selling company.
   a. true
   b. false

8. Most of the better known ERP software systems perform equally. Some have additional functionality that is unnecessary and undesirable.
   a. true
   b. false

9. The software switches on the front end of most popular ERP software systems need to be thoroughly understood. They can generally affect
   a. linkage to the general ledger.
   b. handling of inventory allocations.
   c. human resources records.
   d. all of the above
   e. a and b

10. An example of an inventory strategy is
    a. salvage sitting at the machine.
    b. make to order.
    c. real-time location balances.
    d. none of the above

# 14

# EDUCATION AND TRAINING IN LEAN MATERIALS MANAGEMENT

## IMPORTANCE OF EDUCATING ALL PARTIES

To get everyone on the same track right from the beginning, there needs to be shared goals, a common glossary of terms, and a shared vision. The goals are accomplished most successfully through education. Don't think of it as teaching "old dogs new tricks." Instead, regard it as reorganizing the group's thoughts into a central and shared focus—like light shining through a magnifying glass. When the whole team is on the same path, change can occur quickly. This is the goal— make it happen as quickly as possible while keeping the spirit of the goal clearly in front of the team.

There is probably an opportunity to educate in several areas: Enterprise Resource Planning (ERP), lean, and eventually Six Sigma. Top management education is perhaps the most critical. Each of the topics usually takes about 4-6 hours for the overview and is normally performed in one setting per topic over time. In the first session there is significant emphasis on top management's role to ensure a successful implementation. Included are the Sales and Operations Planning (S&OP) process roles, management system roles, and walking the talk. Frequently, outside experts conduct this meeting simply because top management people do not always listen as attentively to insider direction. Also, by completing the education early in the process, top management people easily position themselves as the champions of this process implementation, which is a powerful sig-

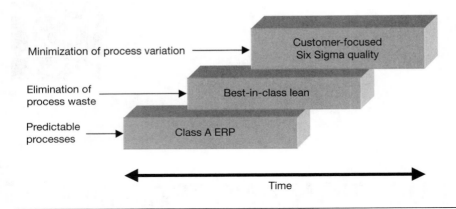

**Figure 14.1** Multi-Step Performance Process

nal to send to the organization. The focus is on the multi-step performance process goal (figure 14.1).

Education of the remainder of the team comes in waves. Middle management must own the implementation at least as much as top management, and without proper understanding, that cannot happen. Typically each plant has its own core team headed by a process improvement champion for that plant. Education in these teams is completed in several ways. The most effective and easiest way for the company, perhaps, is to have the education delivered by professionals that cannot only explain the basics, but can also give examples of their experiences with other companies. This can be especially effective in the early stages as converts and advocates of change are won over. Content of the core training includes detailed education on topics matching the processes in the Class A ERP business model (figure 14.2), lean, and eventually Six Sigma. Timing depends on the ability to process and apply the learning.

Everyone in the company is eventually introduced to the concepts of process improvement. The last level of education is most effectively delivered by the managers of the people being trained. This approach puts special emphasis on the management team understanding the basics of process improvement. It also sends a strong message that it is important and not just another "float in the parade," one that "might miss me if I keep my head down." Purchased video education is helpful in this regard, using managers for facilitators; however, outside education offers an especially effective alternative for the facilitation if needed. The video resources make facilitating easier and require less expertise at the front of the class.

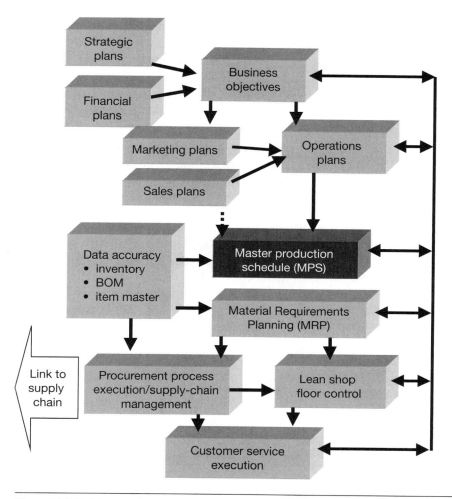

**Figure 14.2** Training and ERP Business Model

## TRAINING

Following the educational process, implementation begins. Processes are changed and invented, steps are eliminated, and cycle times reduced. Each change requires that the documentation is updated. The documentation becomes the vehicle for the training of new hires and transferred employees. The difference between education and training is easily understood. I think of education as the "why" around business process and training as the "how" (figure 14.3).

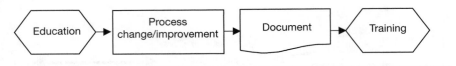

**Figure 14.3** Flow Chart of Education and Training

Companies that believe human capital is worth the investment, and demonstrate that, are most often the more successful companies. People skills are frequently the difference between success and mediocrity or even failure. You can have the best machinery and tools, but if the people are less than competitive, the company will suffer. Successful lean materials management is no magical ride. Success is based on understanding and shared goals.

Among these shared goals must be a belief in accountability. Accountability must be part of the fiber of the company culture. The support of top management is essential. It normally manifests itself in the management systems of the organization. This includes the monthly, weekly, and daily systems detailed in this book. With these in place, there is reason to be optimistic. Now go do it. I bid you Godspeed!

## DISCUSSION QUESTIONS

1. Education and training are important in changing the culture of an organization.
   a. true
   b. false

2. Education is generally explaining "how" to do a task.
   a. true
   b. false

3. All personnel need some exposure to education and training.
   a. true
   b. false

4. Education and training are normally considered investments in human capital.
   a. true
   b. false

# ANSWERS TO DISCUSSION QUESTIONS

## CHAPTER 1

1. d
2. c
3. b
4. b
5. c
6. c
7. d
8. d
9. a
10. a
11. e

## CHAPTER 2

1. f
2. d
3. c
4. a
5. c
6. b
7. a
8. d
9. a
10. a
11. a
12. b
13. a
14. a
15. e

## CHAPTER 3

1. d
2. a
3. d
4. e
5. b
6. c
7. b
8. b
9. b
10. b

## CHAPTER 4

1. b
2. b
3. b
4. d
5. d
6. c
7. a
8. a
9. b
10. a

## CHAPTER 5

1. d
2. b
3. e
4. b
5. e
6. a
7. c
8. b
9. a
10. d

## CHAPTER 6

1. a
2. a
3. c
4. b
5. b
6. c
7. d
8. c
9. a
10. e

## CHAPTER 7

1. b
2. a
3. e
4. b
5. a
6. b
7. b
8. a
9. c
10. b

## CHAPTER 8

1. a
2. c
3. b
4. a
5. b
6. b
7. e
8. a
9. b
10. b

## CHAPTER 9

1.  e
2.  a
3.  b
4.  b
5.  a
6.  c
7.  b
8.  d
9.  b
10. g

## CHAPTER 10

1.  b
2.  a
3.  b
4.  b
5.  b
6.  a
7.  c
8.  b
9.  d
10. b

## CHAPTER 11

1.  e
2.  b
3.  e
4.  b
5.  e
6.  a
7.  d
8.  a
9.  a
10. b

## CHAPTER 12

1.  c
2.  e
3.  e
4.  b
5.  a
6.  b
7.  f
8.  a
9.  a
10. a

## CHAPTER 13

1.  d
2.  b
3.  a
4.  c
5.  b
6.  a
7.  a
8.  a
9.  d
10. b

## CHAPTER 14

1.  a
2.  b
3.  a
4.  a

# INDEX